Understanding the Infrastructure of Online Social Networks

Richard

Copyright © 2024 by Richard

Table of Contents

I   Introduction and Objectives   1

1   Introduction

   1.1   Motivation . . . .

   1.2   Objectives . . . .

   1.3   Structure of the book . . . .

   1.4   Publications List . . . .

   1.5   Research Projects . . . .

II   Selected Papers   12

2   Review of Privacy Mechanisms for Social Network Services

   2.1   Introduction . . . .

   2.2   Privacy decision-making process . . . .

   2.3   Advances on privacy mechanisms . . . .

      2.3.1   Preferences-centered requirement . . . .

      2.3.2   Sensitivity inferring requirement . . . .

      2.3.3   Multi-user privacy requirement . . . .

      2.3.4   Relationship inferring requirement . . . .

    2.3.5   Scope inferring requirement . . . .

    2.3.6   Fine-grained requirement

    2.3.7   Automation requirement . . . .

    2.3.8   Privacy-preserving requirement . . . .

    2.3.9   Explainable requirement . . . .

2.4   Open challenges . . . .

    2.4.1   Privacy-related metrics . . . .

    2.4.2   Validated model for automation . . . .

    2.4.3   Explainable, argued, and reflective privacy policy solutions . .

    2.4.4   Adaptation to user's modifications . . . .

    2.4.5   Co-privacy . . . .

    2.4.6   Content-fading solutions . . . .

2.5   Conclusions . . . .

3 **Estimation of Privacy Risk through Centrality Metrics**   **48**

3.1   Introduction . . . .

3.2   Related work . . . .

3.3   Privacy risk scenario . . . .

3.4   Privacy Risk Score (PRS) . . . .

    3.4.1   Calculation of the PRS metric . . . .

    3.4.2   PRS metric in OSN . . . .

3.5   PRS and centrality metrics . . . .

3.6   Experiments . . . .

    3.6.1   Simulation environment . . . .

    3.6.2   Settings . . . .

    3.6.3   PRS and global centrality metrics . . . .

    3.6.4   PRS, local, and social centrality metrics . . . .

3.7   Conclusions . . . .

4   Metrics for Privacy Assessment when Sharing Information in Online Social Networks   76

4.1   Introduction . . . .

4.2   Related Work . . . .

4.3   Privacy Threats in OSN .

4.4   Privacy Risk Metrics when Sharing Information

    4.4.1   Metrics Calculation . . . .

4.5   Experiments . . . .

    4.5.1   Experiment settings . . . .

    4.5.2   Privacy Metrics in Different Network Topologies . . . .

    4.5.3   Correlation between privacy metrics and structural properties

4.6   Conclusions . . . .

5   Empowering OSN Users about the Sensitivity of their Data through Nudge Mechanisms   102

5.1   Introduction . . . .

  5.2   Literature review . . . .

    5.2.1   Definition of personal data . . . .

    5.2.2   Quantifying the value of personal data . . . .

    5.2.3   Sensitivity in the OSN domain . . . .

5.3   Proposal . . . .

  5.4   Experiment . . . .

    5.4.1   Methodology . . . .

    5.4.2   Results . . . .

5.5   Discussion . . . .

5.6   Conclusions . . . .

6   "Who should I grant access to my post?": Identifying the most Suitable Privacy
Decisions on OSNs   120

6.1   Introduction . . . .

6.2   Literature review . . . .

6.2.1   Privacy calculus theory and privacy decisions . . . .

6.2.2   Information disclosure and benefit . . . .

6.2.3   Privacy cost and overexposure . . . .

6.3   Research model and hypothesis development . . . .

6.3.1   Channel factors . . . .

6.3.2   Sensitivity of the message . . . .

6.3.3   Differences between types of receivers . . . .

6.3.4   Online Social Well-being . . . .

6.4   Methodology . . . .

6.4.1   Research settings . . . .

6.4.2   Data collection . . . .

6.4.3   Measurement . . . .

6.4.4   Sample characteristics . . . .

6.5   Analysis and results . . . .

6.5.1   Measurement model assessment . . . .

6.5.2   Structural model assessment . . . .

6.6   Discussions . . . .

6.6.1   Theoretical implications . . . .

6.6.2   Practical implications . . . .

6.6.3   Limitations and future research . . . .

6.7   Conclusion . . . .

6.A   Appendix . . . .

6.A.1   Measurement instrument . . . .

6.A.2   Descriptive statistics, reliability and validity results . . . .

7   Enhancing the Privacy Risk Awareness of Teenagers in Online Social Networks through Soft-Paternalism Mechanisms   149

7.1   Introduction . . . .

7.2   Related work . . . .

7.3   Nudging Mechanisms . . . .

7.3.1   Privacy Risk Score (PRS) . . . .

7.3.2   Nudges . . . .

7.4   Experiment . . . .

7.4.1   Platform . . . .

7.4.2   Setup . . . .

7.5   Results . . . .

7.5.1   Demographics and activity . . . .

7.5.2   Participants' posting behavior . . . .

7.5.3   Research questions and hypothesis testing . . . .

7.5.4   Participants' perception about nudges . . . .

7.6   Discussion . . . .

7.7   Conclusions . . . .

8   Assessing the Effectiveness of a Gamified Social Network for Applying Privacy Concepts: An Empirical Study with Teens   182

8.1   Introduction . . . .

8.2 Literature review . . . .

    8.2.1 Educating teenagers about OSN privacy . . . .

    8.2.2 Social networks and Gamification in education . . . .

    8.2.3 Individual differences . . . .

8.3 Experimental design . . . .

    8.3.1 Study site . . . .

    8.3.2 Instruments . . . .

    8.3.3 Participants . . . .

    8.3.4 Procedure . . . .

    8.3.5 Measures and data analysis . . . .

8.4 Results . . . .

    8.4.1 Privacy-seeking behavior . . . .

    8.4.2 Social network engagement . . . .

    8.4.3 Gender & Age behavior differences . . . .

8.5 Discussion . . . .

8.6 Conclusion . . . .

III Discussion   **208**

9 General Discussion of the Results

9.1 Results on open research lines about privacy . . . .

9.2 Results of the definition of a privacy risk metric . . . .

9.3 Results of the proposed sensitivity metric for social network publications

9.4 Results on users' benefit-cost trade-off in privacy decisions . . . .

9.5 Results on nudging users with privacy risk and sensitivity metrics . . .

9.6   Results of educating teenage users about privacy with social gamifica-
        tion items   . . . .

10 Conclusions and Future Work   **218**

Part I

Introduction and Objectives

## CHAPTER 1

INTRODUCTION

1.1   Motivation   3
1.2   Objectives   7
1.3   Structure of the **book**   8
1.4   Publications List   10
1.5   Research Projects   12

1.1   Motivation

Online social networks (OSNs) have become a mainstream cultural phenomenon for millions of Internet users, being its usage one of the most popular[1]. Independently of the context or type of the social network (e.g., professionals, dating, focused on instant messaging, based on video content, etc.), all of them have a set of common features. Users[2] normally have a (self-constructed) profile that represents their self-presentation to others and communication mechanisms that enable users to be pseudo-permanently "in touch". The usage of these networks provides users benefits such as influencing others, increasing their reputation, receiving support, getting brand offers, connecting with a huge community, etc. These benefits may differ depending on the network type and the user's motivations. However, the flip side of using social networks is the loss of privacy and the potential consequences of it.

According to Alan Westin, privacy is defined as *"the claim of individuals, groups, or institutions to determine for themselves when, how, and to what extent information about them is communicated"* [278]. However with the emergence of new technologies, new meanings and broader categories of the term have emerged. These meanings/categories applied to network domain are based on (i) a security approach that explores the architectures (P2P vs. Client-Server) and communication protocols of the online social networks to protect users' privacy from vulnerabilities and attacks [135, 199]; (ii) the users' linkage among different online social networks and how it affects their identity anonymity, personal space privacy, and communications [135, 90, 199]; (iii) the social network service providers policies towards the selling and/or sharing of users' information to other companies (e.g., third-party applications) [135, 199]; and (iv) the users' privacy behaviors towards other users and the privacy policies set via privacy mechanisms [90]. This **book** work is focused on the last privacy category which is related to the privacy decision-making process (i.e., information disclosure and privacy policy choice).

In the OSN environments, any action that users perform stems from the need for getting social benefit [118] and is always preceded by a privacy decision or a privacy acceptance that limits the potential costs/risks of the action. This constitutes the privacy decision-making process, and users make these decisions in social networks millions of times. Depending on the OSN site, different types of privacy mechanisms are provided to users to make privacy decisions. These privacy decisions differ in their type and granularity, e.g., users of OSNs like Instagram manage their followers and decide whether they want their profiles public or private; but others OSNs like Facebook allows finer granularity with mechanisms to select groups, personalized access lists, or even members individually to grant or deny the access to the information for each post. This variability among social networks may be a challenge for users. Furthermore, due to the complexity of the privacy concept [231] and the number of factors to assess (e.g., the number of friends, the relationship type, the context of the information, etc.), users have difficulty in assessing potential risks of disclosing information [5]. Therefore, they tend to relax or restrict too much their decisions which finally end up with the posting in a wide audience or the not posting, respectively. In turn, this is translated into potential privacy risks or loss of benefits [270], respectively.

In recent years, privacy concerns have led to improved privacy mechanisms and policies in social networking services. Examples of these improvements can be found on Facebook with the smart access lists and direct access to general privacy settings [238]; on Twitter with private profiles and the possibility of sharing information by directly selecting the users who are going to receive it. Even so, privacy leaks continue to affect users' real lives [270]. For example, job layoffs due to comments or photos shared on social networks; or the appearance of "stalkers", people dedicated to spying on others through social networks. This is because users might not able to understand the different mechanisms they have available to manage their privacy, nor they completely understand the risks their actions have on privacy. There is still a long way to go towards privacy mechanisms that fully protect users' privacy and interests, and prevent privacy leaks.

Artificial intelligence techniques and feature extraction methods applied to social networks are powerful tools to enhance privacy mechanisms. Current research work extracts characteristics from social networks, user interactions, and user preferences to develop all kinds of privacy tools, mechanisms, and metrics. Most approaches rely on automation to calculate privacy policies aligned with user preferences, providing users with privacy policy recommendations [86, 262, 34, 244]. However, the consideration of using only the user's preferences as a reference is not an appropriate approach. The reason is that users make disclosure actions that then regret because they are not able to evaluate all possible risk scenarios. As for other works that attempt to focus more on preserving user privacy [49, 129, 178], these also produce a recommendation for the user. The problem with both approaches is that the user remains unaware of the reason for the solution provided, and it is he/she who has to finally accept the recommendation or not.

Research in business and economic studies has proved that an individual always assesses the cost-benefit when facing a decision [210]. For avoiding the regret of the decision, an individual needs as perfect information as possible for properly assessing the cost-benefit of the decision. Real experiments in online social networks have demonstrated that individuals seldom have perfect information for deciding [5]. To address the lack of users' information, promising research lines are working on quantifying the privacy risks and social benefits produced by these actions, and on designing user interfaces (UIs) to present that information to users. However, the ways users interpret a piece of information differs, and might be linked to cognitive limitations, so their decisions underlie different biases. For example, the same issue can be expressed through text or pictures resulting in different perceptions of the content among individuals. Therefore, it is important how a piece of information, a message, or a set of choices is presented to users [222].

The discussion above raises several questions that this research is intended to answer:

Q1. Are the current mechanisms/solutions in the privacy decision-making process good enough for users to make privacy decisions that represent their wishes and do not cause regrets?

Q2. Which additional requirements should meet the next generation of privacy mechanisms to ensure the improvement of users' decisions?

Q3. How can be measured and quantified the privacy risks that a user's action in online social networks can cause?

Q4. Which features empower the users' scope in a social network and how these impact on the privacy of users?

Q5. Which types of information are most sensitive than others and how can be quantified the information sensitivity of a social media publication?

Q6. Which is the user's trade-off between cost and benefits when face perfectly informed privacy decisions in social networks?

Q7. What are the best UIs for the privacy decision domain in social networks and how information should be introduced to users for not limiting their decisions?

Q8. What will be the effects of these explainable mechanisms on users' privacy decisions in a real environment?

For this reason, we plan this book work in the way of improving the metrics to estimate privacy risks, compute privacy solutions, and provide users with understandable explanations before making privacy decisions.

This work is also motivated by the research lines of the Valencian Research Institute in Artificial Intelligence (VRAIN), where the Ph.D. student works. Among other areas of AI, the institute is interested in online social networks, users' behaviors and interactions, users' privacy protection, the mining of social information, and the development of privacy mechanisms. This book work is being developed in the context of the following national research projects: PESEDIA (TIN2014-55206-R), and AI4PRI (TIN2017-89156-R). The PESEDIA project proposes algorithms and metrics for analyzing privacy risks in social networks, and a rapid transfer of the results for customizing privacy mechanisms, and proactively training people on the value of their privacy. In the framework of this project and my Master's book [15], the social network prototype called PESEDIA was implemented. The outcomes of the PESEDIA project and this Ph.D. book work were materialized in the social network PESEDIA. The second project, AI4PRI, is intended to the inference of social norms, emotions, and arguments, for developing a multi-agent system integrated into the social network PESEDIA with which to improve the control of the user's privacy. Both projects are aimed at the vulnerable group of young people who are initiating in social networks and have limited abilities for self-regulation and complex decision-making.

1.2   Objectives

This **book** proposes the design and use of privacy mechanisms that besides considering the users' preferences, also considers the users' privacy-preserving approach and the informed assistance during users' privacy decisions. By considering the users' privacy-preserving approach, we try to quantify the amount of users' personal information that is overexposed in social networks and it is not making a significant benefit for the owner user. By considering the explainability of privacy decisions, we try to educate users in a well-informed way about the potential privacy risks of their decisions. The final goal of this **book** is to improve the current privacy mechanisms of online social networks for users could choose better privacy policies and reduce the regrets of their actions. Therefore, this **book** proposes the following objectives detailed below:

- Review of the whole privacy decision-making process in online social networks and the current privacy mechanisms in order to identify advantages and lacks in previous approaches.

- Specification of a list of requirements that a privacy decision mechanism and its solutions would have to meet in order to address the current problems and reduce the regrets of users' actions.

- Research into users' overexposure to social networks and the perception of their actions to compute users' privacy risk metrics.

- Development of privacy metrics that assess the risk of re-sharing information in social networks, taking into account the visibility and importance of users in the network.

- Development of privacy metrics that assess the sensitivity of users' information in social networks, taking into account other approaches and the specificity of the OSN domain.

- Development of a research model to understand the user's trade-off between benefit and cost, and his/her choice of the different elements of online communication during disclosing decisions.

- Development of explainable privacy mechanisms that take into account those privacy metrics to show users the potential effects of their decisions and educate them on privacy.

- Validation of the developed privacy mechanisms, the effect on users' privacy behaviors, and the users' acquisition of conscientiousness via well-informed mechanisms.

1.3 Structure of the **book**

Considering the motivation and objectives of this book, the rest of the document is structured as follows:

- **Part I. Introduction and Objectives:** In this part, the motivation and objectives of this book, as well as the structure of the document are presented. Moreover, this chapter also stresses the projects that supported the research of this book work and all the contributions that were produced in the context of it.

- **Part II. Selected Papers:** This part presents a selection of the most representative articles supporting this book objectives (set in Section 1.2) which were published in conferences and journals.

  Chapter 2 (under review state in the ACM Computing Surveys journal) presents in detail the current problems of users' privacy from the perspective of the pri-vacy decision-making process in the social network domain. The paper identi-fies from those problems a list of requirements that privacy mechanisms have to meet in order to reduce users' privacy problems and potential regrets. From the requirements, we make a review of current advances from OSN providers and researchers in privacy mechanisms and we highlight the open challenges that could improve users' decisions.

  Chapter 3 (previously published in [11]) proposes a privacy metric for assessing the privacy risk score that a user of a social network has. The metric is based on epidemic models to estimate the user's risk of reaching other users. This paper takes information from network centrality properties (closeness, betweenness, etc.) and previous information flows (usually emerged from intimacy among users, time spent on the network, etc.). In this regard, we test the validity of approximating the privacy risk score metric with centrality metrics. This privacy metric differs from other proposals because takes into account the daily users' activity (dynamic metric) instead of the profile items (static metric).

  Chapter 4 (previously published in [13]) proposes an extension of the privacy metric with new metrics that estimate the depth and width of users' dissemination power. In this case, these metrics can be adapted to users' privacy concerns and perceptions.

Chapter 5 (previously published in [14]) details the review of all the tries to compute/quantify the sensitivity value of information, especially personal information. In this work, the inclusion of information sensitivity from the social network approach is also discussed, which is related to users' reputation. As a result, a sensitivity metric is proposed that it is the mean of all other approach proposal values. The paper also includes a study of the empowerment of users and the effects on privacy decisions by knowing the sensitivity value of their publications during those decisions.

Chapter 6 (under review state in the Internet Research journal) proposes a research model of users' cost-benefit trade-off for disclosure actions in social networks. This research work evaluates the relationships between the elements of online communication (especially the channel, the message, and the receptor), the personal information disclosure, and the privacy trade-off in the social network context. As a result, our model is able to explain a considerable percentage of the relationship between the considered factors during users' information disclosure action.

Chapter 7 (previously published in [12]) presents different kinds of privacy mechanisms based on soft-paternalistic mechanisms (i.e., nudges) that inform users about the potential consequences of their privacy decisions. In this work, the privacy mechanisms are developed and integrated into the social network PESEDIA and are finally tested in a study with real users. The study is carried out during a one-month course about social networks where users had complete access (24/7) to the social network PESEDIA to interact among them. The study validates the significant effect of customized nudge mechanisms on users' behavior.

Chapter 8 (under review state in the IEEE Transactions on Learning Technologies journal) presents the advantages of integrating gamification elements in a social network in order to educate on social networks and raise awareness of users regarding their privacy. In this work, two configurations (with and without gamification) of the social network PESEDIA are tested with 387 teenage participants for one month. The comparison of both configurations highlights the advantages of applying gamification in the users' common activity in networks, empowering their capacity to make privacy decisions.

- **Part III. Discussion:** This part presents a final review and discussion of published work and results, as well as future directions for further research.

1.4 Publications List

In this section, all the international publications related to this book are listed. They have been classified according to their type (journals or international conferences) as well as whether they are listed in JCR or in CORE, respectively. Those publications which have been included in this document are marked with **(*)**.

- Journals listed in JCR:

    - <u>Under Review</u> R. Ruiz-Dolz, J. Alemany, S. Heras, and A. García-Fornes. *On the Prevention of Privacy Threats: How Can We Persuade Our Social Network Users?*. **User Modeling and User-Adapted Interaction** (2020) **Impact Factor: 3.400.**

    - **(*)** <u>Under Review</u> J. Alemany, E. del Val, and A. García-Fornes. *Review of Privacy Mechanisms for Social Network Services.* **ACM Computing Surveys** (2020) **Impact Factor: 6.131.**

    - **(*)** <u>Under Review</u> J. Alemany, E. del Val, and A. García-Fornes. *"Who should I grant access to my post?": Identifying the most Suitable Privacy Decision on OSNs.* **Internet Research** (2020) **Impact Factor: 4.109.**

    - **(*)** <u>Under Review</u> J. Alemany, E. del Val, and A. García-Fornes. *Assessing the Effectiveness of a Gamified Social Network for Applying Privacy Concepts: An Empirical Study with Teens.* **IEEE Transactions on Learning Technologies** (2020) **Impact Factor: 2.315.**

    - **(*)** J. Alemany, E. del Val, J. Alberola, and A. García-Fornes. *Metrics for Privacy Assessment When Sharing Information in Online Social Networks.* **IEEE Access** Vol. 7, pp. 143631-143645. (2019) **Impact Factor: 4.098.** DOI: *https://doi.org/10.1109/ACCESS.2019.2944723*

    - **(*)** J. Alemany, E. del Val, J. Alberola, and A. García-Fornes. *Enhancing the privacy risk awareness of teenagers in online social networks through soft-paternalism mechanisms.* **International Journal of Human-Computer Studies** Vol. 129, pp. 27-40. (2019) **Impact Factor: 2.006.** DOI: *https://doi.org/10.1016/J.IJHCS.2019.03.008*

    - **(*)** J. Alemany, E. del Val, J. Alberola, and A. García-Fornes. *Estimation of privacy risk through centrality metrics.* **Future Generation Computer Systems** Vol. 82, pp. 63-76. (2018) **Impact Factor: 3.997.** DOI: *https://doi.org/10.1016/J.FUTURE.2017.12.030*

- S. Valero, E. del Val, J. Alemany, and V. Botti. *Enhancing smart-home environments using Magentix2.* **Journal of Applied Logic** Volume 24 B, pp. 32-44. (2016) **Impact Factor: 0.838**. DOI: *https://doi.org/10.1016/J.JAL.2016.11.022*

- Other international journals:

  - E. Agente, E. Vivancos, J. Alemany, and A. García-Fornes. *Educando en privacidad en el uso de las redes sociales.* **Education in the Knowledge Society** Vol. 18, N. 2, pp. 107-126. (2017) DOI: *https://doi.org/10.14201/EKS2017182107126*

  - J. Alemany, S. Heras, J. Palanca, and V. Julian. *Bargaining agents based system for automatic classification of potential allergens in recipes.* **Advances in Distributed Computing and Artificial Intelligence Journal** Vol. 5, N. 2, pp. 43-51. (2016) DOI: *https://doi.org/10.14201/ADCAIJ2016524351*

- International conferences listed in CORE:

  - <u>Under Review</u> R. Ruiz-Dolz, J. Alemany, S. Heras, and A. García-Fornes. *Transformer-Based Models for Automatic Identification of Argument Relations: A Cross-Domain Evaluation.* The 2020 conference on **Empirical Methods in Natural Language Processing**, EMNLP (2020) **CORE ERA-2018 Rank: A.**

  - (*) J. Alemany, E. del Val, and A. García-Fornes. *Empowering users regarding the sensitivity of their data in social networks through nudge mechanisms.* 53rd **Hawaii International Conference on System Sciences**, HICSS Vol. 2020, pp. 2539-2548. (2020) ISBN: 978-0-9981331-3-3. **CORE ERA-2018 Rank: A.** DOI: *https://doi.org/10.14201/10.24251/HICSS.2020.310*

- Other international conferences:

  - R. Ruiz-Dolz, J. Alemany, S. Heras, and A. García-Fornes. *Towards an Argumentation System for Assisting Users with Privacy Management in Online Social Networks.* 19th Workshop on **Computational Models of Natural Argument**, CMNA Vol. 2346, pp. 17-28. (2019) *http://ceur-ws.org/Vol-2346/paper2.pdf*

  - J. Taverner, R. Ruiz-Dolz, E. del Val, C. Diez, and J. Alemany. *Image Analysis for Privacy Assessment in Social Networks.* 15th International Conference on **Distributed Computing and Artificial Intelligence**, DCAI Vol. 802, pp. 1-4. (2018) Print ISBN: 978-3-030-00523-8. Online ISBN: 978-3-030-00524-5. DOI: *https://doi.org/10.1007/978-3-030-00524-5_1*

  - J. Alemany, S. Heras, J. Palanca, and V. Julian. *An Agent-Based Application for Automatic Classification of Food Allergies and Intolerances in Recipes.* 14th

International Conference on **Practical Applications of Agents and Multi-Agent Systems**, PAAMS Vol. 9662, pp. 3-12. (2016) Print ISBN: 978-3-319-39323-0. Online ISBN: 978-3-319-39324-7. DOI: *https://doi.org/10.1007/978-3-319-39324-7_1*

– J. Alemany, S. Heras, J. Palanca, and V. Julian. *Automatic Detection System for Food Allergies and Intolerances in Recipes*. 14th International Conference on **Practical Applications of Agents and Multi-Agent Systems**, PAAMS Vol. 9662, pp. 235-238. (2016) Print ISBN: 978-3-319-39323-0. Online ISBN: 978-3-319-39324-7. DOI: *https://doi.org/10.1007/978-3-319-39324-7_20*

– S. Valero, E. del Val, J. Alemany, and V. Botti. *Using Magentix2 in Smart-Home Environments*. 10th International Conference on **Soft Computing Models in Industrial and Environmental Applications**, SOCO Vol. 368, pp. 27-37. (2015) Print ISBN: 978-3-319-19718-0. Online ISBN: 978-3-319-19719-7. DOI: *https://doi.org/10.1007/978-3-319-19719-7_3*

1.5 Research Projects

The research work presented in this Ph.D. book was carried out in the context of the following research projects:

- **Privacy in Social Educational Environments during Childhood and Adolescence (PESEDIA)**

    – Funder: Ministerio de Economia y Empresa *(TIN2014-55206-R)*

    – Lead Applicant: A. García-Fornes, and A. Espinosa.

    – Years: 2015 - 2018

- **Intelligent Agents for Privacy Advice in Social Networks (AI4PRI)**

    – Funder: Ministerio de Economia y Empresa *(TIN2017-89156-R)*

    – Lead Applicant: E. Argente, and A. García-Fornes.

    – Years: 2018 - 2021

Part II

Selected Papers

## CHAPTER 2

REVIEW OF PRIVACY MECHANISMS FOR SOCIAL NETWORK SERVICES

*— (Under review status) by **Jose Alemany**, **Elena del Val**, and **Ana García-Fornes** in the ACM Computing Surveys*

2.1 Introduction 16
2.2 Privacy decision-making process 17
2.3 Advances on privacy mechanisms 25
2.4 Open challenges 45
2.5 Conclusions 49

2.1 Introduction

Online social networks (OSNs) have become a mainstream cultural phenomenon for millions of Internet users, being its usage one of the most popular[1]. There are different types of online social networks (e.g., professionals, dating, focused on instant messaging, based on video content, etc.), but they all have a common set of properties that allow users to interact with others. Users[2] normally have a (self-constructed) profile that represents their self-presentation to others and communication mechanisms that enable users to be pseudo-permanently "in touch". The usage of these networks provides users benefits such as influencing others, increasing their reputation, receiving support, getting brand offers, connecting with a huge community, etc. These benefits may differ depending on the network type and the user's motivations. However, the flip side of using social networks is the loss of privacy and the potential consequences of it. Therefore, the suitable usage of social networks is the one that balances the user's social benefits with the potential risks.

Privacy problems associated with digital communication and network technologies are constantly reported [290]. In online social networks, each action users do represents a personal action due to can be linked to personal data[3] (from fulfilling a profile field or sharing a new photo to joining a group or liking a publication). All these actions have a visibility/access component on the network that, in some aspect, is decided by users via a privacy policy[4]. It is here where privacy issues may appear and might be translated into regrets and real consequences for users [270, 88]. Those privacy policy choices are made using a privacy mechanism, which is a tool with some kind of user interface where users choose or accept a privacy policy.

Alan Westin defined privacy as *"the claim of individuals, groups, or institutions to determine for themselves when, how, and to what extent information about them is communicated"* [278]. Even so, in the online social network domain, there are broad categories for the privacy concept. These categories are based on (i) a security approach that explores the architectures (P2P vs. Client-Server) and communication protocols of the online social

networks to protect users' privacy from vulnerabilities and attacks [135, 199]; (ii) the
users' linkage among different online social networks and how it affects their identity
anonymity, personal space privacy, and communications [135, 90, 199]; (iii) the social
network service providers policies towards the selling and/or sharing of users' information to other companies (e.g., third-party applications) [135, 199]; and (iv) the users'
privacy behaviors towards other users and the privacy policies [90]. In this article, we
focus on the last privacy category which is related to the privacy decision-making process (i.e., information disclosure and privacy policy choice). Our review work differs
from others [32, 135, 90, 199, 266] because it takes notice of all the decisions that users
make during the whole privacy decision-making process and reviews the mechanisms
proposed in the literature to aid users to make these decisions. As a consequence, this
article produces the following contributions: (i) a detailed description of all the decisions that users make during the whole privacy decision-making process in online
social networks; (ii) a representation of the potential problems arising from each of
the decisions of the online communication elements; (iii) the identification of a set of
essential requirements for the design of privacy mechanisms to address these potential
problems; (iv) a review of the current advances on privacy mechanisms; and, finally, (v)
a discussion of the open challenges in designing and implementing privacy mechanisms
and some tips for addressing them.

The remainder of the article is structured as follows. Section 2.2 describes the complexity and problems of users' privacy policy decisions, remarking the factors that produce
those problems and providing a series of possible requirements for the design of future
privacy mechanisms. Section 2.3 reviews the current advances made in each of those requirements. Section 2.4 discusses the future lines to deal with the open issues detected.
Finally, Section 2.5 presents some concluding remarks.

2.2   Privacy decision-making process

Any action that users perform in a social network environment stems from the need for
getting social benefit [118] and is always preceded by a privacy decision that limits the
potential costs/risks of the action. These privacy decisions are classified into two kinds:
1) the acceptance of a predefined privacy policy or 2) the choice of a specific privacy
policy. For the case of the first kind of privacy decisions, the acceptance of predefined
privacy policies, some of these are established in the general privacy policy statement
by the OSN service provider (e.g., the profile picture on Facebook that is compulso-
rily public nature). By joining a social network site, users have to accept the general
privacy policy statement and they face their first decision by providing their personal

information and accepting the predefined privacy policy for these data. Once their social account is created, they have several privacy decisions on their privacy settings that variate among the different social networks. Privacy options not included in the privacy settings, like possibly the visibility of mentions or tags, are part of the predefined privacy policies of the social network. We can find them in the general privacy policy statement or sometimes are summarized on informational pages provided by the OSN service providers (e.g., Facebook Help Centre[5], and Instagram Help Centre[6]). In other cases depend on the privacy decision made by other users. For example, when a user comments on another user's posts on Facebook or Instagram, the commenter user is accepting the privacy policy that the other user chose for the post. Depending on the social network, the number of predefined privacy policies changes, so users can make more or fewer privacy decisions. In all of these cases, if the user wants to complete the action, he/she is required to accept these conditions. It is usual that users accept them either by ignorance/unconsciousness (i.e., a lack of knowledge about these predefined privacy policies) or by unconcern (i.e., they do not think about the consequences). For the case of the second kind of privacy decisions, that are the rest of the actions in social networks, these actions require the users' choice of a privacy policy via privacy mechanisms for the content that they share. Independently of the privacy decision type, both cases have the same elements as traditional communication: a transmitter (the user), a message (the publication), a channel (the social network), a receiver (the audience), and feedback (likes, comments, etc.). It has been proved in business and economic studies that an individual always assesses the cost-benefit when facing a decision [210]. For avoiding the regret of the decision, the individual should have as perfect information as possible for properly assessing the cost-benefit of the decision. So, the privacy choice should consider the influence of the online communication elements in the estimation of cost-benefit. In addition, this cost-benefit should be aligned with the user goals or intentions (i.e., reach as many users as possible, share information only with trusted users, etc.). However, users do not have perfect information and/or a full understanding of all the possible risks [5]. Next, we introduce an example of a scenario to illustrate the problematics and complexity of privacy decisions. Figure 2.1 depicts the whole privacy decision-making process map of a user split by the individual decisions of communication elements, the problems raised from these choices, and the factors of the elements that are involved.

Step 0: Desire to share something. *"Bob wants to share a piece of information (e.g., an opinion about some topic, a lived experience, etc.) for getting a social benefit. Users' benefits* *are diverse and may be motivated by influencing others, increasing their reputation, receiving support, getting brand offers, connecting with a huge community, etc."*

The transmitter-user, who owns and decides to share the message, is who retains full responsibility for his/her actions in the OSN, even if multiple users own it. The risks are usually generated by his/her wrong decisions in choosing the other communication elements. The *personality* of the transmitter, his/her grade of *concern* about privacy issues, and his/her motivation for using social networks [248] are the basis for understanding the relationship with the other elements towards the assessment of the cost-benefit relationship. For example, people with a high value of openness are positively correlated with the number of users' likes, group associations, status updates, and they express emotions more frequently. However, they are negatively correlated with dense social networks (i.e., they tend to have friends who are more disperse socially) [19]. That is because their benefit is related to these kinds of actions. Conversely, there are users that are more aware of and thus more jealousy about their privacy. Therefore, they prefer to disclose their information only with close friends or, as other research works state, they do not disclose it because they are jealous of their privacy and they do not trust privacy mechanisms [240, 216]. The other factor of the transmitter is his/her usage *motivation*. It has been detected several usage motivations on social networks (enjoyment, self-presentation, relationship building, keep up with people and news) [151]. Depending on the transmitter's motivation, some actions could report more or less cost/benefit. So, it is important to consider all of these aspects of the transmitter or be able to remember them to the transmitter for avoiding possible future regrets of his/her privacy decisions.

Step 1: Choose a channel.   *"Followed by Bob's desire for social disclosing. The first decision Bob has to make is choosing the channel."*

The channel is the environment where the information is going to be transmitted (see Figure 2.1, step-1 column). In this work domain, it refers to an online social network but also the communication way within the network, i.e., a user's wall publication, a story, a direct message, etc. The choice of this element is mainly motivated by *popularity* (i.e., if Bob's friends are in the social network) and *trust* (i.e., Bob's trust towards the social network) [151]. A nice indicator of a social network's popularity may are the number of active users that use it, or from the users' perspective, the number of their friends and acquaintances that are on it. Regarding trust on a social network, it usually involves behaviors such as protection and usage that the social network does towards users' information (i.e., their privacy). Privacy risks such as unauthorized access [207] are caused by vulnerabilities in the social network and/or by human errors

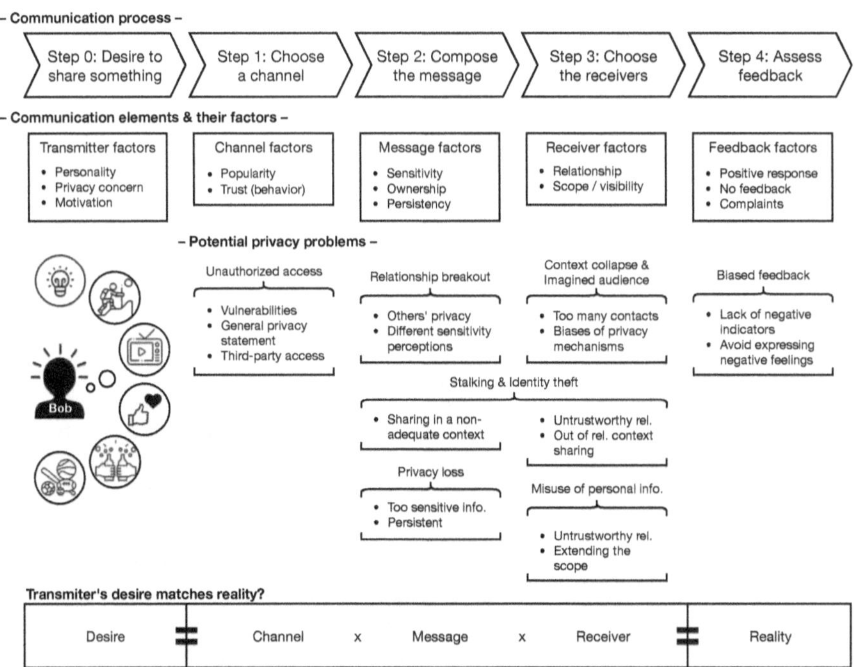

Figure 2.1: Privacy decision-making by steps, highlighting the involved communication elements, their factors, and their potential privacy risks.

of the social network provider. Others are related to the treatment of personal data and how third-party companies have access to them [159]. However, the only indicators of social network mistrust are the news about information leakages, attacks, or company bad behaviors, and not all this information reaches common users. To remedy this situation, user-friendly metrics should be developed that objectively evaluate the behavior of social network providers. Even so, as we stated in Section 2.1, this article does not focus on analyzing privacy aspects that involve privacy and security of systems, so we assume that channel decision is already made and we just consider the users' perceptions toward the social network. For example, trust as an indicator of usage. The higher the user's trust in the social network, the higher the user's participation and engagement to the social network [151].

Step 2: Compose the message. *"Once the channel is decided, Bob has to choose the specific piece of information to disclose. This piece of information may be personal information (in several*

*ways and sensitivity grades) and it can be related to Bob; or related to other users, which makes
the privacy decision harder. In addition, Bob has to give it a format (text or graphics) to compose
the final message that will be shared (i.e., a social network post)."*

The message is an important and (in turn) complex element in online communication (see Figure 2.1, step-2 column). The message may contain *sensitive* information and that information usually remains permanently online until the owner decides to delete it. Generally, this information refers to personal data about the transmitter and sometimes about other users (co-*ownership*), e.g., in party photos or group selfies, which increases the complexity of sensitivity estimation. Other users could have different perceptions of their privacy or other goal motivations, so the trade-off between social benefits and privacy costs have to be made and combined with all users involved. Furthermore, the sensitivity of a piece of information has, for some kind of information, an ambiguous value and depends on the user's interpretations and socio-cultural factors [221]. For example, religion is highly sensitive in areas where there is a high degree of sectarian conflict. Most of the privacy risks and privacy regretted decisions are related to the sensitivity of the message or to the context associated with the information [270, 88]. When users share too much information about themselves to others or the information is too sensitive, there is a risk of privacy loss with potential consequences for users as relationship breakouts, bad reputation, loss of job/educational opportunities, etc. Other risks available online associated with the information contained in the message are potentially related to stalking [170], identity theft [33], and the misuse of personal information [104]. All of these risks could be reduced with a lower exposition in social networks (i.e., reducing the details about the information disclosed).

Moreover, the *persistence* of information over time is another remarkable factor. Generally uploaded information is online indefinably and that can cause privacy issues because users forget their items with time and later new relationships could have access to them. It has been shown that posting old memories in social networks has generated privacy conflicts [242]. Fading privacy policies, i.e., reducing the final audience or even hiding the content completely (only accessible for the owner) could be a good alternative. In fact, a new way of disclosing information has raised in popularity in the last years in all the social network services, the Stories. Stories are effectively another news feed, but one that relies on visual rather than written information. Once posted, a story stays viewable for 24 hours, which allows users to break the idea of posting only perfect information. After that, the story disappears.

Step 3: Choose the receivers. *"At the time Bob is going to disclose the post, the social network
requests Bob to choose a privacy policy using the social network privacy mechanism. Most com-*

mon and used privacy mechanisms are based on social circles with the following options: Public, Friends, Specific friends/lists, and Only me. In this step, Bob's decision will be about the receiver users who will have access to the Bob's message."

In this case, the receiver is another important and complex element in social networks due to online communication usually is directed to multiple receiver-users (see Figure 2.1, step-3 column). Deciding which privacy policy to set up for a message implies deciding which receivers will have access to the publication in social networks. Nowadays, social network users manage a huge number of user's relationships. On Facebook, the average number of friends is 338[7]. According to Dunbar's theory [78], an individual is cognitively able to manage a limited number of people with whom he/she can maintain stable social relationships. Dunbar proposed a number of 150 stable relationships. This huge difference between real facts and the user's cognitive possibility may be a cause of privacy problems. Moreover, *relationships* might be of different nature and strength. Dunbar proposed an explanation for this difference with a relationship hierarchy of concentric groups (based on the strength tie): relations that exceed the 150 stable relationships refer to acquaintances or unknown people; the group formed by the 150 refers to the tribe of the individual (casual friends); around 50 of these are identified as the individual's clan, people the individual would consider his/her close friends; the following 15 refers to very good friends and family with whom the individual might spend his/her free time; while the first 5 refers to the best and more intimate relations.

Regarding the receiver-users, once they interact with the others' messages, they give them visibility. The *scope* of a receiver-user might extend too much the information of the transmitter (especially due to re-sharing actions), losing the transmitter's privacy and/or reaching an unexpected audience. To have influencing characteristics—whether personal attributes like credibility, expertise, or enthusiasm, or network attributes such as connectivity or centrality—are advantages in the information dissemination process [11]. Influential users can initiate and conduct the dissemination of a sharing action more efficiently than "normal" users [20]. Therefore, influential users in networks are normally more responsible for large cascades of information diffusion and contribute to increasing the privacy risk. Even so, the transmitter has to assess the privacy decision for each receiver-user in his/her list of contacts and for each message he/she decides to disclose on the social network. That requires matching the factors regarding the receiver such as their relationship and the receiver's actions scope/visibility with the factors regarding the message such as sensitivity, ownership of the information, and persistence. Bad matches of receivers and messages could facilitate privacy issues as exposed above (stalking, identity theft, and misuse of personal information).

This is a very hard and heavy task for social network users because of the number of required assessments and their complexity.

Another aspect of deciding the receivers of a publication is related to the privacy mechanisms provided by most of social networks. They are based on social circles and contexts concepts for determining the audience, i.e., which users will receive (have access to) the owner's post (*Bob* in our case). The borderline that defines and isolates them is more clear in offline communications than in online communications. Due to the excessive simplification of privacy mechanisms of social networks, these mechanisms have biases that generate that users usually have only one social circle (Friends on Facebook, Followers on Instagram, etc.). These social circles are predefined by the social network (via user acceptance of relationship connection), are created by users that selected each of their members, or are automatically generated by relationship-inferring techniques [181, 165] (Facebook Smart Lists[8]). The most common biases of privacy mechanisms of nowadays social networks are the *context collapse* and the *imagined audience*. The *context collapse* is produced by the default social circles provided by social networks [68]. Examples of these social circles are the "followers" audiences on Instagram, the "friends" social circle on Facebook, and the "followers" (users) on Twitter, where users from family, work, and friendship contexts (even unknown users) are inside them. The *context collapse* occurs when different social groups with their own rules and routines of information merge with each other in a default group. A potential example of this problem is when a user decides to share a picture on social networks of her/him-self on a party smoking or drinking some alcoholic beverage and uses a default social circle. This picture might be potentially accessible by the user's family, coworkers, acquaintances, friends inside the party context, and other friends outside to the party context. This scenario may generate the following risks: legal risks, in the case that the user does not have enough age for alcohol consumption; family issues, in the case that his/her family do not accept the user smoke habit; relationship breaking, in the case that a friend was not invited to the party; etc. An opposite example of this problem is that users known the *context collapse* bias and they share nothing to avoid potential risks, losing also the opportunity of making benefits. Therefore, if users would have biases-free privacy mechanisms, they could make more suitable privacy decisions. Another bias produced is known as *invisible audience* or *imagined audience* [31]. This bias is slightly related to *context collapse*. It refers to the audience the user is not aware of, or the user did not know they could see his/her publications [176]. Previous works have shown that users are not capable to remember or identify all their social network friends [65], and they think that the privacy policy chosen for sharing an item matches their desired audience (imagined). However, the imagined audience does not actually fit with the privacy policy chosen, and other undesired users are included in it. Moreover, prior work has shown that privacy mechanisms are often difficult to understand and use, and users do not have full knowledge and enough time to evaluate all potential scenarios [5].

Step 4: Assess feedback. *"Once Bob made the privacy decision, he starts to receive feedback from other users in the form of likes, comments, supports, or regrets if someone does not agree with Bob's post or Bob has violated another's privacy."*

The feedback/responses received by the transmitter's contacts is an element to take into account because it provides real facts about the social benefits and/or privacy risks of the transmitter's decisions made (see Figure 2.1, step-4 column). Nowadays, social networks provide more facilities to express *positive feedback* and support to others than to express *negative feedback* or conflicts among them. In addition, users avoid expressing these negative feelings until there are serious conflicts [270]. Therefore, some content could have a cost for the users and might not be detected by current social network indicators. New indicators for estimating the effect of a message in a social network could help users to balance the cost-benefit trade-off offering them more complete information about the privacy decision-making process. These indicators could be estimated from previous actions on social networks as indicators of potential benefits or costs. Furthermore, these indicators could also provide to the users' privacy decisions greater explainability of their adequacy to users' interests.

Repetition. *"Bob repeats this cycle each time he wants to interact in social networks."*

A recent report about social media[9] (2019) shows that users generate a huge amount of traffic of personal data, around 18 millions of text posts and 2 millions of media posts per minute. Therefore, users are confronted a lot of times per day with the privacy decision-making process without having perfect information or understanding fully all the possible risks of their decisions. Additionally, privacy is a complex and messy concept for social network users due to all the involved factors [231]. Most of users perceive the privacy risks as being abstract and psychologically distant, and more related to the distant future. For these decisions regarding privacy, the social network services do not provide any support for them, which produces users to put privacy in the background. Whether social network providers facilitate users with clear and understandable information about privacy, users could better make their decisions about privacy. Social network providers have tools for identifying others on pictures, sensitive content on messages such as nude photos, offensive text but they do not use them to aid on users' decisions, they just use them for banning specific content. An interesting (and maybe needed) point of view might be the combination of metrics and human-computer interfaces to depict and thus complete the information needed for users to make a non-regrettable decision regarding privacy. This could be particularly interesting for vulnerable or novice/amateur users such as teenagers who are initiating in their usage and have limited abilities for self-regulation and complex decision-making [10]. Furthermore, research works such as [179] have shown that most of the time users regret a message seconds later of sharing it (immediately or later during the conversation). Therefore, the information provided could give users enough time to reflect on the privacy decision.

From the whole privacy decision-making process in online social networks, we have summarized in Table 2.1 for each of the above steps all the potential problems including the relationship of identified factors that raise them and the expected requirements that should be addressed by privacy mechanisms. We refer factors as the properties of the online communication elements that in some way promote and/or are responsible to produce the problems and regrets of users' privacy decision-making. Regarding requirements, we refer them as the properties that privacy mechanisms and privacy policy solutions should be fulfilled to reduce and/or minimize the problems and regrets of online social network users.

2.3 Advances on privacy mechanisms

This section reviews the most relevant privacy models proposed for online social networks. In each subsection, we focus on one of the above identified requirements (see Table 2.1) to introduce the advances made by previous works.

2.3.1 Preferences-centered requirement

Each time users share a photo, comment on a post, give like to some content, interact with another user, etc. they do it by their interests [151]. These interests variate in a wide range (self-presentation, maintaining a relationship, building new relationships, influencing others, reputation, enjoyment, etc.) and a huge number of factors could be involved in a permit/denial action for a user and a specific piece of infor-

Step	Problematics	Factor	→	Requirement
#0	Differences on users' motivations	Transmitter's motivation	→	Preferences-centered
#1	Unauthorized access	Channel's behavior	→	*(out of the work scope)*
#2	Privacy loss, Stalking,	Message sensitivity	→	Sensitivity inferring
	Identity theft,	Message co-ownership	→	Multi-user privacy
	Relationship breakout	Message persistence	→	Message-fading
#3	Stalking, Identity theft,	Rel. nature & strength	→	Relationship inferring
	Context collapse,	Receptor's scope	→	Scope inferring
	Imagined audience, Misuse	Audience biases	→	Fine-grained
	of personal information			
#4	Lack of negative indicators	Feedback biases	→	Privacy risk inferring
Rep.	Complexity of privacy	Transmitter's burden	→	Automation
	decisions, Differences on	Transmitter's privacy	→	Privacy-preserving
	users' perceptions,	Transmitter's understanding	→	Explainable
	Non-privacy-expert users,			
	High repetition			

Table 2.1: Summary of the requirements identified in the privacy decision-making process considering the factors of the communication elements and reported problematics.

mation. This information is collected or estimated by some research works as users' preferences. There is no consensed way to collect this kind of information. Some works such as the Yang et al. [288] work uses the users' preferences as a weighted parameter of their model that customizes the utility function calculation. There is no information about how these preferences are defined or estimated. They use them to balance the users' perception of their social benefits and privacy concerns. However, other research works (as those based on rule-systems [49, 147]) consider the knowledge and the derived rules as the users' preferences. Another way of representing the users' preferences is by assessing personal features like the stubbornness and the comfort of users when sharing information to negotiate a privacy policy as in the case of Rajtmajer et al. [212] work. However, there is not a comparative work that tested which users' characteristics better represent their preferences or the effect they have on users' information disclosure.

Finally, other research works like [93, 241] use the social circles/privacy groups of traditional privacy mechanisms as users' preferences (i.e., *Private, Friends, Friends of Friends,* or *Public*). This perspective allows their metrics to be more precise because they minimally modify users' privacy decisions. Despite that, the privacy mechanisms that provide recommendations do not consider adaptative or agreed-on results with the user.

They just present the solution to users who finally accept or reject it. These solutions are
mostly based on a computed recommendation that maximizes the user's social utilities.
However, as Hu et al. [117] state, these proposals may not always work well in practice, as they do not capture the social idiosyncrasies considered by users in the real-life
and users' behavior is far from perfectly rational as these game-theoretic approaches
assume. We only found in the literature the work of Fogues et al. [94] where they consider several iterations for the recommendation. In each iteration, new features are
taken into account to improve the current and future recommendations but this scenario is just considered for multi-party decisions and users only can accept or reject
the recommendation (they do not propose). It could be interesting that privacy mechanisms could not only recommend, but also adapt the recommendation to specific user
demands via user's proposals. Moreover, by providing indicators and explainability
about privacy solutions, users will have more sense of this agreed-on solution.

2.3.2 Sensitivity inferring requirement

Privacy issues emerge mainly by disclosing personal information. The identification
of the individual is a strong requirement to talk about personal information, without
his/her identification, it is more difficult to link that information to a physical person.
However, the identification is possible with some specific anonymized personal information [188], so, any information is still valuable if it is linked to other information
and it is possible to deduce or extract new data. In the online social network domain,
identification is usually a common feature because it maximizes the benefits that social
networks provide (communication, support, self-presentation, influence, etc.). There,
users become identifiable by sharing their real names and photographs. Until recently,
social network services did not put too much interest in developing message sensitivity
inferring mechanisms for users. Social networks developed tools for detecting offensive
or sexual content, but they just used them for banning specific content. These tools are
mainly internal and are not available to users. In the case of Flickr, the popular social network for photo sharing, users have the possibility of tagging their content and
define different privacy policies based on these tags, but no one intelligent mechanism
is provided to them to protect their personal information. In the last year, only Instagram introduced an advisor tool[10] for preventing content that can support bullying
activities.

With the new features of data mining and the interest in social networks and privacy, new (and still scarce) approaches on feature extraction have been applied to analyze the sensitivity of users generated content. Some of these approaches estimate the emotions or stress that produces the shared content to determine its sensitivity, while more interesting ones (we will focus on them) distinguish personal from non-personal information. All of these works converge to a clear premise: not all of the personal information has the same value. Legislation such as the GDPR[11], NIST[12], or UKAN[13] (which emerged from the need to protect users' data) distinguishes different levels of data sensitivity. Companies that buy, sell, and exchange users' data as an economic resource also consider different values for data based on the kind of information provided and whether they can link it to other data [172]. Companies have included data as part of their business model in a data-driven economy. However, all the attempts to estimate a sensitivity value of information (by companies, researchers, and legislators) had the next issues. On the one hand, there is no agreement about the sensitivity value that each piece of information has. Furthermore, new questions arise such as which value has a piece of information if it is linked to another piece? or how should be expressed this value of sensitivity? On the other hand, users are not completely aware of the value or sensitivity of their data. Moreover, they have different perceptions of sensitivity for their personal data depending on socio-cultural factors [221]. For this reason, most works request the sensitivity of data as an input of their models, while a few works make simple approximations of the sensitivity value of data for automatically recommend privacy policies or for warning users about the information they are going to share.

We have reviewed relevant works that made some advances in this field, highlighting their strengths and weaknesses. Table 2.2 summarizes these works based on the techniques used to infer the sensitivity of the information and the properties of the sensitivity value solutions. Misra and Such [182, 183] built an agent for recommending personalized access controls in single and multi-party privacy conflicts considering the content of a publication to make a privacy decision. In these works, they highlight the difficulty of the content analysis automation due to is still far in terms of accuracy. For this reason, they use user-generated tags about their content (which reveal topics and contexts about information). The authors' agent uses them to deny or allow access for each potential information receiver. The approach adopted by the authors is similar to Flickr, where the popular social network for photo sharing employs users to classify their pictures according to their type. The authors' work could be able to sometimes deduce sensitive information and allow access only to trusty users if this were the reg-

---

[11]European General Data Protection Regulation
[12]National Institute of Standards and Technology
[13]UK Anonymisation Network

	Research works				
	[182, 183]	[261]	[50]	[120, 263]	[291]
Sensitivity inferring way					
- user's intervention	✓				
- ML techniques	✓	✓	✓		✓
- information content				✓	
- text analysis		✓	✓		
- image analysis					✓
Sensitivity properties					
- binary value		✓	✓		✓
- categories	✓	✓			✓
- continuous value				✓	

Table 2.2: A comparison of research works focused on the detection of personal information and its sensitivity, remarking the detection technique and the properties of the computed solution.

ular user's behavior. However, this perspective lacks personal information detection and cannot always protect users' privacy.

There are other works that use *Machine Learning* (ML) text categorization techniques to detect sensitive content. For instance, Vanetti et al. [261] propose an automatic generated rule system that analyzes the shared textual information to filter wall messages. They automatically assign categories of personal information for each publication. Specifically, they distinguish between personal and non-personal information. In addition, for the personal information, the authors distinguish violence, vulgar, offensive, hate, and sex categories. The accuracy of their classifiers makes their system a reliable one. Therefore, using these categories plus relationship information among user's contacts improves the protection of the user's privacy in social networks. However, their categories are not enough wider, so, users could share highly sensitive information such as his/her health condition, credit card number or passport number without any response of the system. Another example is from Caliskan et al. [50], they developed a more complex and wider textual detector of personal information also based on ML techniques. They combine topic modeling, named entity recognition, privacy ontology, sentiment analysis, and text normalization to represent privacy features. In this way, they are able to detect a wide range of categories and information topics that they finally converge to the following 9 categories: location, medical, drug/alcohol, emotion, personal attacks, stereotyping, family/association details, personal details, personally identifiable information, and neutral/objective. Moreover, they make one more distinction in these categories distinguishing between self or other users related information. The detector was used to provide privacy scores about social network users comparing the proportion of personal messages with the total of their posted messages. This promising application only was used (to the best of our knowledge) to depict their users' population, while it could be easily extended for advising users about the sensitivity of their publications or for recommending privacy policies that balance privacy risks and social benefits. Furthermore, a distinction of sensitivity values for these categories could be done. Weights could be used to assess better the privacy risks for disclosing this kind of information. Still, their work can be continued because they released their software and ML models to the community without restrictions.

Information Content (IC) theory, which measures the inverse of the appearance probability of a term in a corpus, has been also used to distinguish between general and specific terms. This idea was used in [120, 263] to propose a system for automatic semantic annotation by using knowledge bases and linguistic tools. Their system is able to make distinctions between values of the sensitivity of the information. The premise of this theory is that most general terms appear more times than specific ones and, in turn, these have less sensitivity value. A simple example is the *disease* term, this term provides a less informative value than a specific disease like *cancer* and, in turn, than a specific type of cancer like the *carcinoma*. Despite the specificity that this approach provides in terms of sensitivity assessment, it lacks weighted categories (as the previous work [50]) that specify the maximum and minimum sensitivity value for this kind of information. Besides, another problem emerges because this approach requires a "perfect" textual corpus, that means an updated, free of biases, and balanced corpus.

Taking into account the popularity of multimedia content generated in social networks, the analysis of sensitivity has been also applied to images. Yu et al. [291] address the privacy protection of this kind of content via the analysis of images. Using deep multi-task learning techniques, they detect the underlying privacy-sensitive objects to applying a blurring filter to them. This work considers any object in an image and then classifies the objects in categories where finally distinguishes between sensitive and non-sensitive objects. Even so, it needs a strong support of which objects have more sensitivity value than others and a formal definition of other factors related to the privacy decision-making process (e.g., about the potential audience, user's preferences, etc.). Another factor that this work as well as most works do not take into consideration is the suggestion of privacy policies. Most works recommend policies based on previous users' decisions and preferences. However, many users do not make a proper use of the mechanisms provided by social networks to establish their privacy policies [5]. Therefore, it is required also privacy-centered instead of mechanisms only transmitter's preference-centered.

2.3.3 Multi-user privacy requirement

One of the requirements for current privacy mechanisms is the management of the privacy settings of items shared among users of the social network that affect the intimacy of several individuals. This requirement has become indispensable due to each time more media content where several individuals appear is shared and their privacy is also involved (e.g., group photos). At present, OSNs leave the responsibility of setting the proper privacy policy for the shared item on the hands of the item's owner. This decision may suppose a threat to the privacy of the other involved users. In this subsection, we review the advances taken on providing support for choosing the appropriate privacy policy to publications in which content is co-owned by more than one user.

As Such and Criado [240] state, multi-party privacy is a very complex problem because it requires (i) identifying the users whose information is related to them in some way, (ii) negotiating a privacy solution that satisfies all of the parts before sharing the item, and (iii) solving conflicts emerged from discrepancies on users' preferences. The identification of users involved in some way with the information has been not addressed yet in the literature. There are only a few research works [126, 242] that have analyzed which kind of multi-party privacy conflicts are given online in order to find out the ways users are involved in a co-owned publication. In all of them, they concluded that the understanding of co-ownership is crucial to design tools for managing co-owned items. For example, Such et al. [242] performed an empirical study to analyze which kind of conflicts are produced on multi-party privacy situations. Through this work, they found out new ways of multi-party privacy conflicts such as (i) uploader-users being co-owners of the publication in spite of not being themselves in the photo, or (ii) co-owners who were not in the photo themselves but something of them was in the photo (their car, house, room, pet, etc.) or someone they felt responsible for (e.g., their children). These findings, in turn, reveal that the co-owners identification may be a more difficult task than one might think at first.

Conversely, most research works have focused their efforts on providing multi-party privacy solutions based on recommendations with automatic negotiations and potential conflicts solving. For instance, Mester et al. [178] developed a framework where agents interact to reach a consensus before publishing a post. A user agent is aware of the privacy concerns, expectations, and friends of the user. When the user is about to post new content, its agent reasons on behalf of the user to decide which other users would be affected by the post and contacts with their users' agents. The authors' proposal was focused on fulfilling the following properties: automation, which is minimizing the number of interactions with users; fairness, by maximizing the users' satisfaction with the reached agreement; concealment, that refers to not exposing the reasons of the disagreement; and protection, which means not allowing access to the information until an agreement is reached. However, these properties were just validated by case-based scenarios without real user experimentation, so this study lacks a realistic validation. Furthermore, they do not mention how the user's preferences are collected or estimated and neither how the co-owners of a publication are identified. They do not also explain how their proposal can be adapted to new changes or user's preferences, which have shown a high variability [117]. Another example of multi-party privacy solutions based on recommendations with automatic negotiations is proposed by Rajtmajer et al. [212]. They propose a privacy evolutionary model where all the users involved in a publication negotiate for allowing or denying the access to users of the potential audience. Authors characterize the users' properties with a set of features (such as their comfort and stubbornness towards a solution) and the content sensitivity. Using the well-known game-theoretic solution concepts such as the Nash equilibrium, they compute an iterative solution, that converges to a balanced risk-benefit value for all the involved users. This solution reduces all users' interests into two features: communicative motivation and stubbornness. This approach lacks validation of these features for the user's daily privacy decisions in the social networks domain. Moreover, the users' representation is too vague and may not represent all the social idiosyncrasies considered by users in the real-life [117]. Another remarkable example of multi-party privacy solution is the proposal of Such and Criado [239]. Their proposal consisted of a mediator that detects privacy conflicts based on users' preference vectors and resolves the conflict. For that, the mediator estimates the item sensitivity, the relative importance of the conflict, and the user's willingness. Finally, it suggests a solution according to three main principles that combine the users' traditional and well-known multi-party coping strategies: the uploader overwrites, majority voting, and veto voting. The main issue of work is that they are just focused on the transmitter preferences to compute the solution (i.e., transmitter preferences-centered approach) instead of also promoting solutions that preserve users' privacy (i.e., privacy-preserving approach).

Finally, there are interesting solutions that propose argued negotiations and recommendations of privacy policies. These solutions provide some kind of explainability to the computed solutions. On the one hand, Kokciyan et al. [147] propose an argumentation approach for solving privacy disputes in online social networks. They model users' preferences and privacy constraints as semantic rules. This proposal is based on a previous work [178], where authors also assessed the properties of persuasion, in a way that a user can question and rebut a specific claim of another user during the negotiation;

and external consultation, that allows agents to consider rules from other agents to
extend their knowledge base. However, the evaluation of this proposal has been done
through interviews and scenario-based cases. Therefore, as the majority of works, they
lack integration of their privacy mechanism in a social network where the real effec-
tivity of their proposal is assessed with users' interactions. On the other hand, Fogues
et al. [93] propose also the use of argumentation, in addition to the traditional features considered relevant for privacy decisions such as context of the information and
the relationships, user's preferences, and information sensitivity. In this case, they use
four argumentation schemes for the negotiation that consists of arguments from good
consequences, bad consequences, an exceptional case, and popular opinion. However,
they just consider three possible privacy policies in their approach (i.e., share with all,
common, themselves) which limits the capabilities of their proposal in real scenarios
and has a high risk of biases like *context collapse*.

2.3.4   Relationship inferring requirement

Online social networks try constantly to differentiate between users and the nature of
their relationships. However, users are usually either friends or strangers, there are no
intermediate or specialized relationships between them. This approach does not faith-
fully reproduce the real human relationships. Some social networks such as Facebook
have mechanisms to distinguish communities or groups through users' profile information, e.g., users who studied in the same high school, users who lived in the same place,
etc. This information is usually used to organize contacts in access lists, which can be
used by users to set the privacy policy for their posts. Furthermore, a user can also
make different specializations for their contacts from acquaintances to best friends
which bring his/her contacts different access permissions to his/her activity registry.
This feature allows users to define new contexts and setting, in a discrete way, the tie
strength of a relationship. The main problems of this approximation are the following:
(i) it just uses the group/community detection feature for allowing or denying access
without considering the tie strength between members; (ii) it requires users to complete
their profiles; and (iii) these features are not very well-known, understandable or easy
to use, so, only experienced users are able to use and configure them in their benefit.

In this research field, there are a lot of works that have explored ways to esti-
mate/compute the relationship strength and type between users of a social network.
Most of them take information from the users' interactions [130, 91] and consider users
who are similar in socially significant ways (i.e., homophily) [282, 91]. On the one
hand, it has been shown that the higher the number of interactions between users, the

	Research works								
	[130]	[282]	[91, 92]	[289]	[262]	[233]	[261]	[182, 183]	[287]
Relationship inferring way									
- interactions metadata	✓	✓	✓	✓	✓	✓	✓	✓	✓
- homophily		✓	✓						
- blacklists							✓	✓	
- network structure	✓		✓				✓	✓	✓
- text analysis				✓					
Relationship properties									
- tie strength	✓		✓	✓	✓	✓	✓	✓	✓
- multiple relationship types								✓	
- community			✓			✓	✓	✓	
- trust loss									✓

Table 2.3: A comparison of research works focused on relationship properties detection for managing privacy decisions, remarking the detection technique and the properties of the computed solution.

stronger the relationship. On the other hand, homophily states that the more two people have in common (job, friends, hobbies, etc.), the more likely it is that these two people have a strong relationship. Moreover, homophilic information is also used for context detection in relationships. Although the estimation accuracy is moderately high, these works do not differentiate the kind of interaction, i.e., whether the interaction among users is a neutral, an irritating or a pleasant communication. Some works explore new ways of computing relationship properties that extend the traditional ones, mainly based on analyzing the user-generated content [289]. This point of view turns out interesting by the popularity of social networks centered in graphical content (e.g., Instagram), by exploring the features of graphics that could provide new (and potentially relevant) information. Nowadays the works that address the image analysis use graphic features directly and in a simplistic way for tagging graphical content with a default privacy policy [46, 253, 142].

Once the users' relationship properties are inferred, the privacy mechanisms proposed by research works make different approximations combining them with other factors to compute the best audience. Below, we highlight the most relevant works that use users' relationship properties. A summary of these works is also included in Table 2.3. First, we highlight the work presented by Vidyalakshmi et al. [262]. They introduce a framework for calculating a privacy score metric considering users' personal attitudes towards privacy and communication information. This work uses the relationship data as the input of a cubic bezier curve function with four points represented as (i) the origin point stated at zero coordinate, (ii) the user's privacy attitude, (iii) the user's communicative attitude, and (iv) a threshold point. However, authors just

compute the relationship property as an approximation of the frequency of user interactions without considering more relationship features. The work proposes the use of a
function as a balance between users' benefits and privacy risks. Even so, it is not clear
the meaning of the privacy score value given to the user's contacts. Second, another
interesting work is the PriMa framework for users' privacy protection introduced by
Squicciarini et al. [233]. The work includes a very complete formalization where the
relationship properties are used to compute an access score as the balance between
these relationship properties and a risk score for the action. The relationship properties used are composed by the type of relationship (represented as a common weight)
and a trust/reputation value. The main problem of this approximation is that the relationship definition is too vague and, to the best of our knowledge, the framework was
not finally tested. Third, we reviewed a proposal of Vanetti et al. [261] of an automatic
generated rule system. The system analyzes shared textual information, relationship
properties, and previously privacy decisions made to filter wall messages. An interesting approach of this work is that the authors use not only the relationship type
and the tie strength value, but also the distance between not connected users to infer
more complex relationships. However, we consider their approach is limited because
little knowledge is taken from the *publisher* user, who has high variability in his/her
motivations and his/her behavior is far from perfectly rational [117]; and because no
relationship context is considered, which can distinguish different friend groups. Moreover, the evaluation made on their system lacks a final user's validation. Fourth, the
proposal of an agent for recommending personalized access controls is presented by
Misra and Such [182, 183]. The agent extracts information mainly from relationships
(types and strength), blacklisted contacts, and tagged content (which reveals topics
and contexts about information). In these works, they used a well-tested algorithm to
detect overlapped communities in social networks, the *Clique Percolation Method* (CPM).
However, that algorithm does not give clues about the context of these communities
or social contexts. Therefore, users must indicate them. Finally, Xu et al. [287] provide
a new trust evaluation point of view oriented to multi-party privacy scenarios. They
consider that relationships could have negative values. At the moment, the other works
had considered only positive interactions between users to measure their tie strength.
In their work, Xu et al. consider interactions among users with negative intentions or
results. These negative interactions are mainly based on privacy issues and conflicts
generated by the uploader user with the rest of the co-owned users. The last two research works propose interesting privacy management mechanisms, but we consider
that they do not cover some of the requirements highlighted in this work such as the
adaptation to the user's interests, and the explainability of the solutions.

2.3.5 Scope inferring requirement

The sharing-action of information implies indirectly the loss of control of that piece of information. In offline communication, information dissemination is produced by mouth-to-mouth which sometimes may generate a loss of details. Nevertheless, in online communication, users can re-share the original user's post and, thanks to the facility of technology, it can spread rapidly and become viral [56]. Most social networks provide users with mechanisms to re-share information, but they do not check if the action produces a privacy violation. Current research works focused on social media behaviors and information dissemination analyze which are the factors and the specific conditions that cause this behavior [39, 162], but only a few researchers analyze that behavior from a privacy point of view and propose solutions. Below, we review the most relevant research works.

Yang et al. [288] present a privacy recommender system that computes a trade-off between users' privacy risks and social benefits. In their metric computation, they associate the re-sharing action, the low trust values, and the potential values a user's information may have (i.e., if someone posts a selfie, then the gender values that could reveal are male or female) as an indicator for predicting information leakages. Their risk estimation metric computes as an important factor for assessing the privacy risks of the action. Specifically, they adopt the information-theoretic framework [224] (based on the entropy principle) which is widely used to measure the amount of information leaked in secure systems. For that, the authors use the amount of all the possible information values in a publication, the probability of performing a re-sharing action, and the relationship strength toward a specific user to quantify the information that a sharing action leaks. This computation has limitations because each piece of information could have an infinite range of values. Conversely, Squicciarini et al. [233] present the PriMa framework for users' privacy protection, where they used another way to measure the users' scope. In their work, authors also use the scope as an indicator of the privacy risk of the action. In this situation, the scope is measured using a centrality metric which reflects the number of reachable users and also measuring the visibility of previous interactions. Then, the algorithm compares the difference between the post's author scope value and the potential receiver's scope value to estimate if there is a privacy risk. However, this proposal has not been proved on simulations or via real users' usage, so there is no data about its performance in real scenarios.

2.3.6 Fine-grained requirement

Fine-grained privacy policy solutions consist of providing different audiences for different kinds of messages and different transmitter intentions. Nowadays, this requirement is not fulfilled by current social network privacy mechanisms due to the high number of users' contacts and the documented biases on current privacy mechanisms. Regarding advances proposed by researchers, this requirement is theoretically fulfilled by the majority of works analyzed in this survey. This requirement is achieved as a consequence of fulfilling other requirements such as automation, relationship inferring, etc. where the audience is automatically computed and individually assessed. However, we put a note of emphasis on the "theoretically" adverb because none of these previous works have actually tested this requirement in a real social network environment.

2.3.7 Automation requirement

The privacy decision-making is a burdensome and complex task for users, and they have to make it several times per day with the use of social networks. It is natural that emerge solutions (from research works and social network services) that try to partially or completely solve the privacy decision-making in an automatic way, thus reducing the burden of users and helping them to protect their privacy. Most of the research works included in this survey study provide some kind of automation. In this subsection, we review the most relevant works that use automation splitting them into three groups depending on the base of their automation: rule-check, machine learning, and utility functions. Moreover, we also classify them depending on the result of the automation: an indicator value or a recommendation; and on the source of knowledge extraction: what others do, user's previous behavior, or principles and tested theories. Table 2.4 depicts the classification of the reviewed research works into these categories.

Rule-based automation

This kind of research works uses the rules specified by users and the automatic generation of rules to check which users have access to specific information. Current work examples that use this kind of automation are Calikli et al.[49] and Kokciyan et al. [147]. The first work presents *Privacy Dynamics*, an adaptive architecture that learns users' privacy norms. Their system acts as a middleware layer between the OSN platform and the user, analyzing all the information (relationships, history of sharing ac-

	Research works						
	[49]	[147]	[86]	[225]	[164]	[262]	[288]
Automation type							
- rule system	✓	✓					
- ML techniques	✓		✓	✓			
- utility function					✓	✓	✓
Automation based on							
- user's pre-behavior	✓	✓	✓				
- what other do		✓		✓			✓
- principles & assumptions					✓	✓	✓
Automation for							
- metric evaluation					✓	✓	✓
- feature extraction	✓		✓	✓	✓	✓	
- recommendation	✓	✓	✓	✓			✓

Table 2.4: A comparison of research works focused on the automation of some part of the privacy decision-making process.

tions, content analysis) to infer norms that detect and prevent conflicts. So, it learns from previous sharings' actions made by users. Finally, the solutions of their system are introduced to users in the way of a recommendation. The second work proposes an argumentation approach for solving privacy disputes in online social networks based on semantic rules. They model users' preferences and privacy constraints as semantic rules, differentiating them as inference rules and privacy rules, respectively. However, they do not focus on how the semantic rules are specified or how new ones are inferred. Their work is also dependant on an ontology that properly represents the knowledge. The main limitation of rule-based systems lies in the knowledge representation and the generation of new rules. These systems require a perfect representation of the knowledge with a complete ontology and systems capable to infer and generate new types of rules. Currently, rule-based systems are far from that utopia, their representation is usually incomplete and/or may generate inconsistent norms.

Machine learning automation

Most research works that use machine learning techniques use them to learn from previous experiences (i.e., datasets of publications labeled with a privacy policy) or to extract features from users' posts (mostly text and photos features). Fang and LeFevre [86] present a privacy wizard that suggests privacy policies to users for different items of their profiles such as real name, address, and birthday. They consider the previous

labeling process of friends as the input for their classifier. Then, the wizard infers labels
for the other remaining friends. Since their proposal is based on supervised learning,
users' participation is needed. Besides using machine learning for the classifier, they
also use it for feature extraction, especially for the detection of communities and other
profile data. Authors consider mutual friends as a community feature, while hobbies
or fan pages that a user likes are activity features. With a feature-vector representation, they learn the privacy policy for a specific user. The main idea of this work
is that users label a low portion of privacy decisions, and the wizard does the rest of
privacy decisions. Their evaluation results show that the wizard behaves better when
only communities are considered. The main restriction is that their proposal is just
applicable to profile data, not being considered the content of publications (text and
photos) neither activity interactions like comments and likes. So, other elements such
as images or videos are also excluded. That requires to enhance the wizard system to
consider new features of items. Shehab et al. [225] propose an approach based on the
assumption that similar or nearby users should have similar privacy permissions. Similarity is computed using both the users' profile attributes and social network metrics.
Authors use an iterative semi-supervised learning technique to provide privacy policy recommendations. This machine learning technique requires users to label a small
set of their friends and privacy policies for facilitating the labeling propagation. They
modeled the privacy labeling problem as a two-class classification problem giving each
user an allow/deny label for each item. This solution make the labeling automation in
a fine-grained way. However, accessing not only to their information but also to their
privacy policy decisions for that information could be considered a privacy violation
of the own individual. Conversely, other research works focus on using machine learning techniques to extract features of information, users, and relationships as the works
reviewed in subsections 2.3.4, 2.3.2, and 2.3.5.

Utility-function-based automation

Finally, other research works base their automation on the computation of self-
developed utility functions which assess relevant aspects for the privacy decision-
making, measuring and balancing also the potential social benefits of the action. For
instance, Liu and Terzi [164] developed mathematical models and algorithms for computing the privacy score of users in online social networks. The mathematical models
are created on the support of premises like "the more sensitive information a user reveals, the higher his/her privacy score". Authors estimate the score according to the
sensitivity of information users' reveals and the visibility that the information has in
the social network. To estimate sensitivity and visibility values, they use concepts from

Item Response Theory (a psychometric theory evaluation method). This work is mainly focused on the analysis of users' profile items to compute their privacy score, while privacy issues related to daily activities such as status updates, likes or comments are not taken into account to compute the users' privacy score. Even so, this is a clear example of a research work that uses utility functions to automatically assess a privacy-related concept. Another example is the work of Vidyalakshmi et al. [262]. They present a framework for calculating a privacy score metric considering users' personal attitudes towards privacy and communication information. They estimate a Privacy Index (PIDX) which is offered as a service to help users on privacy decisions. The PIDX values range from 0 to 100 and are also computed using the IRT (Item Response Theory) for the profile data and the user's ego-subnetwork (i.e., the subnetwork composed by the root user, their contact users, and their relationships). With all this data, they apply a function based on a cubic bezier curve to draw a smooth curve where data is represented as points and a final privacy score is resultant of this function. Finally, they tested the proposal with a synthetic experiment. From experimental results, we can deduce that estimating the different factors included in the utility function is not easy and the distribution of the real values could do not match with the used cubic bezier curve. An interesting utility-function design that assesses the social benefits and the privacy risks of social network decisions was proposed by Yang et al. [288]. For defining privacy risks, they consider two assumptions: (i) the more sensitive information a user shares, the greater its privacy risk, and (ii) the more information is predicted to be leaked to unintended recipients and untrustworthy friends, the greater the user's privacy risks. For defining social benefits, they consider the following aspects: (i) a user gains social benefit if his/her information is seen by his/her selected social circles, and (ii) the social interactions emerged by an action or decision also increase the user's benefit. The design of this utility function was validated through experiments, although not reliable results can be extracted because they made the experimentation via simulated data and assuming normal distributions. Finally, the usage of this function is focused on producing recommendations of privacy policies, including the users who could access to a piece of information (i.e., access lists). Although the above automation works evaluate privacy management from a more privacy-related perspective via metrics which are mainly based on principles and basic assumptions of social networks and communication, they did not test the combination of these principles and basic assumptions on users' real behavior. For example, the general principle "the more sensitive information a user reveals, the higher his/her privacy score" could be not right if a user shares a sensitive content with intimate contacts.

2.3.8 Privacy-preserving requirement

As we stated, users' privacy refers to determining when, how, and to what extent information about themselves is communicated [278]. A great number of research works take as data sources previous sharing behaviors [86, 225] and users' preferences [93, 241] to compute/recommend privacy solutions. However, it has been shown that users do not always choose suitable privacy policies. Following the above definition, any users' accepted privacy decision is valid in privacy terms. Despite the definition, it has been shown that users regret their own privacy decisions because they have make them with incomplete or unknown information. Furthermore, users perceive privacy risks as abstract and psychologically distant, and more related to the distant future, which makes users do not consider all possible consequences during their privacy decision-making process [109]. Because of these reasons, research works have focused on defining new metrics for assessing the privacy-preserving attitude of an OSN user and/or the privacy-preserving level of a specific privacy solution [266].

Some approaches like the Liu et al. [164] work proposes a model to estimate both the sensitivity and the visibility of information items. The model computes the privacy score as a combination of the partial privacy scores of each one of the user's profile items. The privacy score considers the privacy settings of users with respect to their profile items as well as their positions. This approach can be considered as privacy-preserving because it computes privacy-related aspects such as sensitivity and visibility of information that can be used to provide users with full information to face privacy decisions. A similar approach is presented by Nepali and Wang [189]. They propose a social network model, SONET, for privacy monitoring and ranking. The authors consider a privacy risk indicator that is used to describe an entity's privacy exposure factor based on the sensitivity and visibility of the attribute. Another work is the proposed by Talukder et al. [249]. They developed a service called Privometer that computes the privacy-risky of a user's account of social networks. It reviews all the user's information and his/her privacy policy considering the sensitivity of data and suggests self-sanitization actions to regulate the amount of leakage. It also considers that malicious apps installed in the user's friends profiles could be trying to gather user's information. All these proposals seem interesting in reviewing periodically the users' accounts, but none of these have considered being included in privacy mechanisms to assist in the users' privacy decision-making process.

Other approaches [263, 120] have considered preserving the users' privacy through the sanitization of the content shared. These research works use machine learning techniques to analyze textual posts, extract features of them, compute their sensitivity value, and sanitize the text changing the sensitive words for less specific and descriptive words. They adapt the normalization taking into account the tie-strength and type of relationship of the owner towards the potential information receiver. Although these works try to preserve users' privacy, it seems too complex that users set up different levels of sensitivity for different types of audiences or at least reach an agreed-on solution.

Regarding research works where recommendations are made based on the privacy-preserving statement, just a few works meet this requirement. On the one hand, the privacy solution of Squicciarini et al. [233] computes an access score function for disclosing the user's traits with his/her contacts. Each user has a threshold that determines, using the access score value, which users are or are not allowed access to a publication. The way their solution preserves user's privacy is through the assessment of the contact's visibility compared to the owner besides of the assessment of the spreading capacity of a user based on his/her structural centrality metrics (this assessment is a part of the access score computation). On the other hand, Yang et al. [288] designed a set of metrics grouped into metrics for predicting social benefits and metrics for predicting privacy risks. The metrics that predict benefits consider the potential positive social interactions that can be caused. Conversely, the metrics that predict privacy risks consider three relevant aspects: the sensitivity of the information, the probability of a re-sharing action, and trust towards the information receiver. In their solution, they balance both metrics (benefit and risk). If the result is positive (i.e., there are more reasons to share) the recommendation is to share with those contacts, otherwise the recommendation is not to share. The analyzed works [288, 233] consider the transmitters' preferences (preferences-centered approach) but also the users' privacy (privacy-preserving approach). However, both lack a strong validation of their proposals with real users, sharing information and interacting with other users.

Finally, to the best of our knowledge, no one privacy-preserving solution was found for multi-party privacy cases except by Xu et al. [287] work. They provide a trust metric that considers negative values for relationships. At the moment, the other works had considered only the positive interactions between users to measure the tie strength among them. In their work, authors consider interactions among users with negative intentions or results. These interaction problems are mainly based on privacy issues. Moreover, their proposal of privacy management that uses the trust metric is collaborative. The proposed trust metric can be used to asses a trade-off between data sharing and privacy-preserving.

2.3.9 Explainable requirement

A great drawback that users find when deciding the privacy policy on online social networks is the difficulty of having a complete view to take a suitable solution. Sometimes they do not know how or what personal information is disclosed through online social networks. This can be caused by internal (e.g., the user's contacts, the user's personal information) and external factors to the user (e.g., others' reactions) that are usually considered in the decision and users do not have enough resources to do it. In fact, the internal factors that are more closely related to users such as their contact list should be easier to be assessed by users during privacy decisions, but it has been shown that they normally do not even remember the users that compose their contact list [65].

Among the proposed solutions reviewed, we remark the following by its interesting perspective. Lipford et al. [160] explore the role of interface usability in current privacy settings. For that, they propose a new interface for Facebook called AudienceView that offers users the possibility to observe how their profiles are seen in the third person (i.e., from a perspective of search, network, and friend). Their proposal was evaluated by 16 participants that commented it helped them to understand better the actual consequences of their privacy settings. This approach was included on Facebook (View As Public) but only the network perspective. Mazzia et al. [177] present PViz, an interface that is focused on helping users understand the visibility of their profiles. PViz depicts the social structure of the user's contacts in a graphical way. Contacts are automatically grouped in communities using the idea of modularity optimization. The higher levels of the hierarchy have groups of users that are loosely connected and share fewer attributes, the lower levels of the structure represent groups of users that share many common friends, tastes, and demographic data. The authors empirically evaluated PViz comparing it with AudienceView [160] and the Facebook standard interface. Their results showed that participants preferred PViz over the other two options; some participants even suggested that a combination of AudienceView and PViz could create a better solution. However, this kind of solution was not designed for helping users during privacy decision-making, but to give them attention marks. These tools are only useful for sparking the users' concerns in privacy and make them doubly check their decisions about privacy to avoid potential regrets. Moreover, there is a huge distance between users' concerns and their final privacy behavior (known as the Privacy Paradox) as it has been shown in [24].

New approaches focused on informing users about privacy for privacy decision-making have recently raised popularity. Mostly focused on nudging about privacy and security, they use these mechanisms to improve decision-making processes where a lack of information or cognitive overload may unfavorably affect user privacy [21]. These mechanisms are known as soft paternalistic interventions (i.e., nudges). They attempt to influence decision making to improve individual well-being, without actually limiting users' ability to choose freely (because of all options are still available), thus, preserving the users' freedom of choice [7]. In a 6-week experiment with 28 Facebook users, Wang et al. [273] present their results with nudge mechanisms. They introduced three types of nudges: *audience nudge* (contains textual and visual information of the audience), *timer nudge* (introduces a visual delay of 20 seconds after a user clicked the "post" button before publishing the submitted post), and the combination of the two. The results concluded that participants that use Facebook to post personal opinions perceive the nudges as being more beneficial than those who use it to broadcast news articles or for commercial purposes. Moreover, the users that have experience in the configuration of privacy settings considered that the nudges could be more useful for people without experience in social networks. However, in the case of the audience mechanism the privacy risk that a user could have if the expected audience re-share the user's publication is not considered. This information could provide him a broader view of the potential reachability of his publication. The results of the experiment suggest that these mechanisms can be useful for people who are starting to use social networks (e.g., children and adolescents). A similar 12-day experiment with 21 participants was carried out by Wang et al. [272]. The authors propose different nudging mechanisms to be integrated into Facebook. The first mechanism *audience nudge* provides images of the audience that could see the post. Similarly to the audience mechanism proposed in Wang et al. [273], this mechanism also does not take into account the potential audience in the case of a user with permissions re-shares the publication. The second mechanism *timer nudge* includes a time delay before a user posts a message on the social network. The third mechanism *sentiment nudge* consists of an estimation of the sentiment associated with the post that the user is going to publish. The authors analyzed the data collected from the experiment (i.e., number of changes in online privacy settings, number of canceled or edited posts, post frequency, and topic sensitivity) and the data of a questionnaire after the experiment. They found clear evidence of changes in posting behavior for some of the participants. The participants mentioned that the *audience nudge* was useful for thinking about customized groups. For the *timer nudge*, the users mentioned that the mechanism provided them the opportunity to stop and think about the publication. In general, the *sentiment nudge* was perceived as being a less useful nudge than the others. The authors mention that the reasons could be associated with the sentiment algorithm that was used. Indeed, as this kind of works seems to work well in the privacy domain, other research works have been done to increase the effectiveness of nudges personalizing them to users [222, 218]. Even so, all

these works converge to the same conclusion: providing users with customized nudge
messages could increase further their effectiveness. Therefore, we think that combining
nudge mechanisms with indicators (of privacy risks) and factors (about users' scope,
information sensitivity, etc.), that are currently assessed by some research works, could
provide argued explanations to users about privacy that, in turn, they would improve
the explainability of privacy solutions.

2.4   Open challenges

Although works reviewed in this survey cover some of the requirements that privacy
mechanisms and their privacy solutions should have, we have identified possible lines
of future research to improve the current proposals. In this section, we discuss these
possible future directions in the research field of users' privacy decision-making in online social networks. Addressing the following research lines could shed light on users
privacy understanding and be used as a valuable support for privacy decisions, thus
reducing the probability of regretting their decisions. In addition, this will train users
towards safer and/or more specialized decisions, which could lead to an increase in
their participation in online social networks.

2.4.1   Privacy-related metrics

As we highlight in the review about privacy requirements and solutions, most of the analyzed research works follow a transmitter preferences-centered approach were factors
of trustworthiness and transmitter preferences are assessed for setting privacy policies.
Just using these factors is not the only thing to consider due to (i) users do not always remember the audience who compose their contact list or the information they
shared, (ii) users are not always able to evaluate all the possible scenarios because they
work with incomplete or unknown information, and (iii) users perceive privacy risks
as an abstract problem, psychologically distant, and more related to the distant future. Other factors must be taken into account, factors related to the other elements
involved in the communication. For this reason, privacy-related metrics should be designed as indicators of potential privacy issues. In this survey, we have remarked some
proposals that try to cover this problem. However, they could be improved and refined
providing clear and understandable information to users during the privacy decision-
making process. Moreover, none proposal following the privacy-preserving approach
was proposed for multi-party privacy scenarios. Among the factors that could measure
potential privacy risks in online social networks, we find the following: the user's per-

ception of sensitivity towards information, and the user's exposition, scope, influence level, and identification level. However, these ones depend on better estimators of information sensitivity and users' scope capacities. Below, we discuss some improvements that can be made to enhance these estimators.

Information sensitivity

Currently, we have found several ways (from the literature works) to estimate information sensitivity. These approaches are mainly based on: (i) laws and regulations, referred to which types of users' information require more protection than others by companies that stores them [256]; (ii) market valuation, referred to the value of data from indicators such as the market revenues obtained per data record, the market prices for data, the cost of a data breach, and data prices in illegal markets [196, 172]; (iii) individuals' valuation, referred to individual's willingness to pay to protect data [217, 221]; and (iv) linguistics, referred to words-level analysis and frequency of appearance [263, 120]. The comparison and implementation of a model that provides a combined approach of sensibility (adapted to online social networks domain) for the different information types could help to define better risk indicators. But this is not enough because the publications shared in social networks are composed of several types of personal information. Therefore, deep analysis and discussions about the sensitive value of information when several pieces of information appear together are required. For example, knowing that Bob is male is probably worth less than knowing that Bob is a male, 27-year old living in Valencia and he is interested in climbing, traveling, and movies. To the best of our knowledge, no one has analyzed exhaustively this property for making a serious proposal.

Scope of the user in the social network

Regarding the users' power of dissemination, there are a lot of factors that influence the visibility of their actions on the network. Some works were based on the privacy policy given to specific profile items [164], others on re-sharing probabilities [288], and others on users' time spent on social networks [56]. Current researches in the field of information dissemination are focused on detecting these users for strategic marketing proposes [131]. They merge social network factors with epidemic models to estimate the information spreading [276]. An interesting research line could be to use them as a tool for determining the risk a user has when share (or re-share) a personal piece of information due to the user may give too much visibility to the information. Metrics

based on measuring, the depth and width of cascades caused by re-sharing actions
could help users to understand the potential risks regarding privacy.

2.4.2   Validated model for automation

Automation has been used in many privacy research works reviewed in this survey.
On the one hand, some works collected information about users' behaviors to replicate
them. However, this could not be the most suitable solution due to the Privacy Paradox
(i.e., users' attitudes and concerns about privacy do not match their actions). On the
other hand, other works use some basic principles such as "the more sensitive information a user shares, the greater her privacy risks" and/or "the user gains social benefit if
her information is seen by information receiver" to design their metrics. However, the
designed functions do not consider factor combinations and they do not follow any
reasoned or validated psychological behavior. For this reason, we reviewed works in
the psychological field focused on self-disclosure in online social networks to find any
works that consider the online communication elements (transmitter, receptor, message, channel, and feedback) and how they influence privacy aspects. However, all of
them were made following the users-centered approach without analyzing the potential information receivers or the message properties. Therefore, we consider interesting
to work in a research line centered on analyzing the psychological behavior of users to
validate the individual's reasoning model during online communication. This would
allow researchers to create a complete model that considers the influence of online
communication elements in privacy and could be used for automating the computation of the trade-off between users' social benefits and privacy costs/risks.

2.4.3   Explainable, argued, and reflective privacy policy solutions

Nowadays, privacy mechanisms provided in online social networks tend to be basic
and include biases that (i) are responsible for causing privacy issues by disclosing information with silent listeners (i.e., users out of the *imagined audience*) and (ii) decrease
the users' disclosure by the incapacity to specify the desired audience (*context collapse*).
So, many of the research works analyzed try to automatically compute the best privacy
policies for the users, decreasing the users' burden and trying to improve their interests
(e.g., self-presentation, relationship maintenance, creating new relationships, privacy
protection, etc.). All these works mainly offer recommendations to users who finally
decide to accept or not accept them. However, some of these recommendations (i) are
not translated into an understandable format or language for users and (ii) the reasons

why the recommendation excludes/includes a user into the audience are not provided. Therefore, we consider that explainable, argued and reflective privacy solutions could facilitate the users' understandability of privacy mechanisms proposed and the transition between the recommendation and the final privacy policy decision. There are some research works that already considered nudging mechanisms as a way to educate and make users reflect about privacy decisions, but they were only applied to current social network privacy mechanisms. Moreover, no one included information about privacy metrics considered to compute the recommendation. This information could be useful to nudge users and make them reflect on their priorities. Hence, we think that new research on the explainability of privacy decisions considering also ethics and other users' privacy preferences, and consequently decreasing regrets by privacy decisions.

2.4.4 Adaptation to user's modifications

Based on the works analyzed, we observed that most of them offer closed recommendations, i.e., users have to accept or reject them without the possibility to modify them. We believe that this requirement is needed due to users have different interests and motivations that could change, being the users' behavior far from perfectly rational [117]. Therefore, future research should consider variations in users' privacy policy recommendations linking them to explainable characteristics. This new approach could provide better privacy mechanisms.

2.4.5 Co-privacy

For addressing the co-privacy issue, we already mentioned that huge advances have been done in the way of detecting and solving multi-party privacy conflicts. However, these solutions are mainly centered on balance users' preferences instead of considering privacy metrics that protect all's privacy. Furthermore, another important point could be preventing multi-party privacy conflicts instead of solving them. To address the prevention of these conflicts, the analysis of nudging mechanisms about others' privacy could shed light on ways of prevention.

2.4.6 Content-fading solutions

There is content published on social networks that were appropriate in a certain context but over time it may not be as appropriate as it used to be. The problem is that users forget that they published it and keep it accessible. When these users create new relationships, there is a chance that these new contacts can access these previous postings. Hence, we consider that it would be interesting that users have the possibility to provide an expiration date to their content or that privacy mechanisms, depending on the risk of the publication (taking into account the sensitivity of the content, the target audience, etc.) recommend associating an expiry date with the publication. Nowadays, there is no enough research on the users' old publications or the effect/benefit of new mechanisms such as Instagram Stories that fade their content. Researches about this requirement could be an interesting research line for improving privacy mechanisms.

2.5   Conclusions

The possibilities of interaction and social benefit that online social networks offer have raised their popularity. Any application or service of the lasts years has been designed following a social approach, usually linked to other online social networks. In this connected world, controlling which information and who has access to it is of paramount importance. The current mechanisms of online social networks to control the users' privacy could be improved, and the privacy solutions provided lack mainly on explicability. Hence, privacy mechanisms that fulfill the lack of current approaches remarked in this survey work will be the subject of future research during the next years.

In this survey work, we have explored the privacy decision-making process highlighting the drawbacks and the current issues of privacy mechanisms, in addition to the potential privacy problems that could emerge. To improve privacy mechanisms, we proposed several requirements that arise as a result of potential problems during the privacy decision-making process. Some of these requirements are almost fulfilled, but others related to the explainability, privacy-preserving, adaptation, and co-privacy still need deeper research. Above all, we understand the complexity of the design of a privacy mechanism that fulfills the entire set of requirements. For that reason, we need to produce clear and convincing results to attract the attention of online social networks to develop new privacy mechanisms. We think that this approximation may need a redesign of the user layer to include advanced and explainable/understandable privacy management.

## CHAPTER 3

ESTIMATION OF PRIVACY RISK THROUGH CENTRALITY METRICS

*— Published by **Jose Alemany, Elena del Val, Juanmi Alberola**, and **Ana García-Fornes** in the **International Journal of Future Generation Computer Systems** [11]*

3.1	Introduction	52
3.2	Related work	53
3.3	Privacy risk scenario	56
3.4	Privacy Risk Score (PRS)	57
3.5	PRS and centrality metrics	63
3.6	Experiments	67
3.7	Conclusions	77

3.1 Introduction

The popularity of mobile devices and applications that are related to online social networking has changed the way we communicate. People now share their opinions, ideas, photos, etc. in online social networks (OSN) [74, 60]. When sharing information, users are not often aware of who will or will not have access to what they have just published. This uncertainty creates a risk in the privacy of the user, which in some cases may have negative consequences if the scope of the publication reaches people who were not in the original audience. Applications related to OSN offer the possibility to configure options that are related to the privacy profile of users. However, this is often a tedious task and is usually focused on protecting the information related to the user profile and not to the privacy of the user's publications [164, 189, 225]. Some works try to address these issues with the automation of privacy settings [86, 262, 34, 244]. However, these proposals usually require an initial intervention by the user and do not solve the problem of increasing privacy awareness. Other approaches deal with the improvement of the awareness of users regarding the misalignment of users' expected audience with the actual audience [49, 129, 178]. However, these approaches do not deal with the problem that a publication might produce if the expected audience performs sharing actions among their contacts. Assuming this scenario, there is still a potential privacy risk that should be considered.

The topological location of a user in a network is one of the main factors that influences the scope that a certain sharing action can reach [101]. The scope of a sharing action can be seen as the effect of a diffusion process. In the area of Complex Networks, spreading processes such as epidemics or information diffusion have been analyzed [153, 163, 71, 66]. Several works have studied spreading dynamics and influential or relevant individuals in these processes based on structural properties [205, 277, 169, 226, 25]. From the point of view of determining the privacy risk associated to a user's sharing action, it is interesting to determine if there are influential users in the path that information follows who increase the privacy risk score if they perform a re-sharing action. Influential users can initiate and conduct the dissemination of a sharing action more efficiently than "normal" users. Therefore, influential users in networks are normally more responsible for large cascades of information diffusion and contribute to increasing the privacy risk. Traditionally, centrality metrics such as degree [201], pagerank [169], k-core [141, 205], closeness [41], or betweenness [97, 96, 158, 98] have been used to detect these relevant users in networks [38, 226, 156].

Not all users have the same perception of risk [185, 61, 237]. On one hand, there are some users who are more comfortable with the possibility that their information can be

seen by others and are even interested in achieving that effect. On the other hand, there
are users that have greater privacy concerns and prefer not to disclose information
that could be seen by users beyond their direct friends [89]. Depending on the users'
concerns, different levels of risk perception should be considered.

In this article, we propose a Privacy Risk Score (PRS) for measuring the privacy in
social networks, which provides the following major contributions:

- The privacy is oriented to the reachability of a user-sharing action instead of being focused on the misalignment of the users' expected audience with the actual
  audience.

- The measure provided is not only global, but it is also adjustable to the risk
  perception of each individual.

- The PRS does not require the user to provide information explicitly since it takes
  into account the paths that the publications follow in the social network.

- We provide an estimation of this measure for those scenarios in which information related to flow paths is not available. This estimation is based on an analysis
  of the relationship between global, local, and social centrality metrics and the
  proposed measure.

The rest of the paper is structured as follows. Section 3.2 presents previous approaches
that are related to privacy score metrics. Section 3.3 exposes the privacy risks in social
networks with an example of scenario and proposes a solution. Section 3.4 describes the
concept of friendship level and presents the PRS. Section 3.5 describes a set of global,
local, and social centrality metrics to estimate the PRS. Section 3.6, presents a set of
experiments that were performed to evaluate the suitability of centrality metrics to
estimate the PRS in synthetic and real network topologies. Finally, Section 3.7 presents
conclusions.

3.2   Related work

In the literature, there are works that try to tackle the problem of improving the awareness of the effect of communicative actions from different perspectives. Table 3.1 provides an overview of relevant contributions in this area, which are classified according
to the dimensions of focus.

There are approaches that provide wizards to facilitate the management of privacy profile settings. Liu et al. [164] propose a mathematical model to estimate both the sensitivity and the visibility of information items. The model computes the privacy score as a combination of the partial privacy scores of each one of the user's profile items. The privacy score considers the privacy settings of users with respect to their profile items as well as their positions. A similar approach is presented by Nepali et al. [189]. They propose a social network model, SONET, for privacy monitoring and ranking. The authors consider a privacy risk indicator that is used to describe an entity's privacy exposure factor based on the known attributes (the sensitivity and visibility of the attribute). Shehab et al. [225] present a privacy policy recommendation approach that is based on the idea that nearby users should have similar labels (permissions). The approach requires users to label a small set of their friends. These labels are propagated over the social network to provide users with privacy policy recommendations. Fang et al. [86] present a privacy wizard that considers previous labelling processes of friends as the input for their classifier. The wizard then infers labels for the other remaining friends. Vidyalakshmi et al. [262] present a framework for calculating a privacy score metric considering users' personal attitude towards privacy and communication information. Bilogrevic et al. [34] propose an information-sharing system that decides (semi-)automatically whether to share information with others. They consider a vector that encodes whether or not the information is shared based on user decisions, and then a logistic classifier makes the remaining decisions. These approaches require user intervention and assume that users are privacy aware of the consequences of their decisions. They are focused on a local view of the social network and do not evaluate other collateral effects such as information diffusion processes.

Some approaches focus on providing information about which people have or may have received information that was not addressed to them initially. These works help them to increase their privacy risk awareness and better define their social groups more carefully. Calikli et al. [49] propose an adaptive architecture that provides sharing recommendations to users as well as assisting them to re-configure the users' groups. Their proposal is based on social contexts and conflicts. This approach depends on the provision of accurate user's social contexts and conflict rules. Kafali et al. [129] provide an approach that is based on model checking that checks whether certain properties hold. The system uses as input privacy agreements of the users, user relations, the content they upload as well as some inference rules. The system specifies whether the property of interest can or cannot be violated in a given social network. Mester et. al [178] developed a platform where agents interact to reach a consensus on a post to be published. The agent is aware of the user's privacy concerns, expectations, and the user's friends. When a user is about to post new content, the agent reasons on behalf of

| | Type of information | | | User intervention | Privacy risk estimation |
| | Profile items | Actions | | | |
		Audience	Reachability		
Liu et al. [164]	✓				✓
Nepali et al. [189]	✓				✓
Shehab et al. [225]	✓				
Fang et al. [86]		✓		✓	
Vidyalakshmi et al. [262]				✓	✓
Bilogrevic et al. [34]		✓		✓	
Calikli et al. [49]		✓			
Kafali et al. [129]		✓		✓	
Mester et al. [178]				✓	
Yang et al. [288]					✓
Our work			✓		✓

Table 3.1: Overview of approaches related to privacy in social networks. We considered three main features: (i) the type of information considered to evaluate the user's privacy risk (i.e., the user's profile items or actions). In the case that the approach considers actions, the goal can be to determine if the information shared was received by the intended audience or to estimate the reachability of the information; (ii) if the approach requires user intervention as input for the privacy risk estimation; and (iii) if the approach provides a privacy risk metric to the user.

the user to decide which other users would be affected by the post and contacts those users' agents. However, the privacy concerns of a user should be predefined. Yang et al. [288] present a privacy metric of user i sharing information with a neighbor j as a trade-off between user i's concerns and incentives of sharing information with j. They present privacy risk as an individual metric, without considering other potential users that might re-share information.

From our point of view, privacy risk does not only concern the problem that information might reach people who were initially not expected to receive it. Assuming that people who received the information are part of the target audience, it must also be taken into account that there is still a problem if one user of this intended audience re-shares the information. Then, the original user loses control over the scope of the information. For this reason, it is important to consider the privacy problem from a network perspective instead of individuals alone. The audience that is allowed see the information that a user publishes is influenced by the structure of the social network. Network models that mimic the patterns of connection in real networks (i.e., Erdös-Rényi [81, 257, 37], Barabási-Albert [22, 48], and Watts-Strogatz [274, 51]) facilitate the analysis of the implications of those patterns [190]. Small-world, Scale-free, and Random models are very common structures in social networks. The Small-world model is characterized by the transitivity in strong social ties and the ability of weak ties to reach across clusters. The Scale-free model exhibits a power-law degree distribution where there is a small set of vertices with a degree that greatly exceeds the average. The random model assigns equal probability to all graphs with exactly the same number of edges.

In this paper, we deal with this problem with the proposal of a Privacy Risk Score (PRS) that is focused on the risk of potential re-sharing actions from the expected and unexpected audience that might receive the message. The main contributions of this work are the following: (i) the proposed PRS metric considers the paths that information follows as a result of sharing actions without the user's intervention; (ii) the calculation of the PRS metric for different users' risk perceptions; (iii) we provide and evaluate a set of centrality metrics to estimate PRS values in scenarios where there is a lack of a global view of the network and/or data about the users' sharing activity.

3.3 Privacy risk scenario

Privacy risk not only concerns the problem that information might reach people who were initially not expected to receive it, but it also involves the problem of losing control over the scope of the information. In Figure 3.1, we describe this privacy risk problem in online social networks.

The social network is structured into nine communities (see Figure 3.1a). Nodes represent users and the node color corresponds to a community. Gray nodes represent isolated users (i.e., they do not belong to any community). In Figure 3.1b, the user represented by the node encircled in red shares a message on his/her wall. The user determines the audience depending on his/her selected privacy policy (e.g., *friends*). Therefore, only their friends can see the message (see Figure 3.1c, nodes encircled in green). If a node encircled in green performs a sharing action, the message could reach other communities causing a privacy problem.

The Privacy Risk Score metric proposed in this paper deals with this problem by providing information about the potential privacy risk of an action. The PRS aims to increase the users' awareness about the reachability of their publications in the social network even though they have restricted the visibility of their publications. Figure 3.2 shows the workflow phases for calculating the PRS. First, the activity in the social network is monitorized (specifically, the path followed by user messages). This information is used to establish the reachability of the actions performed by each user and

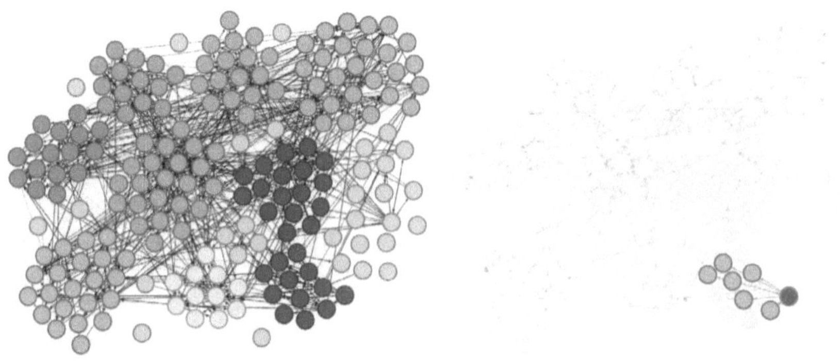

(a) A social network structured into communities.   (b) Sharing action initiated by the node encircled in red.

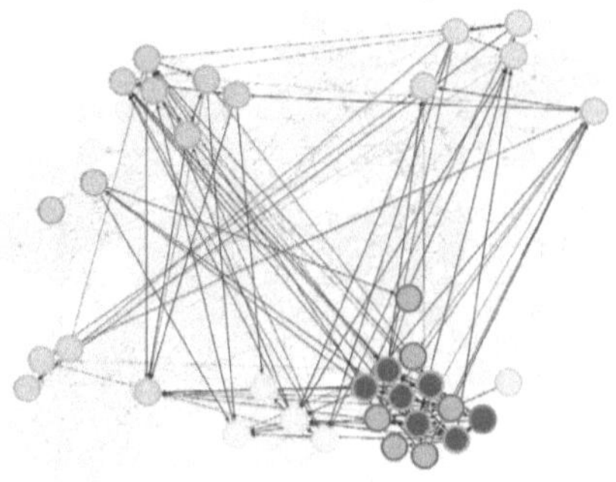

(c) Potential audience in level 2.

Figure 3.1: Example of a potential privacy risk in online social networks.

to calculate the PRS value. Then, when a user is going to post a message, the PRS values analyzed until that moment are shown to the user. The PRS of a user would provide him/her with an estimation of the visibility of an action at different levels of friendship or in general. By taking into account their privacy risk perception and their PRS, users could make better decisions about sharing or not sharing a message on their walls.

3.4   Privacy Risk Score (PRS)

To define how our proposed PRS metric works, first we are going to explain some important concepts. We assume that there is a social network $\mathcal{G}$ that consists of N nodes, where every node $a_i \in \{a_1, ..., a_m\}$ represents an agent (i.e., a user of the social net-

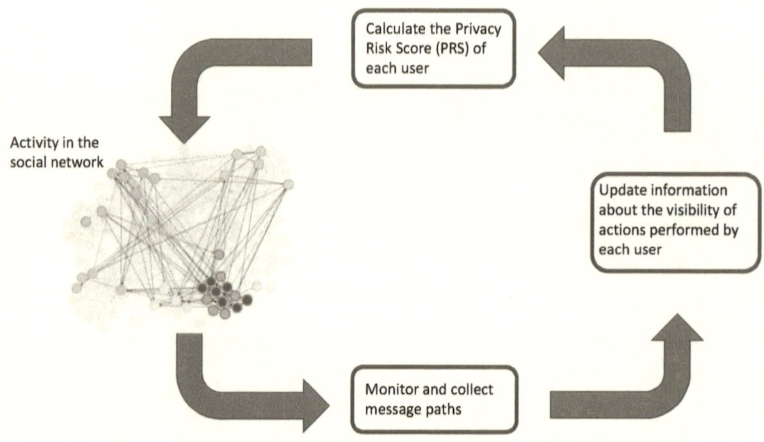

Figure 3.2: Flow chart of the phases for calculating the PRS in a social network.

work). Agents are connected through links that represent friendship relationships and correspond to the edges $E \subseteq N \times N$ of $\mathcal{G}$. We assume that friendship links are bidirectional, and, therefore, the social network is undirected. We define the adjacency matrix $\mathbf{A}$ to represent these links. Given two agents a_i and a_j, if there is a link between these agents, we represent this as $\mathbf{A}_{a_i,a_j} = 1$ and $\mathbf{A}_{a_i,a_j} = 0$ if there is not a link. Considering an agent a_i, we define a level L as the subset of agents whose shortest distance to a_i is l:

$$L_{a_i}(l) \subseteq N, \forall a_j \in L_{a_i}(l) : d(a_i, a_j) = l \wedge \nexists d'(a_i, a_j) < d(a_i, a_j)$$

We define the Privacy Risk Score (PRS) for an agent a_i that performs a message diffusion action (i.e., publishes a message m on its wall, comments on an existing post, shares a post, etc.) as an indicator of the potential risk of this message to be diffused over the social network (i.e., potential visibility). The higher the PRS value, the higher the threat to agent a_i's privacy.

3.4.1 Calculation of the PRS metric

In a social network $\mathcal{G}$, there is a set of paths that messages follow more frequently than others [39, 115]. If an agent is in these paths and performs a diffusion action, it has a higher privacy risk than another agent that is out of these paths. Therefore, an agent's position in the network is relevant to the privacy risk. Furthermore, not all users have the same view of risk when sharing information. As an example, some users may consider that sharing information with friends of friends might be risky, while others may consider that the true risk is at the next level of friendship. Therefore, the estimation of the PRS for an agent a_i should be provided in friendship levels in order to deal with different levels of risk perception.

In addition, according to the information diffusion model SIR (Susceptible, Infected, and Removed) [277], the time instant in which a diffusion action of a message is performed is also important for measuring the privacy risk. This model states that the privacy risk related to the diffusion of a message is higher during the initial stages than when the message has already been diffused through the social network. In other words, the diffusion risk of a message is higher when an agent diffuses a new message since no other agents have viewed it yet. Therefore, the calculation of the PRS also includes the stage of the message in which an agent a_i interacts as a diffusion action. To represent this, we define $T = \{1, 2, \ldots, n\}$ as the stages of the message, which are the product of the diffusion process of the message. This variable is represented for each message and indicates the number of steps from its creation. The value of the variable T (and also of the variable L) is limited by the network diameter. Therefore, if its value is not too high, the network diameter is a good approximation of T and L. For the sake of simplicity, we assume that an agent can carry out a single message diffusion action (i.e., re-share a message, comment on a message, etc.), allowing other agents to see this message at that time instant.

Considering the above two factors (friendship level and risk of initial stages), we define a $T \times N$ reachability matrix γ_i associated to each agent a_i to represent the number of messages that an agent a_i has diffused in a certain stage t and have been seen by other agents. The rows of this matrix represent the diffusion actions that a_i carries out over messages in the same stage, while columns represent the agents of the social network. We use $\gamma_{i_{t,a_j}}$ to refer to the entry in the tth row and a_jth column of γ_i. This value represents the number of messages diffused by a_i in stage t that were seen by a_j. Note that the a_ith column of each row t ($\gamma_{i_{t,a_i}}$) represents the messages diffused by a_i in stage t that were seen by a_i (i.e., all of the messages published by a_i in t).

Given a stage t and a set of agents of level l, we define $p(a_i, t, l)$ as the average number of agents of this level that saw a message published by a_i in stage t:

$$p(a_i, t, l) = \frac{\sum\limits_{a_j \in L_{a_i}(l)} \gamma_{it,a_j}}{\gamma_{it,a_i}} \tag{3.1}$$

Taking into account the above value, we estimate the PRS for an agent a_i at level l as the percentage of agents of that level that potentially see a message published by a_i at any stage. This can be calculated as:

$$PRS(a_i, l) = \frac{1}{T} \sum_{t=1}^{T} \left(\frac{p(a_i, t, l)}{|L_{a_i}(l)|} \right) \tag{3.2}$$

In a general view, by taking into account the whole population of the social network $\mathcal{G}$, we can estimate a general value of PRS for an agent a_i as the percentage of agents of the social network that potentially see a message published by a_i at any stage. This can be calculated by combining Equations 3.1 and 3.2:

$$PRS(a_i) = \frac{1}{T} \sum_{t=1}^{T} \left(\frac{\sum\limits_{a_j \in N} \gamma_{it,a_j}}{\gamma_{it,a_i} \cdot |N|} \right) \tag{3.3}$$

Figure 3.3 shows a scenario where the privacy risk score is calculated for agent a_1 in a social network. This scenario represents an example of a social network with interactions between agents. We assume that all of the agents in $\mathcal{G}$ have the privacy policy that only their direct friends can see their walls. As indicated in the definition above, the maximum value for parameters T and L cannot exceed the network diameter. Therefore, for this example of PRS calculation, we use the value 3 for parameters T and L.

The message diffusion actions performed in this scenario are the following. (1) Agent a_1 publishes a message m_1 on its wall. Therefore, agents a_2 and a_3 can see the message. Since the interaction of agent a_1 with the message m_1 is in its initial stage, stage t is 1. The information about the agents that can see m_1 is stored in γ_1. (2) Agent a_3 then decides to share m_1 on its wall. Agents a_4, a_5, a_6, a_7, and a_8 can see message m_1. As in the previous case, the information about the agents that can see message m_1 is updated in γ_2. The interaction of agent a_3 with message m_1 occurs after agent a_1

shares it (i.e., the interaction is produced in the next stage $t = 2$). Note that the values of γ_1 are updated at $t = 1$ because agent a_1 interacts with the message in this stage, and in γ_1 we are measuring the reachability of the messages when agent a_1 interacts with it. (3) Agent a_8 then shares m_1 publishing it on its wall. Agents a_3 and a_9 can see it. Therefore, γ_8 is updated at $t = 3$, and γ_1 and γ_3 are updated in their corresponding t's (i.e., $t = 1$ and $t = 2$). (4) Agent a_1 then publishes a new message m_2 that agents a_2 and a_3 can see at stage $t = 1$. Then, γ_1 is updated at $t = 1$.

With the information stored in the γ matrix, the proposed PRS is calculated for each agent. In the scenario described in Figure 3.3, we show the values of PRS for agent a_1

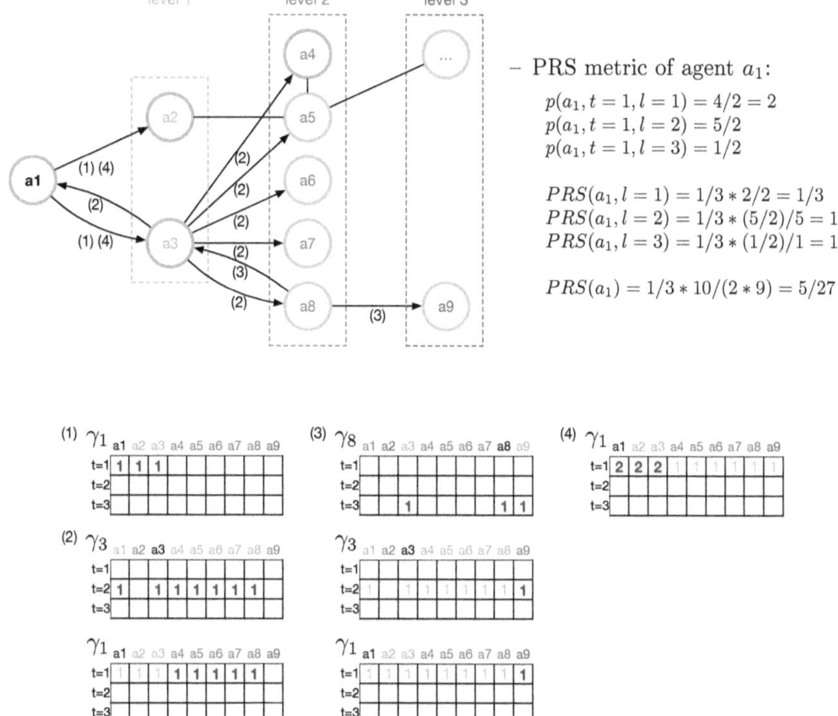

– PRS metric of agent a_1:

$$p(a_1, t = 1, l = 1) = 4/2 = 2$$
$$p(a_1, t = 1, l = 2) = 5/2$$
$$p(a_1, t = 1, l = 3) = 1/2$$

$$PRS(a_1, l = 1) = 1/3 * 2/2 = 1/3$$
$$PRS(a_1, l = 2) = 1/3 * (5/2)/5 = 1/6$$
$$PRS(a_1, l = 3) = 1/3 * (1/2)/1 = 1/6$$

$$PRS(a_1) = 1/3 * 10/(2 * 9) = 5/27$$

Figure 3.3: Example of social network activity and the PRS calculation process. The activities carried out on the social network are as follows (in this example, all agents share information with their friends): (1) agent a_1 publishes/shares a message m_1 on its wall; (2) agent a_3 shares the message m_1; (3) agent a_8 shares the message m_1; and (4) agent a_1 publishes/shares a new message m_2.

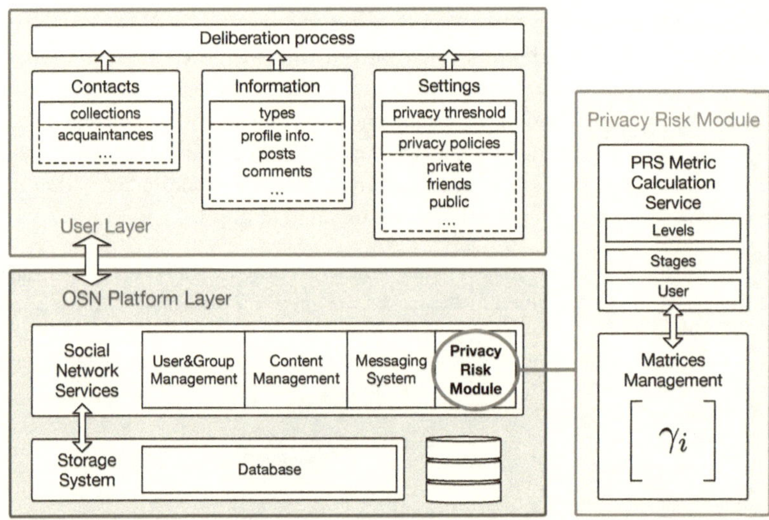

Figure 3.4: Block diagram of the integration of PRS metric as a service in OSN.

at different levels (i.e., $PRS(a_1, l = 1)$, $PRS(a_1, l = 2)$, and $PRS(a_1, l = 3)$) and the general PRS value (i.e., $PRS(a_1)$).

3.4.2   PRS metric in OSN

The integration of the PRS metric in OSN must be done as a service for users. This privacy service will help users to manage their sensitive and non-sensitive information and aware its scope, improving their experiences in OSN. In Figure 3.4, we show a block diagram of OSN where the PRS metric was included as a service in the OSN platform layer. The diagram is composed of a User layer, OSN Platform layer, and Privacy Risk Module. The User layer manages user's contacts, information related to the user (e.g., profile info, posts, comments, etc.), and setting parameters to control who has access to the information when a sharing action is carried out. The OSN Platform layer provides the whole functionality of a OSN (e.g., management of users, messaging system, etc.). The Privacy Risk module is included as a service of the OSN Platform layer. This service is responsible for the PRS metric calculation.

Figure 3.5 shows the workflow to estimate the PRS value of an individual agent when he performs a message sharing action in the OSN. The process starts when an agent a_i sees

a publication or when he creates content for a new publication (m_j). Then, this agent
evaluates the risk of sharing/publishing m_j considering its PRS value ($PRS(a_i)$). If
the value is greater than his individual risk threshold (θ_{a_i}), a_i does not perform the
action. Otherwise, a_i shares m_j, which in turn, could be seen by other agents. In
this case, the matrix γ_i of a_i is updated as well as the matrices of other agents that
previously participated in the sharing process of m_j.

3.5 PRS and centrality metrics

Even though the PRS estimation provides accurate measurements of the privacy risk
associated to a diffusion action, this estimation requires a detailed record of sharing activity in a social network. However, the management of this information is not always
feasible in large networks with high activity, and, in some scenarios, this knowledge
is not even accessible. As a result, in certain circumstances, we would require metrics
that approximate PRS values in a feasible way.

Influential users may play a critical role in paths that information follows. If an influential user sees a publication and performs a sharing action, it is more likely for
the publication to reach more people. It is important to have a reliable and efficient predictor of these nodes based on topological properties. From the area of Complex Networks, there is no consensus on the best metric for predicting this influence.
Researchers have proposed several structural metrics for identifying influential users
[152]. According to the information they used, these metrics can be classified into three
classes: global, local, and social [227].

Global metrics are based on structural properties that require a complete view of the
network structure to be computed. Among the global metrics, we considered the following commonly used metrics: betweenness, closeness, and pagerank. Betweenness
metrics are based on assumptions about the paths that information follows. Shortest-
path betweenness assumes that information is transmitted along the shortest paths. It
is defined as the fraction of the shortest paths between pairs of agents in a network
that pass through the agent of interest [96],

$$\text{bet-sp}_i = \sum_{a_j, a_k \in N} \frac{\sigma(a_j, a_k | a_i)}{\sigma(a_j, a_k)}, \tag{3.4}$$

where $\sigma(a_j, a_k)$ is the number of shortest (a_j, a_k)-paths, and $\sigma(a_j, a_k | a_i)$ is the num-
ber of those paths passing through some node a_i other than a_j, a_k.

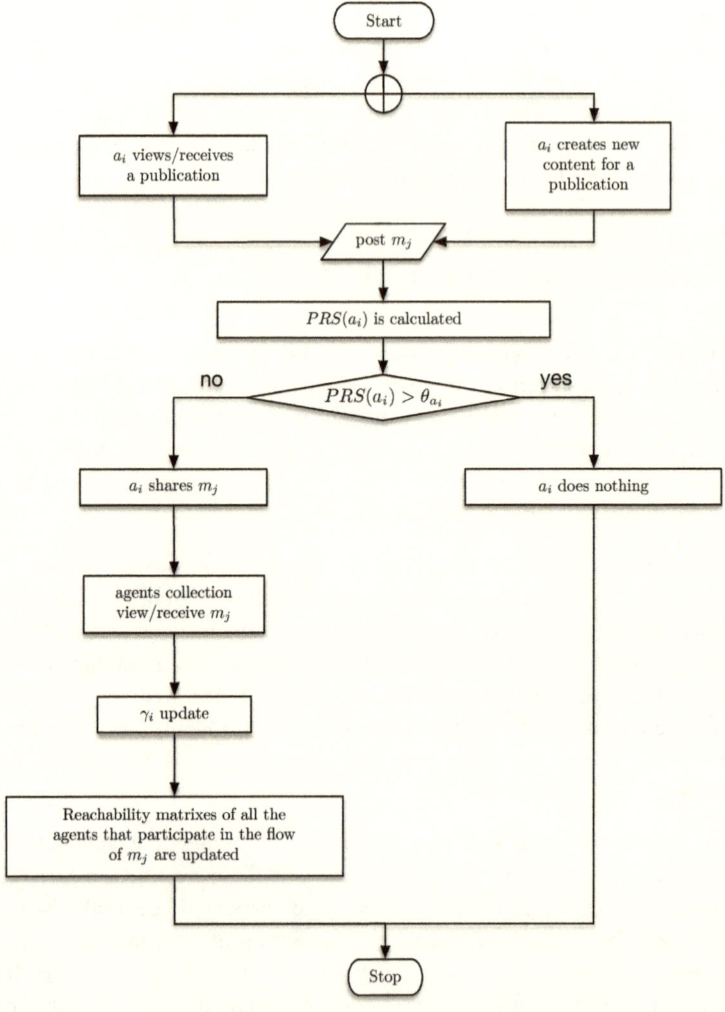

Figure 3.5: Flowchart of the PRS calculation process.

Random-walk betweenness was proposed by Newman [191], and, instead of considering the shortest paths, it considers the number of times a random walk between each
pair of agents passes through the agent of interest. Thus, random-walk betweenness

can be defined as follows,

$$\text{bet-rw}_i = \sum_{a_j, a_k \in N} \frac{\sigma_r(a_j, a_k | a_i)}{\sigma_r(a_j, a_k)}, \tag{3.5}$$

where $\sigma_r(a_j, a_k)$ is the number of random (a_j, a_k)-paths, and $\sigma_r(a_j, a_k | a_i)$ is the number of those random paths passing through some node a_i other than a_j, a_k.

While betweenness centrality measures represent the degree to which an agent is between pairs of other agents, closeness is just the inverse of the average distance to other agents. Closeness is defined as the mean geodesic distance from the agent of interest to the rest of the reachable agents in the network,

$$\text{closeness}_i = \frac{|N| - 1}{\sum_{j=1}^{j=|N|-1} d(a_j, a_i)}, \tag{3.6}$$

where $d(a_j, a_i)$ is the shortest-path distance between a_j and a_i, and $|N|$ is the number of nodes in the network. This metric reflects the efficiency of an agent distributing information to any agent in the network [41].

PageRank is based on the idea that an agent has a high rank if the sum of the ranks of its neighbors are high. The ranks are calculated based on the structure of the links of the agent of interest. Then, pagerank centrality can be defined as follows,

$$\text{pagerank}_i = \alpha \sum_{j=1}^{j=|N|} A_{a_j, a_i} \frac{\text{pagerank}_j}{k_j} + \beta, \tag{3.7}$$

where α and β are constants and k_j is the degree of node j. This metric implies a relatively low computational complexity and has been used to identify pivotal individuals in social networks who lead to quick and wide spreading of useful items [169].

Global metrics can be suitable to estimate the risk of a sharing action in the network since they capture the user's relevance in the transmission of information and do not require data about information flows. The computation of a global metric requires the analysis of structural properties that involve the consideration of the whole social network. However, in real-world scenarios, these metrics are not always computationally affordable and information about friendship relationships is not always accessible. Moreover, some social applications do not facilitate access to users' information to third party applications; therefore, it is not possible to infer the social network structure beyond the first level.

As an alternative, local and social metrics efficiently identify influential agents when there is no global information about network structure and information diffusion [84]. These metrics are focused on the user's ego networks. Ego networks consist of a focal agent (*ego*) and the agents to whom the ego is directly connected to (these are called *alters*) plus the links [175]. Local metrics such as degree and ego-betweenness only use information from the agent itself to be computed. Degree is the simplest centrality measure and considers the number of direct neighbors (*alters*) that the ego is directly connected to,

$$\text{degree}_i = \sum A_i(a_i, a_j).$$

(3.8)

Ego-betweenness is an ego-centric method for approximating the betweenness centrality [105]. This metric calculates the sum of the ego's proportion of times that the ego lies on the shortest path between each part of the alters. Ego-betweenness is the sum of the reciprocal values $A_i^2(a_j, a_k)$ such that $A_i(a_j, a_k) = 0$. Thus, ego-betweenness can be defined as follows,

$$\text{bet-ego}_i = \sum_{A_i(a_i,a_j)=0, j>i} \frac{1}{A_i^2(a_i, a_j)}$$

(3.9)

Social metrics use strictly local information and topological information from an agent's first and second level neighbors. Social degree and Social ego-betweenness metrics consider the sum of the local centrality metrics of neighbors in the first two levels. We have considered the following four social centrality metrics:

$$\text{bet-ego}_{\text{sum}_i} = \sum_{a_j \in L_{a_i}(1)} \text{bet-ego}_j$$

(3.10)

$$\text{degree}_{\text{sum}_i} = \sum_{a_j \in L_{a_i}(1)} \text{degree}_j$$

(3.11)

$$\text{bet-ego}_{2\text{sum}_i} = \sum_{a_j \in L_{a_i}(2)} \text{bet-ego}_j$$

(3.12)

$$\text{degree}_{2\text{sum}_i} = \sum_{a_j \in L_{a_i}(2)} \text{degree}_j$$

(3.13)

Centrality metrics provide mechanisms to estimate the relevance of users in information transmission processes. Influential users play a key role in information diffusion and therefore in the increase of the privacy risk if they perform a re-sharing action. For this reason, considering global, local, and social centrality metrics might be appropriate to estimate the proposed PRS when there is no data available about information flows. Global centrality metrics can be used if the network structure is known. If there is no access to this information, local and social centrality metrics based on ego-networks provide metrics to estimate the relevance of users in information transmission processes.

3.6 Experiments

In this section, we evaluate the relationship between PRS values of an agent and its centrality in the social network. The social networks considered for the experiments can be viewed in terms of the friendship relationships and the activities carried out by agents. We analyze the relationship between the structural features of the friendship layer and the privacy risk resulting from the diffusion actions. We perform a set of experiments in different synthetic and real networks. For the experiments in synthetic networks we use a simulation tool to reproduce information flows in the network, and the proposed PRS metric to measure the individual risk of users. While in real networks, how there are already real information flows, we only measure the PRS values of users.

3.6.1 Simulation environment

We based our simulation environment on the Elgg engine[1] (Figure 3.6). Elgg is a popular open source engine to build a wide range of social environments. For our purpose, we required to collect message tracing information and manage them in matricial structures in order to calculate the PRS metric. Therefore, we needed to extend the functionalities of Elgg in order to fulfill our requirements. Following the Elgg policy, we extended Social Network Services by means of plug-ins. First, we developed the Privacy Risk Module following the structure shown in Figure 3.4, which is a plug-in for PRS calculation according to our requirements. This module was focused on two different purposes: for being used in simulations and with real users.

Second, we developed the Simulation Tool, which is a plug-in for modelling social networks and generating activity. The Simulation Tool was designed to use the services of

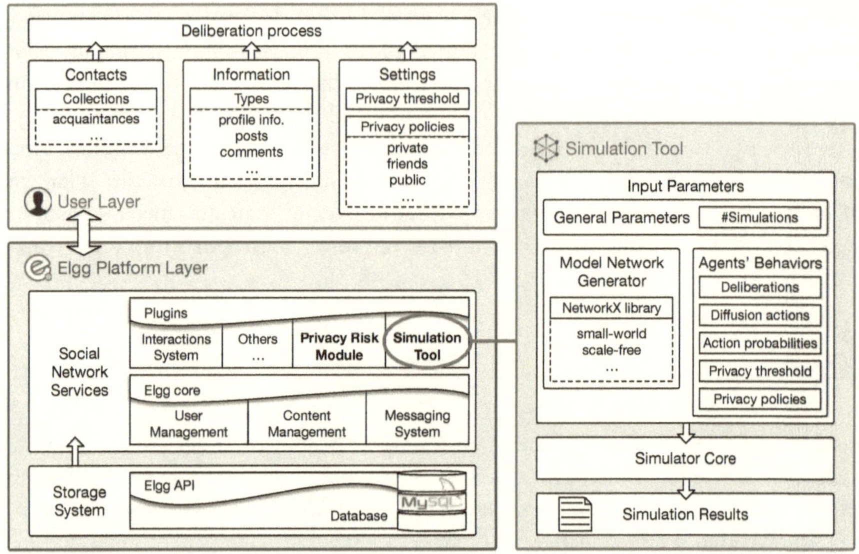

Figure 3.6: Block diagram of the integration of the Simulation Tool developed as a service in the OSN.

the OSN (properly supported by Elgg) such as the creation of users and relationships, message sending, and social interactions. Users are represented as software agents that interact among them in the OSN. Agent-based simulation is widely used in different areas [2]. The Simulation Tool is composed of three main components: Input Parameters, Simulator Core and Outputs. As Input Parameters, the simulation tool allows the definition of the number of simulations, the network model, and the customization of agent behaviours (i.e., message diffusion actions, probabilities, deliberation process, etc.). For modelling social network structures, we used the NetworkX[2], which is a widely tested and recommended library for research purposes in complex networks [134, 194, 8]. The Simulator Core carries out the simulation according to the input parameters. Finally, Simulation Results (i.e., Privacy Risk Score values of each agent) are stored for further analysis. These both plug-ins were integrated into the existing Elgg engine. Since this engine is open source, these plug-ins will be public available.

	Random network	Scale-free network	Small-world network
Nodes	1000	1000	1000
Edges	6464	5875	6000
Density	0.01292	0.01175	0.012
Maximum degree	32	117	21
Minimum degree	3	5	7
Average degree	12.93	11.75	12.00
Assortativity	0.00077	-0.07481	-0.02096
Triangles	631	1022	1963
Diameter	5	5	5

Table 3.2: Structural properties of synthetic networks.

3.6.2 Settings

The experiments carried out using the simulation tool use synthetic networks generated
follow three classic models: Erdös-Rényi [81] (ER, random), Barabási-Albert [22] (BA,
scale-free), and Watts-Strogatz [274] (WS, small-world). The networks are undirected,
have 1000 agents with a diameter of 5, and an average degree of about 12 (see Table
3.2). The number of simulations is 400 per each agent. In each simulation an agent
is randomly selected and the simulation starts if the agent decides to post a message.
Figure 3.7 shows the deliberation process of an agent during the simulation. Each agent
decides whether or not a message diffusion action is carried out (i.e., commenting on
an existing post, sharing a post, etc.) according to his probabilities of performing each
action. If the agent decides to perform a diffusion action, then he selects the privacy
policy for this message. In case that the message was previously received by this agent
or if the agent decides not to carry out a message diffusion action, then, the message
is not diffused by this agent. Each simulation finishes when there is not any message
diffusion action in the OSN.

Simulation parameters are shown in Table 3.3. The #Simulation parameter allows to
define the simulation rounds. Network topology parameter establishes the underlying social network structure (i.e., scale-free, random, small-world). Diffusion action
parameter allows to define the permitted actions in the simulation (i.e., posting a message, sharing a message, commenting a post and liking a post). Action probability parameter establishes the probability of an agent to perform an action. Privacy threshold
parameter specifies the value from which an agent considers that an action is risky for
him. Privacy policy parameter describes the audience of an agent action (i.e., friends),

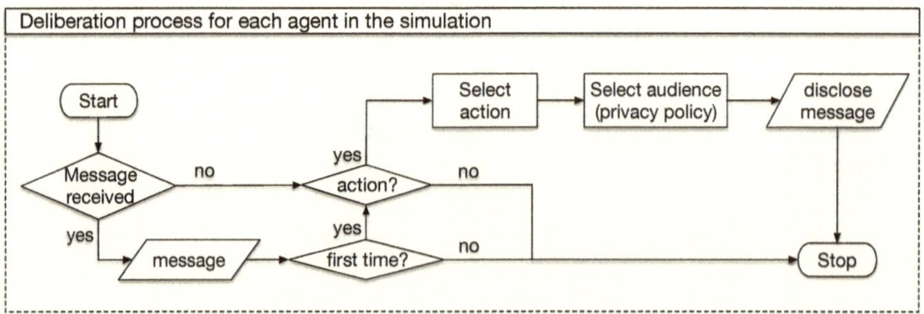

Figure 3.7: Flowchart of the agent deliberation process.

Parameters	Values
#Simulations	400×1000 (agents)
Network topology	{scale-free, random, small-world}
Diffusion action	{publish, share, comment, like}
Action probability	uniform
Privacy threshold	uniform
Privacy policy	friends

Table 3.3: Simulation parameters.

Regarding real networks, we used PHEME dataset[3] that is based on the dynamics of the life cycle of social media rumours on Twitter [297]. The dataset contains 330 conversational threads. We analyzed the PRS and centrality values of the 330 users that initiated a thread through the publication of a message.

To evaluate the relationship between the PRS and structural centrality metrics in synthetic and real networks, we consider message stages from 1 to 4 and also relationship levels from 1 to 4. The reason for the number of relationship levels is based on the analysis presented in [101] where it is reported that most of the cascades in reality are small.

In the next subsections, calculations about agents' PRS based on information sharing activities are used to find a relation with centrality metrics. In this way, approximations using centrality metrics would allow us to calculate agent privacy risks in scenarios where there is no access to data about social interaction, when there is no previous activity, or when new users join the network.

3.6.3   PRS and global centrality metrics

In this section, we analyze whether or not there is a correlation between agents' PRS
(i.e., dependent variable) and their global centrality (i.e., independent variable) in
synthetic networks. Real networks were not considered in these experiments since
the global structures of the rumor networks are not available. We considered the
global centrality metrics described in Section 3.4: random-walk betweenness (bet-rw),
shortest-path betweenness (bet-sp), closeness, and pagerank. The values of centrality
properties are normalized in the range $[0, 1]$. We used analytical regressors to estimate
the dependence relationship between centrality metrics and PRS. We considered the
R^2 coefficient to determine how close the data are to the fitted regression line. In this
case, values close to 1 indicate that there is a high correlation between centrality and
PRS values.

Figure 3.8 displays the comparison between PRS and global centrality values. In 3.8, a
centrality metric is analyzed in each row, and a network topology is considered in each
column. The x axis shows the values of the agents' PRS and the y axis shows the values
of the agents' centrality metrics. Colors represent the number of agents with certain
values of PRS and centrality. The relationship between PRS and centrality metrics is
also shown by the coefficient of determination (R^2). Due to the logarithmic behavior
of the centrality metrics (especially in the case of the scale-free network), a *linear-log*
filter was applied to all of the data.

First, the results reflect the variability of agents' PRS depending on the type of network.
The scale-free BA networks (see Figure 3.8 – first column) favor higher values of PRS
(close to 0.5). In contrast, in the small-world WS networks (Figure 3.8 – third column),
PRS does not reach 0.3. It can also be observed that the type of network reflects the
existence of different groups of agents based on their privacy risk. As an example, in
the scale-free BA networks there is a small group of agents with high values of PRS
(i.e., values that range in the interval $[0.3, 0.5]$), while the rest are distributed between
0.1 and 0.3. In the random ER networks, there is a majority group with relatively high
values (i.e., values between 0.25 and 0.4) and a minority with very low values of PRS.
In the small-world WS network, it can be observed that most of the agents have low
PRS values (between 0.125 and 0.2) compared to other network topologies, and there
are two minorities: one with slightly lower PRS values and another with slightly higher
PRS values.

Second, there is a high correlation between global centrality metrics and the PRS
values (see Figure 3.8). The R^2 value is around 0.9 in scale-free networks (Figure
3.8 – first column [bet.-sp, pagerank]); 0.93 in random networks (Figure 3.8 – sec-

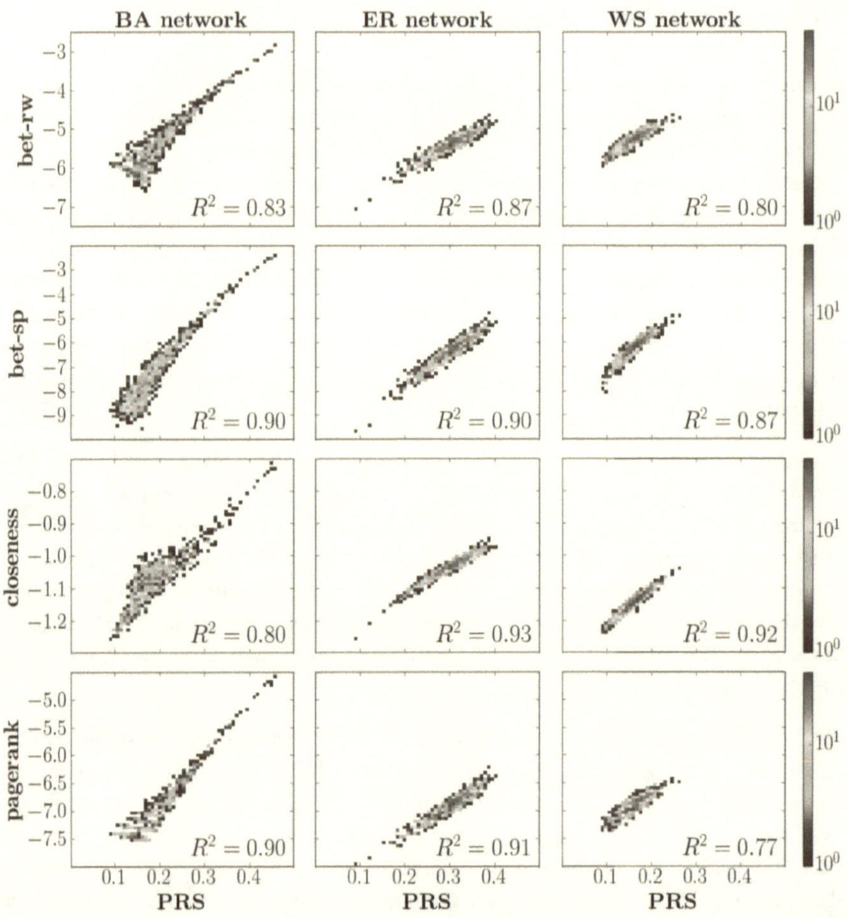

Figure 3.8: Correlation between global centrality metrics and PRS for different social network topologies.

ond column [`closeness`]); and 0.92 in small-world networks (Figure 3.8 – third column[`closeness`]). Thus, we can conclude that PRS values can be approximated through global centrality metrics in scenarios without data about information flows in the social network.

Table 3.4 shows the relationship between PRS and global centrality metrics for each level expressed as the R^2 coefficient. Level 1 (i.e., direct neighbors) is not shown due to its irrelevance, since it corresponds to the agent that initiates the activity (i.e., publishes

Network type	Level	R^2 score			
		closeness	pagerank	bet-sp	bet-rw
scale-free (BA)	2	0.82	0.79	0.75	0.66
	3	0.38	0.29	0.43	0.32
	4	0.82	0.25	0.40	0.18
random (ER)	2	0.93	0.90	0.88	0.83
	3	0.80	0.74	0.77	0.74
	4	0.95	0.82	0.84	0.78
small-world (WS)	2	0.93	0.73	0.87	0.78
	3	0.96	0.74	0.86	0.77
	4	0.78	0.49	0.59	0.50

Table 3.4: Evaluation of the relation between global centrality metrics and PRS by levels for different social network topologies.

a message). As can be seen from the results, the R^2 coefficient generally decreases according to the depth of the target level, except for random ER network topology.

As the results show, the estimation of PRS using global centrality metrics yields promising results. However, as we stated in the previous section, global centrality metrics present several limitations: their calculation requires a knowledge of the whole network structure, and they suffer from performance issues in large networks. Moreover, a recalculation is needed when the network structure changes (i.e., when a new agent joins/leaves the network or a relationship is created/removed). Taking into account these challenges in calculating global centrality metrics, we examine local and social centrality metrics in the following subsection.

3.6.4   PRS, local, and social centrality metrics

In this section, we evaluate the relationship between local and social centrality and PRS values in synthetic and real social networks. First, we analyze degree centrality and the ego-betweenness centrality [105] (i.e., a local approximation of the betweenness centrality metric). Second, we analyze social degree and social ego-betweenness centrality. These experiments have the same settings considered in previous experiments (subsection 3.6.2).

Figure 3.9 shows the results of the linear-log regression analysis to determine if there is a relationship between local centrality and PRS values. Although ego-betweenness

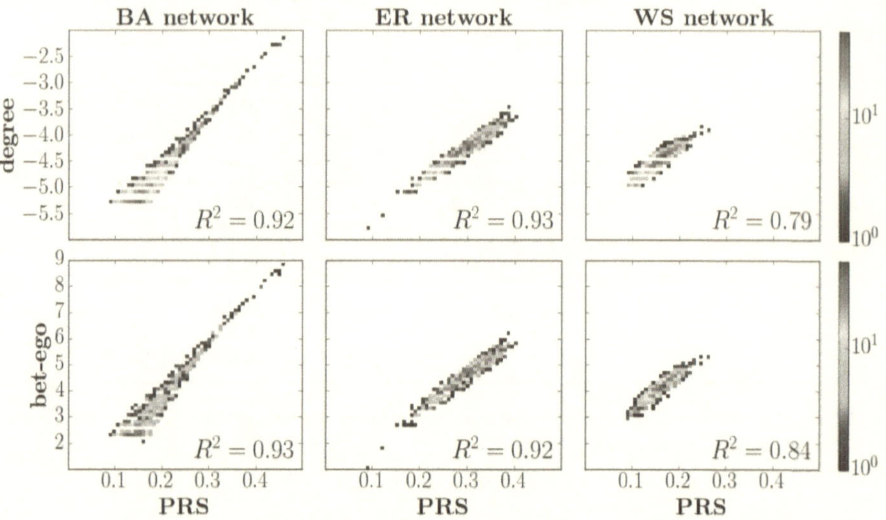

Figure 3.9: Correlation between local centrality metrics and PRS for different social network topologies.

and degree centrality metrics rely on local data, they provide values in scale-free and random network topologies that can be used to provide a fitted approximation of the PRS. Based on agents' privacy risk, both local metrics detect the same groups of agents that were detected with global metrics. The R^2 values obtained with local centrality metrics in some cases improve the results provided by global centrality metrics, or these results are at least as good as those provided by global metrics.

Nevertheless, there are some situations where the degree or ego-betweenness centrality of an agent can be misleading for detecting privacy risk. For instance, an agent a_i can be highly connected to other agents with a low degree of connection and a_i has a high PRS value. However, the message diffusion actions that its neighbors may perform will not have a real risk impact on its privacy. Therefore, it would be interesting to consider not only the local centrality metrics of an agent, but also the centrality values of its neighbors. Hence, in the following experiments, we evaluate the relation between social degree and social ego-betweenness metrics and PRS. Specifically, we examine four measures in the first and second level: bet-ego$_{sum}$, degree$_{sum}$, bet-ego2$_{sum}$, and degree2$_{sum}$ (see Equation 3.10, 3.11, 3.12, and 3.13). We do not consider further distance since the majority of diffusion cascades in reality are small [101].

Figure 3.10 shows the results achieved with social degree and social ego-betweenness

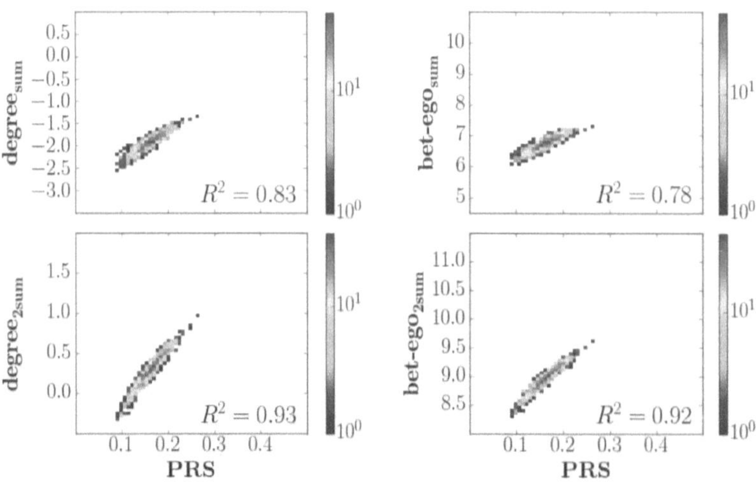

Figure 3.10: Correlation between social centrality metrics (i.e., $degree_{sum}$, $degree_{2sum}$, $bet\text{-}ego_{sum}$, and $bet\text{-}ego_{2sum}$) and PRS for small-world WS network.

centrality metrics for the small-world WS network. The relationship between social centrality and PRS values in scale-free and random structures is not shown since the values obtained were similar to those obtained by using previous centrality metrics. The correlation between centrality and PRS values in the small-world WS network improves considerably for $bet\text{-}ego_{2sum}$ and $degree_{2sum}$, while there is not any improvement for $bet\text{-}ego_{sum}$ and $degree_{sum}$. The reason for this could be that the ability to disseminate information in level 2 (i.e., direct neighbors of neighbors) has a great impact on the final PRS. $bet\text{-}ego_{2sum}$ and $degree_{2sum}$ capture this effect better than $bet\text{-}ego_{sum}$ and $degree_{sum}$.

When analyzing the relationship between the local and social version of degree and ego-betweenness and the PRS values by levels (see Table 3.5), we detect that local centrality metrics have a behavior similar to social centrality metrics. In general, if we compare local centrality with social centrality metrics, we find that the estimation of the PRS by levels improves for the three topologies, especially for deep levels such as level 4. Finally, comparing both social and local centrality metrics, $degree_{2sum}$ obtains a slightly higher degree of correlation with PRS by levels than the other centrality metrics.

Figure 3.11 shows the results obtained in real networks. Most users have low PRS values (i.e., values in the range [0,0.2]). Social and local ego-betweenness are not suitable to

Network type	Level	R^2 score					
		local centralities		social centralities			
		degree	bet-ego	$degree_{sum}$	$bet\text{-}ego_{sum}$	$degree_{2sum}$	$bet\text{-}ego_{2sum}$
scale-	2	0.79	0.79	0.78	0.47	0.63	0.35
free	3	0.33	0.36	0.42	0.36	0.53	0.63
(BA)	4	0.28	0.30	0.83	0.90	0.94	0.88
random	2	0.91	0.90	0.94	0.88	0.93	0.92
(ER)	3	0.78	0.78	0.78	0.72	0.79	0.79
	4	0.85	0.85	0.91	0.89	0.93	0.93
small-	2	0.75	0.81	0.81	0.78	0.95	0.93
world	3	0.77	0.82	0.82	0.79	0.94	0.94
(WS)	4	0.51	0.53	0.59	0.61	0.71	0.70

Table 3.5: Evaluation of the local and social centrality metrics correlation with PRS by levels for different network topologies.

distinguish between users with high or low PRS. The degree of correlation is lower than 0.5 (see Figure 3.11 – second column). However, social and local degree centrality metrics provide better results. Degree and $degree_{sum}$ show a high degree of correlation (i.e., 0.66 with degree and 0.82 with $degree_{sum}$). The results are close to those obtained in synthetic networks, where $degree_{2sum}$ obtained a high degree of correlation with PRS.

The experiments validate the use of centrality metrics to approximate PRS values in scenarios where there is no information about the activity generated in the social network. In scenarios where there is information about network structure, global metrics such as closeness show a high degree of correlation with PRS and PRS in levels. In scenarios where there is only local knowledge, local and social centrality metrics based on ego-networks also provide good results. Specifically, local centrality metrics provide results estimating PRS values that are just as good as those obtained with global metrics or even better in some topologies such as scale-free networks. Social centrality metrics have also been evaluated and the metrics that consider centrality properties based on neighbors of neighbors ($degree_{2sum}$ and $bet\text{-}ego_{2sum}$) obtain the best degree of correlation with PRS and PRS in levels. Finally, we have tested local and social centrality metrics to estimate PRS values with real data from rumor networks. The results show that degree and $degree_{sum}$ provide the best approximation to estimate the privacy risk of an action.

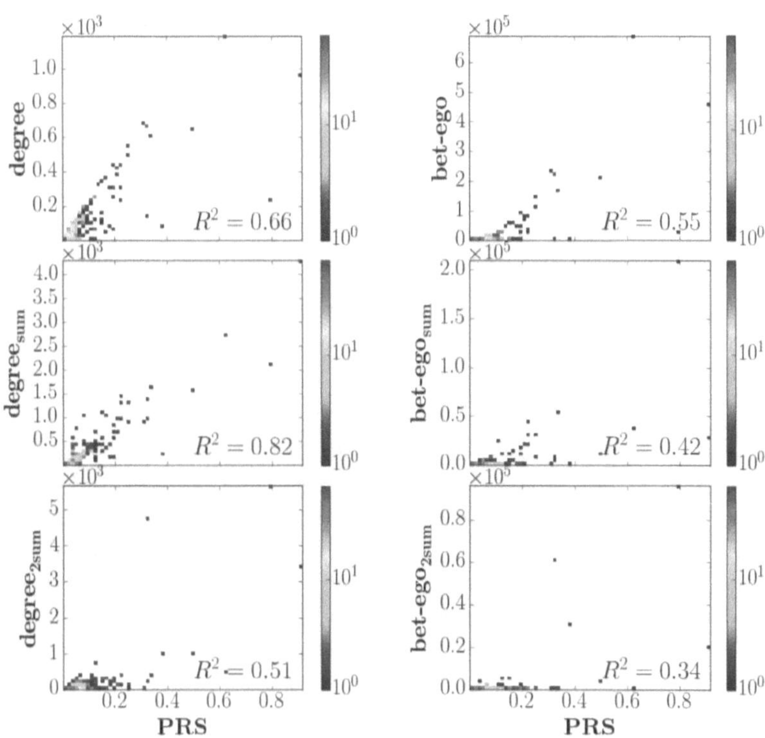

Figure 3.11: Correlation between local (bet-ego and degree) and social (degree$_{sum}$ and degree$_{2sum}$) centrality metrics in rumour social networks.

3.7 Conclusions

Most privacy approaches focus on mechanisms that semi-automatically facilitate the
definition of privacy policies to define the audience that a user expects is going to
receive the information published. However, there is still an open problem of making
users aware of the extent of sharing information on the social network, even if such
information reaches the audience previously defined. In this paper, we have focused
on solving this problem. A measure of the privacy risk of a user-sharing action, PRS,
has been proposed based on the scope of its dissemination in the network with the
following main contributions:

- The PRS is oriented to estimating the reachability of users' sharing actions instead of being focused on the misalignment of their users' expected audience with the actual audience.

- This measure is provided globally and in levels in order to be able to adjust to the user's perception of risk.

- The PRS takes into account the paths that the publications follow in the social network without the need for the user to have to provide information explicitly.

- Centrality metrics have proven to be good estimators in establishing an approximation of the PRS in those social networking environments whose detailed record of the information sharing activity in the social network is not available.

As shown in Section 3.6, despite the topological properties of the network, centrality metrics can evaluate the user's relevance in information transmission processes. We have considered global metrics (i.e., betweenness, closeness, and pagerank) for scenarios where a complete view of the network it is available, and local and social measures (i.e., degree, ego-betweenness) for scenarios where you only have a local view of the structure of the network. To evaluate the relationship between these measures of centrality and the proposed measure of PRS, we have performed a set of experiments in different topologies of synthetic networks and in real networks of rumors. The results showed that in scenarios where there is information about network structure, global metrics such as closeness show a high degree of correlation with PRS and PRS in levels. In scenarios where there is only local knowledge, local and social centrality metrics based on ego-networks provide a suitable approximation to PRS and PRS in levels. The results in real social networks confirm that local and social centrality metrics based on degree perform well in estimating a user's privacy risk and could be integrated in social network applications that offer limited information access.

As future work, we plan to validate the proposed privacy risk score through experiments in real environments. These experiments will provide feedback about the effect of the use of PRS on user behavior in social networks. We also plan to evaluate different methods (i.e., numeric values, text messages, color gradient, etc.) to show PRS values in order to inform the user about the risk of certain actions in the network. We will also evaluate the inclusion of new parameters (i.e., tie-strength between users, user personality, type of content posted, etc.) that may influence the privacy risk in order to obtain more accurate values.

METRICS FOR PRIVACY ASSESSMENT WHEN SHARING INFORMATION IN ONLINE SOCIAL NETWORKS

— Published by Jose Alemany, Elena del Val, Juanmi Alberola, and Ana García-Fornes in the Multidisciplinary Open Access Journal of IEEE Access [13]

4.1	Introduction	80
4.2	Related Work	81
4.3	Privacy Threats in OSN	85
4.4	Privacy Risk Metrics when Sharing Information	86
4.5	Experiments	91
4.6	Conclusions	103

4.1 Introduction

One of the most common online activities in the European Union in 2014 was participation in social networking [83]. According to Eurostat [209] nearly half (46 %) of individuals aged 16 to 74 used the Internet for social networking (i.e., using sites such as Facebook or Twitter). In general, the number of social network users is increasing and it will reach the 2.72 billion in 2019 [245].

There are many users of social networking sites who are not aware of privacy and often share information without considering who will or will not have access to it [128]. The effect of the lack of privacy awareness led users to negative experiences related to privacy [270], and in some cases, there are users who consider leaving as a consequence of inadequate control over their data [99].

Regarding problems with privacy awareness and privacy settings configuration in Online Social Networks (OSNs), the provision of metrics and mechanisms that facilitate the management of individuals' privacy and enhance the awareness of privacy risks become an important issue [292, 265]. Applications related to OSN usually provide mechanisms to configure the users' privacy profile. Nevertheless, the majority of approaches focus on protecting the information referred to user profile and not to the visibility of his/her publications. In the literature we can find proposals that try to address these issues with the automation of privacy settings [86, 262, 34]. However, these usually require some intervention from the user and do not solve the problem of increasing privacy awareness. Other works deal with the improvement of user's awareness about the misalignment of users' expected audience with the actual audience [49, 129, 178]. These latter works facilitate the alignment between the expected and the actual audience. However, there is still an open problem. These proposals do not take into account that users that are part of the target audience might re-share the published information, losing control over the original publication scope.

The structure of the network is one of the main factors that have influence on the scope of a sharing action [101]. This scope can be seen as the effect of a message diffusion process. Spreading processes such as epidemics or information diffusion have been analyzed in the area of Complex Networks [153, 163]. Several works have studied spreading dynamics and influential or relevant individuals in these processes [205, 277].

In social networks, the concept of influential users are referred to those users strategically located in the network, which are responsible of information diffusion since they can efficiently and conduct the dissemination of a message. Since influential users may contribute to increase the privacy risk [136], determining if there are influential users in the path that a user's publication follows would be essential to assess the privacy risk of this publication. Related to this issue, it is widely accepted that structural metrics such as degree [201], PageRank [169], closeness, or betweenness [97, 96, 158, 98] are suitable to detect influential users [38].

The perception of risk may be different from one user to another [185, 61, 237]. Some users are more comfortable with the possibility that their publications can be seen by others and they may be even interested in achieving that effect. In contrast, other users prefer not to disclose their information beyond their direct friends [89]. Therefore, different levels of risk perception should be considered for determining the privacy risk.

Unlike other proposals that present mechanisms to facilitate the alignment between the expected and the actual audience, in this article we focus on the analysis of the potential reach of a publication in social networks as a consequence of re-sharing actions, assuming that the publication was received by the expected audience. We present two privacy metrics: *Reachability* for measuring the user posts probability to reach certain depth level; and *Audience* for clarifying the invisible audience, measuring the percentage of users that really will access to posts. The metrics act as an indicator of the potential risk of user's actions, and are based on information flows and a friendship-layered model that provides information about the reachability of a user publication based on the distance between the user and the potential audience. Finally, to consider scenarios where third applications cannot have access to the traffic of users' messages in online social networks, we analyze if there is a correlation between structural network factors and the proposed metrics. The results obtained in the experiments conclude that local structural properties are correlated with the proposed privacy metrics.

The paper is organized as follows. Section 2 presents previous approaches related to privacy score metrics. Section 3 exposes the privacy risks in social networks with a usual scenario and proposes a solution. Section 4 describes the proposed layered privacy risk metrics. Section 5 presents the experiments that analyze if there is a correlation between structural properties and the proposed privacy metrics. Finally, section 6 presents conclusions.

4.2   Related Work

As communication through social networks acquires greater relevance in our daily social interactions, it is important that users understand the effect of communicative actions using these social tools. Users often see OSN as tools that facilitate communication that has traditionally been face-to-face [17]. However, communication using

OSN does not have the same impact as traditional communication. It is important for users to be aware of the scope of their communicative actions through OSN [234, 114].

Previous works tried to deal with this problem from different perspectives. There are approaches that provide wizards to facilitate the management of privacy profile settings. Fang et al. [86] present a privacy wizard based on an active learning paradigm. Users can assign "labels" (i.e., share or not share) to a set of selected friends. Then, previous labelling processes are used as the input for their classifier. Finally, this wizard determines labels for the remaining friends of these user that are in the same circle. However, this approach assumes that friends in the same social circle have show similar responses of sharing publications. Thus, this approach does not consider that friends can play different roles. Liu et al. [164] propose a privacy score based on user's profile items but without considering the dynamics of how an information item is re-shared through the social network. The authors also propose a recommendation based on a comparison between the user's privacy score and his/her neighbors score. If the score is below that of his/her neighbors, the system can recommend stronger privacy settings. However, not all users in a social network have the same perception of privacy risk. Therefore, a recommendation based only on your neighbors could not fit to your privacy preferences. A privacy score is also proposed by Vidyalakshmi et al. [262]. The authors present a framework for obtaining a privacy score metric from an individual perspective. This metric considers users' personal attitude towards privacy and communication information. Privacy score is estimated using cubic bezier curve that integrates: (i) user's disposition to privacy; (ii) user's attitude towards communication; (iii) a ranking of friends according to their privacy attitude; and (iv) the frequency of communication with friends. The use of a cubic bezier curve facilitates the representation of different types of users' behaviors towards privacy. The inclusion of this privacy score metric could imply a manual sorting process of friends based on the personal view of the user. The proposed score only considers an ego-user view of the social network and does not evaluate other collateral effects such as information diffusion processes in the network. Bilogrevic et al. [34] propose an information-sharing system that decides (semi-)automatically whether to share information with others, whenever they request it, and at what granularity. They consider a vector of 18 features to feed the classifier. The vector encodes whether the information is shared or not. Initially, users make n decisions about features to train the classifier, and then a logistic classifier makes the remaining decisions automatically predicting the users' sharing decisions. The approach requires the user intervention and also assumes that users are privacy aware of the consequences of their decisions.

Some approaches focus on providing information of users that may have received information that was not previously addressed to them. These works help users to increase their privacy risk awareness and to define their social groups/contexts more precisely. Wang et al. [272] focus on the effects of soft paternalistic interventions over users' behavior on information disclosure decisions. This proposal uses three mechanisms that alert users about the risk of sharing information. The mechanisms are: (i) showing images of users that can see the information; (ii) introducing a time delay before sharing information; and (iii) showing a message if the information contains negative words. The effects of these mechanisms were analyzed over a population of 21 users. The authors payed attention to the influence over users' behaviors depending on how the privacy risk information was shown to the users. This study concludes that privacy mechanisms are good to prevent unintended disclosure. However, this mechanisms do not provide accurate information about the reachability of the information sharing action.

Other approaches use norms as a mechanism for defining the different of personal information and reasoning about this information [23]. Calikli et al. [49] propose an adaptive architecture that provides recommendations for sharing information and help users to re-configure user's groups. This proposal is based on two main concepts: social contexts (i.e., group membership information) and conflicts (i.e., privacy norms). Thus, this proposal requires the defintion of accurate user's social contexts and conflict rules. Kafali et al. [129] provide an approach based on model checking for certain properties. This system uses as input privacy agreements of the users (i.e., clauses about which relations are entitled to which privileges), user relationships, the content updated by users, as well as inference rules. The system determines whether or not a property of interest (i.e., whether OSN's commitment to hide a user's information item) can be violated in a given social network. Then, the user use this output to decide his actions. Mester et al. [178] presents a platform where agents interact among them to reach a consensus regarding a message to be published. Agents are aware of user's privacy concerns, expectations, and friends. When a user is about to publish new content, the agent determines which other users would be affected by the message and contacts the respective agents of those users. The negotiation protocol allow agents to discuss constraints and determines a suitable way to publish the content when none of the users' privacy is violated. In this approach, the privacy rules (i.e., privacy concerns of a user) should be predefined using a Semantic Web Rule Language. In addition, this approach is only based on direct contacts and does not consider other levels of friendship that may have access to this information through a friend re-sharing action.

A more flexible approach is presented by Yang et al. [288]. They present a privacy metric of user i sharing information with a neighbor j as a trade-off between user

i's concerns (i.e., potential privacy risks) and incentives of sharing information with j (i.e., potential social benefits). The potential privacy risk of i is based on the re-sharing probability of an information receiver j (i.e., the ratio of the number of times that j re-shares over the number of times that j receives information from a user i) and its trust level (i.e., user i's opinion on j). The social gain considers the receivers that belong to a selected sharing circle and the number of interactions between i and j. They present the privacy risk as an individual metric, without considering the consequences that other potential users might re-share the received information. Pensa et al. [206] propose a privacy metric that includes information sensitivity and the location of a user in the network structure using a centrality metric. Although they metric proposed is interesting, the authors use the page-rank metric without analyzing other centrality metrics that might fit better to the context of information diffusion and might be applied in scenarios where there is no global information of the network.

There are other works focused on the analysis of the effects of information diffusion in social networks using SIR models. Zhu et al. [294] define a privacy protection mechanism based on information sharing in ONS and classify users according to different privacy setting policies. They use a SIR model to describe the dynamics and evolution of information propagation. However, in this proposal the authors classify users based on a static privacy policy. They do not consider that, depending on the information, the privacy policy of a user might change. Similarly, Bioglio et al. [35] use a SIR model to analyze the role of attitude on privacy of a user and her friends on information propagation in OSN. They use an extension of a SIR model that considers the privacy attitude of users using parametric values [36]. In the simulations, the authors consider that all the neighbouring users of the initial user where the diffusion is going to start are going to have the same attitude as the user that starts the diffusion. This is not very realistic due to a user usually have different groups of friends with different attitudes in social networks.

From our point of view, privacy risk does not only concern the problem that information might reach people who were initially not expected to receive it. Previous works focus on this problem providing mechanisms to avoid audience misalignment. In this paper, we assume that users who received the information are in the expected target audience and we focus on the next step. Our proposal is focused on the analysis of the effects over the users' privacy when users from the intended audience re-share the original publication.

The proposal privacy metrics (*Reachability* and *Audience*) improves previous works in the following ways: (i) it focuses on information sharing behaviors instead of static user's profile configuration; (ii) it does not require previous user intervention, norms

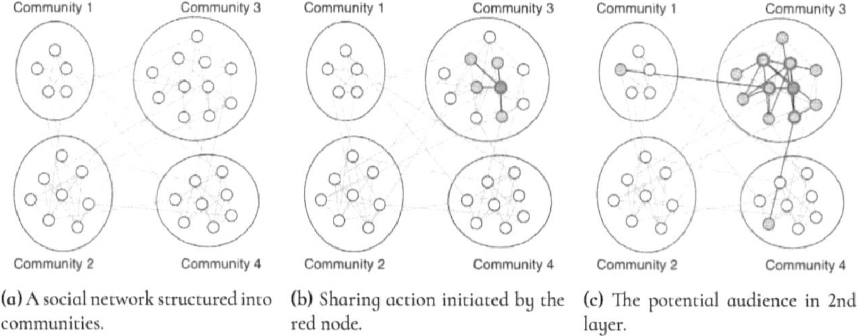

(a) A social network structured into communities.   (b) Sharing action initiated by the red node.   (c) The potential audience in 2nd layer.

Figure 4.1: Example of a potential privacy risk in online social networks.

definition, or manual classification of friends; (iii) the proposed metrics does not provide a unique value to represent the risk of sharing activities; it provides the metrics considering layers of friendship (i.e., confidence) that provides a more accurate view of the disclosure effect over user's privacy.

4.3   Privacy Threats in OSN

Privacy risk not only concerns the problem that information might reach people who were initially not expected to receive it, but it also involves the problem of losing control over the scope of the information. Figure 4.1 describes this privacy risk problem in online social networks. The elements shown have the following meaning: nodes represent users; lines represent friendship relations; scribbled-nodes represent users with content access; encircled-nodes (colored) represent users who share content.

In Figure 4.1a, we show the structure of a social network that is organized into four communities. Figure 4.1b shows the action "sharing message on his/her wall" performed by the red node. The node determines the audience depending on his selected privacy policy (e.g., *friends*). Therefore, only his friends can see the message (i.e., nodes scribbled in green). If a green node performs a sharing action (i.e., nodes encircled in green), the message could reach other communities causing a privacy risk problem (see Figure 4.1c, new nodes scribbled in green in community 1 and 4). The privacy risk of each node variates, as can be seen in the scenario, depending on its position in the social network and his behavior. Therefore, it is important to provide metrics about potential privacy risks to users for improving their control and awareness of the privacy.

Taking into consideration the problem described, there are a lot of moments using social media where this problem may appear. For example, there are situations where users need to use social media as therapy making negatives comments about work, politics or religion [283]. This actions can become viral (or "far-reaching", depending on user's perception) causing privacy risks and users' regret [293]. The use of social media knowing the reachability of users' publications would increase the awareness of users' actions reachability and would reduce users' privacy risk. In addition, there are many articles that analyse silent listeners or invisible audiences and the effect of their actions on users privacy [31, 238]. When users share photos about their holidays with relatives and friends, they may expect that these photos will be seen indirectly by friends of friends; but previous research studies revealed that users are only aware of a small part of the real audience that sees the publication [31].

To deal with the above privacy risk problems, we define two privacy metrics: *Reachability* and *Audience*. These metrics estimate the privacy risk of a user when shares a message in a social network. These metrics can be applied to users' friendship layers. Reachability metric obtains the probability of a message to reach a specific ratio/percentage of users given a specific sharing action. The user can specify this ratio. The Audience metric obtains the percentage of users that will see a message given a specific sharing action and a friendship layer revealing the invisible audience. These metrics aim to increase the users' awareness about the reachability of their publications in the social network even though they have restricted the visibility of their publications.

4.4 Privacy Risk Metrics when Sharing Information

To define how Reachability and Audience work, first we are going to explain some important concepts. We assume that there is a social network $\mathcal{G}$ that consists of N nodes, where every node $a_i \in N = \{a_1, ..., a_n\}$ represents a user. Users are connected through bidirectional and undirected links that represent friendship relationships and correspond to the edges $E \subseteq N \times N$ of $\mathcal{G}$. We define the adjacency matrix A to represent these links. Given two users a_i and a_j, if there is a link between these users, we represent this as $A_{a_i,a_j} = 1$ and $A_{a_i,a_j} = 0$ if there is not a link.

The privacy metrics proposed to evaluate the risk of sharing information actions (e.g., publishing a message in his/her own wall, commenting an existing post, sharing a post, etc.) act as an indicator of the potential risk of the messages diffused over the social network (i.e., potential scope and visibility). The higher the *Reachability* and *Audience* values, the higher the threat to user a_i's privacy by performing a sharing information action.

4.4.1 Metrics Calculation

In the social media context, users perform message diffusion actions that have a potential risk associated with the potential subsequent action that may diffuse the message
over the social network. In addition, another point to take into consideration is that
not all users have the same view of risk when sharing information. Some users may
consider that sharing information with "friends of friends" might be risky while other
users may consider that the true risk is at the next layer of friendship. Moreover, some
users may consider risky that few users (one or two) of a certain layer of friendship
see some information while other users may consider risky only when the majority of
users of a certain layer see it. In order to consider different perceptions of risk in sharing actions in social networks, we have defined the concepts of friendship layer and
information reachability.

Friendship layer is based on the social distance between users. We define the distance
between any pair of users a_i and a_j as the minimum number of links to be traversed
to reach one a_j from a_i and is represented as $d(a_i, a_j)$.

We define a friendship layer $L_{a_i}(l)$ as the subset of users whose distance to the source
user a_i is l:

$$L_{a_i}(l) \subseteq N, \forall a_j \in L_{a_i}(l) : d(a_i, a_j) = l \land \nexists d'(a_i, a_j) < d(a_i, a_j)$$

Therefore, users in layer 1 are those that are direct neighbors of a_i, users in layer 2 are
those that are linked with 2 links from a_i and so on.

We define the information reachability of a user a_i as the number of users that saw
a message m published by a_i. We define a $N \times N$ reachability matrix γ_m for each
message m that is diffused on the social network. The rows and the columns of γ_m
represent users. We use $\gamma_m(a_i, a_j)$ to refer to the entry in the a_ith row and a_jth column
of γ_m, and it has two possible values $[0, 1]$, where 1 represents that message m was sent
by a_i and reached a_j and 0 that did not reach a_j. $\Gamma = \{\gamma_1, ..., \gamma_m\}$ represents the set
of all γ_m associated to each messaged propagated in the network.

Based on the friendship layer and the information reachability, we define two metrics,
Reachability and *Audience*, to provide feedback about the privacy risk of a user when
shares information in a social network.

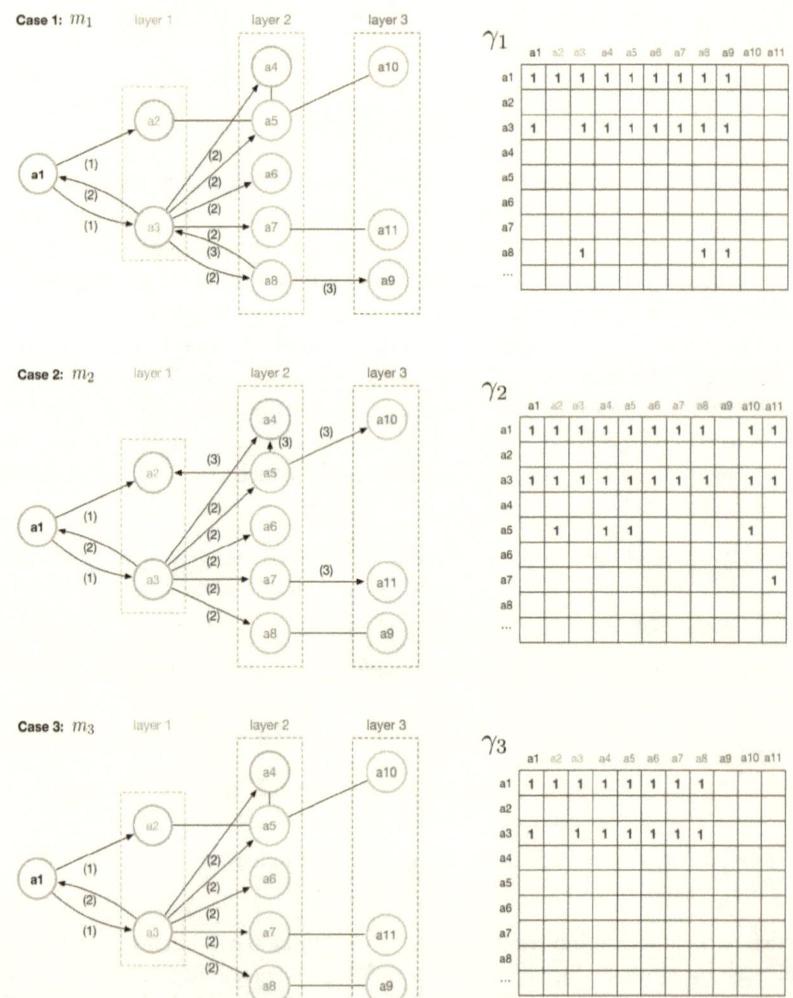

Figure 4.2: Example of social network activity and the calculation process of the Reachability and Audience metrics. In this example, all information shared is visible by users' direct friends. The directed arrows indicate the direction of the message. The number between brackets indicates the stage in the forwarding process of a message. Users perform the following actions on the social network: (case 1) user a_1 publishes/shares a message m_1 on his/her wall and users a_3 and a_8 re-share m_1; (case 2) user a_1 publishes/shares a message m_2 on his/her wall and users a_5 and a_7 re-share m_2; (case 3) user a_1 publishes/shares a message m_3 on his/her wall and users a_3 re-shares m_3.

Reachability ($Re(a_i, l, r)$) represents the probability of a message diffused by a user a_i of reaching a percentage r (i.e., reachability ratio) of users in layer l. Considering $L_{a_i}(l)$ as the set of users in layer l from a user a_i and r as a reachability ratio of users, *Reachability* metric can be calculated as

$$Re(a_i, l, r) = \frac{|\Gamma''|}{|\Gamma'|},\tag{4.1}$$

where Γ' represents the set of reachability matrixes associated to messages in which a_i participated in their diffusion, $\Gamma' \subseteq \Gamma$, such that $\forall \gamma_m \in \Gamma' \rightarrow \exists a_k \, |\gamma_m(a_i, a_k) = 1$; and Γ'' represents the set of reachability matrixes associated to messages in which a_i participated in the information flow and were viewed by a percentage of users of layer l greater than r

$$\Gamma'' \subseteq \Gamma', \text{ such that } \forall \gamma_m \in \Gamma'' \rightarrow \frac{\sum\limits_{a_j \in L_{a_i}(l)} \gamma_m(a_i, a_j)}{|L_{a_i}(l)|} \geq r$$

The *Reachability* metric ($Re(a_i, l, r)$) is appropriate to evaluate the risk that a message shared by a user reaches certain friendship layer. Figure 4.2 shows an example of *Reachability* metric calculation for user a_1, at friendship layer 3, and considering a ratio r of 0.15 ($Re(a_1, 3, 0.15)$). In this scenario, a_1 wants to obtain the probability that a publication in its wall will reach a few users (i.e., $r = 0.15$) at friendship level 3. The value of Re ($Re = 2/3$) means that there is a high probability (greater than 0.5) that the information reaches level 3.

Audience (Au) represents the percentage of users in layer l that is expected to see a message diffused by a_i considering the total number of users of that layer $Au(a_i, l)$ (Eq. 4.2), or considering the total number of users of the network $Au_G(a_i, l)$ (Eq. 4.3). The audience $Au(a_i, l)$ provides a local insight about the risk in a specific layer of the social network. However, the information that $Au(a_i, l)$ provides about the audience that has seen a message in a specific layer could be biased by the number of agents in that layer. Therefore, it could be also interesting for the user to obtain a more global picture of the risk of reaching certain layer considering the whole network. For this reason, we have also proposed the $Au_G(a_i, l)$ metric considering the total of agents of the network.

$$Au(a_i, l) = \frac{\sum\limits_{\gamma_m \in \Gamma'} \left(\dfrac{\sum\limits_{a_j \in L_{a_i}(l)} \gamma_m(a_i, a_j)}{|L_{a_i}(l)|} \right)}{|\Gamma'|} \tag{4.2}$$

$$Au_G(a_i, l) = \frac{\sum\limits_{\gamma_m \in \Gamma'} \left(\dfrac{\sum\limits_{a_j \in L_{a_i}(l)} \gamma_m(a_i, a_j)}{|N|} \right)}{|\Gamma'|} \tag{4.3}$$

The *Audience* metrics are appropriate to evaluate the privacy risk of a sharing action based on the coverage that this action will achieve at certain friendship layer. Figure 4.2 shows the calculation of the *Audience* metrics for messages sent by user a_1 considering the third level of friendship. In this scenario, a_1 wants to know exactly the percentage of users (i.e., the audience) that will see a publication on his wall. Therefore, a_1 will consider the audience metrics.

Figure 4.2 shows a scenario that represents an example of a social network with interactions between users. In the scenario, there are three friendship layers and the reachability matrix associated with each message generated in the social network (i.e., γ_1, γ_2, and γ_3). We assume that all of the users in G have the privacy policy that only their direct friends can see their walls. The message diffusion actions performed in this scenario are the following. In Case 1 (1), user a_1 publishes a message m_1 on his/her wall. Therefore, users a_2 and a_3 can see the message m_1. The information about the users that see m_1 as a result of this sharing action performed by a_1 is stored in γ_1. In γ_1, we are measuring the reachability of the m_1 when a user interacts with the message (2). Then, user a_3 decides to share m_1 on his/her wall. Users a_4, a_5, a_6, a_7, and a_8 can see the message m_1. As in the previous case, the information about the users that can see the message m_1 as a result of the sharing action of a_3 is updated in γ_1. Note that the corresponding row of a_1 is also updated with the new users that see m_1. This update reflects the 'indirect' reachability of user a_1 through the actions of a_3 (3). Then, user a_8 shares m_1 publishing it on his/her wall. Users a_3 and a_9 can see it and the information in γ_1 is updated. As in the previous situation, rows corresponding to users a_3 and a_1 are also updated. In the cases 2 and 3 (i.e., messages m_2 and m_3 respectively), the process performs in a similar way to the case 1. The difference is that the users that re-share the message are different. In the case 2, the users that re-share the m_2 are a_3, a_5 and a_7. In the case 3, the user that re-shares the m_3 is a_3. The corresponding reachability matrixes (i.e., γ_2 and γ_3) are updated accordingly to the sharing actions performed by the users. Following the example, the metric values of Reachability and Audience proposed in this paper of the user a_1 for a three-level depth and a 15% correspond to 0.66 (Re), 0.33 (Au), and 0.09 (Au_G) respectively. A Reachability value of 0.66 means in this case that 2 out of 3 times the message reached more than 15% of the users at third-level depth. An Audience value of 0.33 means in this case that as average 1 out of 3 users on the third-level will have access to the message, that at the same time corresponds to a 10% of the users on the whole network (0.09).

4.5 Experiments

Several experiments were performed to evaluate the privacy risk metrics proposed: *Reachability* and *Audience*. There are two sets of experiments. The first set evaluates the privacy risk metrics in different network topologies considering different layers. The second set of experiments analyzes if there is a correlation between the privacy metrics proposed and structural properties of the networks. The use of structural metrics would facilitate the estimation of the privacy metrics proposed in scenarios where there is no data available about users' information flows.

For both set of experiments, we use a social network simulation tool. This simulation tool was developed using the open source Elgg framework[1] where is possible to build real and virtual social environments. The simulation tool is capable of reproducing social network scenarios such as the creation of users and relationships, message sending, and social interactions.

4.5.1 Experiment settings

The networks generated in the experiments follow three models: Watts-Strogatz [274] (WS, small-world), Barabási-Albert [22] (BA, scale-free), and Erdös-Rényi [81] (ER, random). Table 4.1 shows the set of parameters and properties that characterize each of the networks used for the simulations.

Each simulation run consists of 1000 *seed* messages published by randomly selected agents. These *seed* messages cause that other agents, in turn, perform actions to diffuse the messages throughout the network. The diffusion of a message m occurs when an agent a_i sees a publication. Then, the agent evaluates the risk of sharing m considering the reachability or the audience metrics (Re, Au or Au_G depending on the

Model	Watts-Strogatz	Barabási-Albert	Erdös-Rényi
type	small-world	scale-free	random
# agents	1000	1000	1000
mean degree	12	12	12
diameter	5	5	5

Table 4.1: Networks structural properties.

Parameter	Values
network models	{Watts-Strogatz, Barabási-Albert, Erdös-Rényi}
# agents	1000
privacy policy	friends
layers	2-4
# simulations per network	50
# seed messages per simulation	1000

Table 4.2: Experiment settings.

scenario) values. If the value of the corresponding metric is greater than his individual risk threshold (i.e., a random uniform distributed value in the range [0,1]), a_i does not perform the action, simulating that the agent decided not to propagate the publication. Otherwise, a_i shares the message m. In the latter case, the message could be seen by other neighbor agents and the matrix γ_i will be updated. Figure 4.3 summarizes the specific diffusion model adopted in the simulation which corresponds to a combination of a SIR model with a threshold value.

We perform 50 simulations per each type of network and considering friendship layers $l = 2$, $l = 3$ and $l = 4$ (see Table 4.2). For *Reachability* metric (Eq. 4.1), we considered two reachability ratio values: $r = all$, where the label *all* represents the ratio percentage of 100% in the specified layer (i.e., if the message reaches all the agents of the layer); and $r = one$, where the label *one* represents the ratio percentage to reach one agent in the specified layer. This percentage value will change in each agent since the total number of agents in a layer is not equal for all the agents. For *Audience* metrics (Eq. 4.2 and 4.3), we consider the population of a specific layer Au and the whole population of the network Au_c.

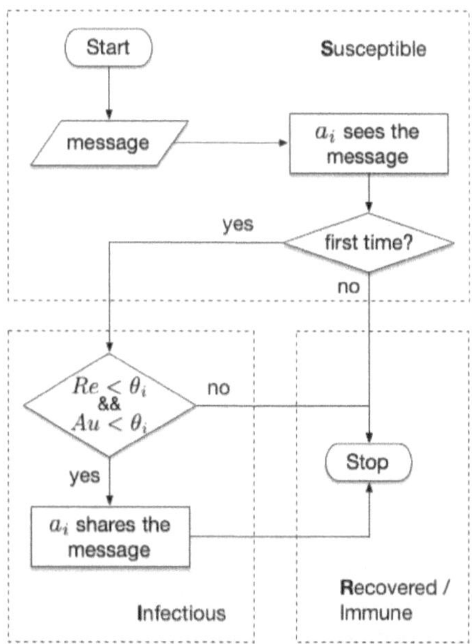

Figure 4.3: Flowchart of the diffusion model followed for each agent in the simulation.

4.5.2 Privacy Metrics in Different Network Topologies

In this section, we analyze the performance of the *Reachability* and *Audience* metrics in the three network topologies considered. Tables 4.3 and 4.4 summarize the results of the simulations.

As it can be observed in Table 4.3, the value of Re for $r = all$ is 0 or a value close to 0 for layers 2-4 in all the networks structures. These results show that it is difficult that a message reaches all the agents in the network. However, the value of Re for $r = one$ increases as the layer increases in the three network structures. Initially, according to the privacy settings of the agents in the network, all direct friends of an agent a_i (i.e., agents in layer $l = 1$) see the publication of a_i. Therefore, the Re in that layer is 1. Then, a subset of these direct friends will re-share the publication. As a result, among all the possible agents at layer 2, only those that are direct contacts of the subset agents that re-shared will see the publication. For this reason, the probability to reach an agent in layer 2 (i.e., $Re(a_i, 2, one)$) decreases to 0.5. In the following layers the Re value increases considerable. The main reason for this is that the publication has been widely propagated in the network and there is a high probability that agents

90

in layers 3 or 4 receive the same publication from different sources (i.e., agents). The values of Re are higher in small-world and random networks due to there is a higher degree of clustering in these topologies than in scale-free networks. Therefore, there is a higher probability that an agent receives the same information from different sources.

The Re metric for $r = one$ captures the idea of the reachability that a publication can achieve in a specific layer. However, this information can be completed with the consideration of the audience in a specific layer. In order to know the percentage of agents that see a message in a specific layer, we calculate the values of *Audience* for the agents (see Table 4.4). The results obtained with Au show a similar trend to the results obtained with Re. The percentage of agents that see the message increases as the layer increases in the three network structures. The highest values of Au are obtained by agents in random networks.

The audience that has seen a message in a specific layer could be biased by the number of agents in that layer. Therefore, we have also analyzed the Au_G metric considering the total of agents of the network. As in the case of Au, the highest values of Au_G are obtained in random networks. In the case of Au_G metric, there is a difference with respect the trend in the values obtained with Au and Re when a message arrives at layer $l = 4$. In the scenario that we have considered for the experiments, the networks have a diameter of 5. When a message arrives at a layer close to the diameter, the number of agents in that layer is usually low. It is very likely that there is an alternative shorter path to the agent that originated the message. Therefore, the number of agents in that layer is low with respect to the total of agents in the network and the values of Au_G are also low.

Taking into account the results of *Reachability* and *Audience* obtained in the experiments, we can conclude that the network topology has a direct effect on the outreach of the information published and therefore, in the proposed metrics. Results also show that there is a high probability that in a scenario where the agents' privacy policy is "friends", a publication reaches a layer $l = 3$, and inside this layer, in the case of random networks, the percentage of agents that could see the publication could arrive close to 30% of the network. The results obtained with *Reachability* and *Audience* metrics reinforce the theories of invisible audiences [31].

In spite of the *Reachability* and the *Audience* estimations provide a suitable measurement of the privacy risk associated with a user's publication action, the calculation of these values presents limitations under certain situations. In real-world scenarios, it is not always computationally affordable the collection and analysis of a detailed record of the sharing activity in an OSN. This becomes more complicated if the OSN frequently

mean $\pm$ std	small-world	scale-free	random
$Re(a_i, 2, one)$	$.514 \pm .121$	$.514 \pm .121$	$.606 \pm .025$
$Re(a_i, 3, one)$	$.901 \pm .054$	$.765 \pm .113$	$.950 \pm .045$
$Re(a_i, 4, one)$	$.945 \pm .038$	$.784 \pm .151$	$.968 \pm .048$
$Re(a_i, \{2, 3, 4\}, all)$	0.0	0.0	0.0

Table 4.3: Statistical analysis of Reachability (Re) values for different network topologies ($mean \pm std$).

mean $\pm$ std	small-world	scale-free	random
$Au(a_i, 2)$	22.56 ± 1.28	13.24 ± 4.37	18.56 ± 0.98
$Au(a_i, 3)$	24.48 ± 2.99	28.77 ± 3.40	42.73 ± 5.37
$Au(a_i, 4)$	39.13 ± 5.36	40.91 ± 9.31	70.51 ± 5.95
$Au_G(a_i, 2)$	2.51 ± 0.57	2.09 ± 1.94	3.66 ± 0.96
$Au_G(a_i, 3)$	14.73 ± 2.87	19.60 ± 3.13	31.24 ± 3.71
$Au_G(a_i, 4)$	10.61 ± 1.59	5.23 ± 3.78	3.63 ± 2.53

Table 4.4: Statistical analysis of Audience (Au) values for different network topologies ($mean \pm std$).

modifies its structure. Moreover, the access to users' information and their activities in some OSN applications to third-party applications is not always possible. It can also happen that even if we have access to the activity of users, there are situations (e.g., when a new user joins the social network) where we do not have information about the previous activity of users. For these reasons, in the following sections, we propose an approximation that evaluates the use of structural network properties to estimate *Reachability* and *Audience* metrics. Specifically, considering the previous results, we have selected the $Re(a_i, l, r = one)$ and Au_G metrics for the following analysis.

4.5.3 Correlation between privacy metrics and structural properties

In this section, we present an approximation based on structural network metrics. This approximation does not use information about the traces of the paths follows by users' messages in OSN. We analyzed the relationship between the *Reachability* and the *Audience* of a user and his centrality values.

Global structural centrality properties

Initially, we considered global centrality metrics to evaluate if there is a relationship between the privacy risk metrics and centrality. These centrality metrics use information about the entire network structure to be computed. Among the global metrics, we have considered [190]: (*i*) *random-walk betweenness* [191] that considers the number of times a random walk between two pairs passes through the agent of interest; (*ii*) *closeness*, that considers the average length of the shortest paths between an agent and all other agents in the network; and (*iii*) *eigenvector*, that gives each agent a score proportional to the sum of the scores of his neighbors. The values of the centrality metrics were normalized in $[0, 1]$ interval.

Using analytical regression, we study how each centrality metric is related to the values of *Reachability* and *Audience*. For this, we performed regression tests where a regressor is launched for each centrality metric. Figures 4.4 and 4.5 show the relationship between *Reachability* (or *Audience*) and centrality values. The point color represents the number of agents with specific values of the metrics. We considered the R^2 coefficient to determine how close the values of the metrics are to the regression model. R^2 values close to 1 indicate that there is a high correlation between *Reachability* (or *Audience*) and the centrality metric. The regression models considered in the experiments are linear, polynomial and logarithmic.

First, we analyze the accuracy of global centrality measures to estimate the *Reachability* metric by layers (see Table 4.5). In general, independently of the layer and the network topology, the best results are obtained by the random-walk betweenness centrality. Figure 4.4 shows the relationship between the Re at layer 3 and global centrality metrics in each network topology considered. We can observe that the polynomial regressor model has slightly higher R^2 values than the linear or the logarithmic. The polynomial regressor model allows adjusting to a linear correlation, especially in the case of the small-world network, whereas in the scale-free network and in some cases the random network its behaviour tends to be curved and therefore it improves remarkably to other adjustments.

Second, we analyze the accuracy of global centrality measures to estimate the *Audience* metric by layers (see Table 4.5). The R^2 coefficient values show that there is a clear relation between closeness centrality and the Au_G metric. Figure 4.5 shows the relationship between the Au_G metric at layer 3 and global centrality metrics in each network topology. The polynomial regressor model provides the best R^2 coefficient values, especially in the case of the small-world network. In the scale-free networks, the correlation values between the global centrality metrics and the Au_G are low, ex-

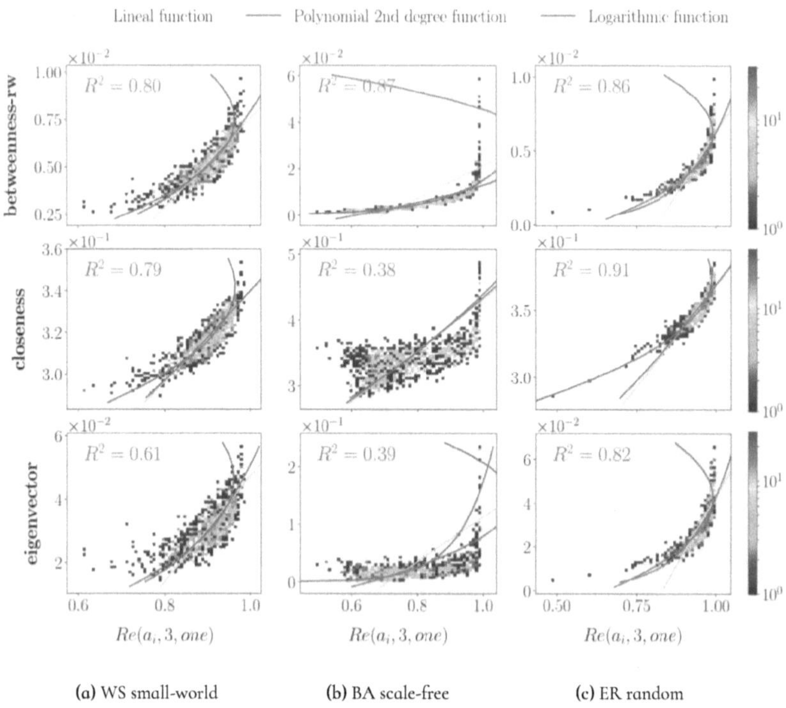

Figure 4.4: Approximation of *Reachability* metric at layer $l = 3$ using global centrality metrics (different network topologies considered).

cept for closeness centrality metric. It can also observed that for agents with high centrality values, their Au_G values are low. The main reason for these results is that in scale-free topologies, when the Au_G is calculated for layers close to the network diameter (d=5), the number of agents that have not been received the message yet is low compared to the total number of agents in the network.

Considering the global centrality measures analyzed, random-walk betweenness metric provides a more fitted approximation to *Reachability* metric, while closeness metric provides a more fitted approximation to *Audience* metric.

Another phenomenon that can be observed is the distribution of agents in different groups depending on network topology and the metrics. In Figure 4.4, we observe that most of the agents in small-world networks have high *Re* values (values close to 0.9)

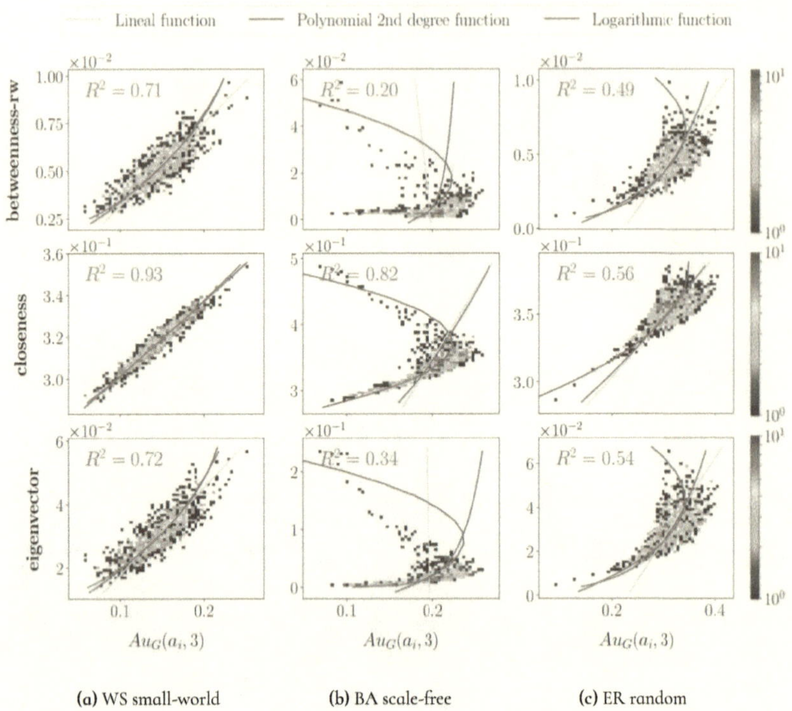

Figure 4.5: Approximation of *Audience* metric at layer $l = 3$ using global centrality metrics (different network topologies considered).

compared to other network topologies, and there are two extreme minorities: one with lower Re values ($[0.6, 0.85]$) and another with slightly higher Re values ($[0.9, 1]$). In the scale-free networks, there is a small group of agents with high values of Re metric ($[0.8, 1]$) while the rest of agents are distributed between 0.6 and 0.8 values of Re. In the random networks, there is a core group with high values (between 0.9 and 1) and a minority of agents with values of Re between 0.7 and 0.9. Therefore, in this scenario, the topologies where there is a large group of agents with a high degree of *Reachability* are random and small world networks.

Something similar occurs in Figure 4.5. In the small-world network for layer $l = 3$, we observe that most of the agents have intermediate Au_G values (i.e., values close to 0.15) compared to other network topologies, and there are two extreme minorities: one with slightly lower Au_G values ($[0.1, 0.12]$) and another with slightly higher Au_G values ($[0.17, 0.22]$). In the scale-free networks, there is a small group of agents with high values of Au_G metric ($[0.15, 0.22]$) while the rest of agents are distributed between 0.1 and 0.15 values of Au_G. In the random networks, there is a core group with relatively high values (0.35) and a minority of agents with very low values of Au_G. Therefore, in this scenario, the topologies where there is a large group of agents that can reach a wider audience are scale-free and random networks.

R^2	small-world			scale-free			random		
	RW_BC	CC	EC	RW_BC	CC	EC	RW_BC	CC	EC
$Re(a_i, 2, one)$	**0.69**	0.48	0.34	**0.85**	0.25	0.24	**0.73**	0.50	0.43
$Re(a_i, 3, one)$	**0.80**	0.79	0.61	**0.87**	0.38	0.39	0.86	**0.91**	0.82
$Re(a_i, 4, one)$	**0.55**	0.51	0.52	**0.67**	0.24	0.34	**0.49**	0.48	0.49
$Au_G(a_i, 2)$	0.81	**0.92**	0.75	**0.97**	0.92	0.90	0.90	**0.96**	0.95
$Au_G(a_i, 3)$	0.71	**0.93**	0.72	0.20	**0.82**	0.34	0.49	**0.56**	0.54
$Au_G(a_i, 4)$	0.53	**0.81**	0.61	0.21	**0.96**	0.83	0.80	**0.96**	0.94

Table 4.5: Dependence strength between global centrality properties and privacy risk (*Reachability* and *Audience*) values measured using the R^2 coefficient. The best adjustments have been highlighted. Header columns correspond with random-walk betweenness centrality (RW_BC), closeness centrality (CC), and eigenvector centrality (EC).

Local structural centrality properties

Global structural centrality properties are suitable for social networking services providers that have access to the network structure. Otherwise, some OSN applications do not facilitate access to users' information to third-party applications, therefore it is not possible to infer the social network structure beyond the first layer. For these reasons, we have also considered strictly local metrics to evaluate their suitability to estimate *Reachability* and *Audience* values in layers.

Considering the limitations to calculate global centrality metrics, in this section we examine local centrality metrics. We considered *degree*, the number of links of an agent; *ego-betweenness*, an ego-centric method to approximate the betweenness centrality; and *effectiveness*, an ego-centric method that measures the number of alters minus the average degree of alters within the ego network, not counting ties to ego network [3]. The effectiveness reflects the links that lead to different people. A high value of effectiveness implies that the agent can lead to a high number of different people.

Table 4.6 shows the results of the analysis of the relation between *Reachability* and local

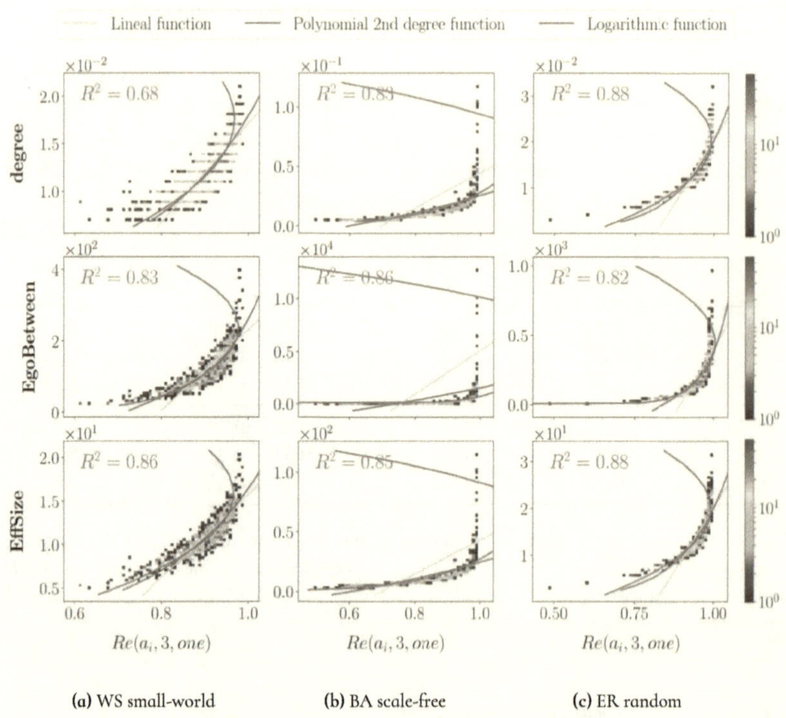

Figure 4.6: Approximation of *Reachability* metric at layer $l = 3$ using local centrality metrics (different network topologies considered).

centrality metrics in different network topologies. It can be observed that the best results are obtained with the effectiveness centrality. Figure 4.6 shows the relation between Re values and local centrality values for layer 3. In small-world networks, ego-betweenness and effectiveness centrality metrics yield good results, in some cases even better than global centrality metrics. In scale-free networks, the relation between Re and local centrality metrics is better than with global metrics. Moreover, we can observe a logarithmic relation between Re and local centrality values, especially in scale-free networks. In random networks, there are no significant differences between global and local metrics and their relation to the Re metric.

Regarding the *Audience* metric, Table 4.6 shows the results of the analysis of the relation between *Audience* and local centrality metrics in different network topologies. It can be

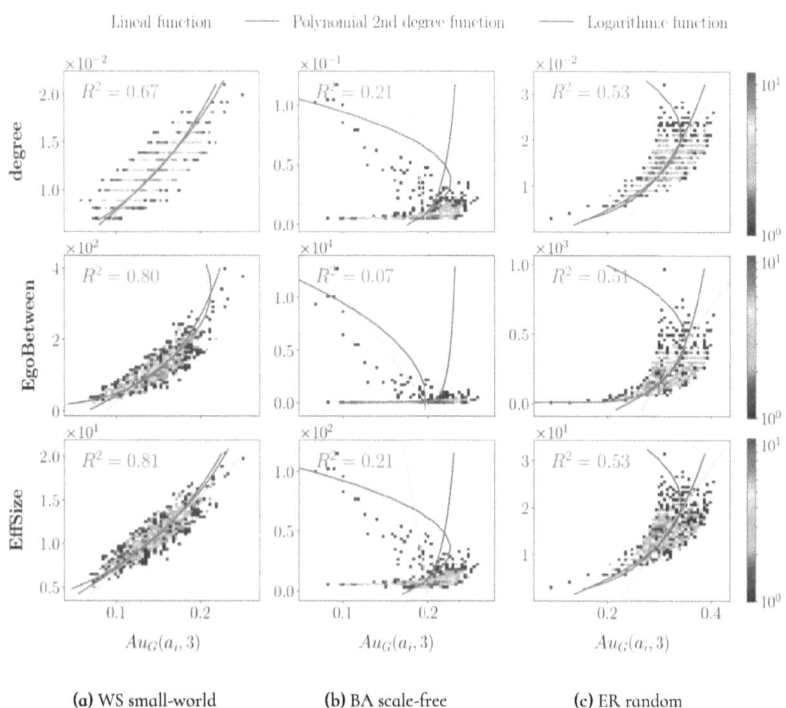

Figure 4.7: Approximation of *Audience* metric at layer $l = 3$ using local centrality metrics (different network topologies considered).

observed that the best R^2 values for small-world and random network topologies are obtained using the effectiveness centrality. In the case of scale-free network topologies, there is only a high correlation values between Au_G and local centrality values for layer 2. Figure 4.7 shows the relation between *Audience* values and local centrality values for layer 3. Ego-betweenness and effectiveness centrality metrics yield good results using a linear regressor. In scale-free networks, the relation between *Audience* and local metrics is similar to global metrics. We also observe a polynomial behavior between *Audience* and local centrality values. In random networks, there are no significant differences between global and local metrics and their relation to the *Audience* metric.

Results show that local centrality metrics offer similar results to global metrics to estimate *Reachability* and *Audience* values. Effectiveness centrality metric provides a

R^2	small-world			scale-free			random		
	D	EGO_BC	EF	D	EGO_BC	EF	D	EGO_BC	EF
$Re(a_i, 2, one)$	0.46	0.58	**0.68**	0.72	0.78	**0.78**	0.65	0.65	**0.65**
$Re(a_i, 3, one)$	0.67	0.83	**0.86**	0.83	**0.86**	0.85	0.88	0.82	**0.88**
$Re(a_i, 4, one)$	**0.57**	0.53	**0.56**	0.69	0.43	**0.74**	0.50	0.41	**0.53**
$Au_G(a_i, 2)$	0.76	0.89	**0.90**	0.98	0.95	**0.98**	0.96	0.95	**0.96**
$Au_G(a_i, 3)$	0.67	0.79	**0.81**	0.21	0.07	**0.21**	0.53	0.51	**0.53**
$Au_G(a_i, 4)$	0.55	0.60	**0.61**	**0.28**	0.25	0.23	0.85	0.79	**0.88**

Table 4.6: Dependence strength between local centrality properties and privacy risk (*Reachability* and *Audience*) values measured using the R^2 coefficient. The best adjustments have been highlighted. Header columns correspond with degree centrality (DC), ego betweenness centrality (EGO_BC), and effectiveness (EF).

slightly higher fitted approximation using the logarithmic regressor model. Results obtained with Effectiveness along with the ease of its calculation allow us to make an estimation of the proposed risk metrics (i.e., *Reachability* and *Audience*) that will assess the user in the publication process of an information item in an OSN.

If we observe the relation between the different values of privacy risk metrics and the centrality measures (global and local), we reach the following conclusions. Regarding the global centrality metrics, closeness metric has a higher correlation with privacy risk metrics, especially with *Audience*, in different network topologies than other global centrality metrics. In the case of *Reachability*, random-walk betweenness provides a higher degree of correlation. Regarding local centrality metrics, effectiveness metric achieves the best results both in the different network topologies and for the different types of privacy risk metrics (i.e., *Reachability* and *Audience*). Specifically, effectiveness metric yields promising results comparable to global centrality measures and close to the proposed privacy risk metrics (i.e., *Reachability* and *Audience*). Moreover, effectiveness facilitates the estimation of privacy risk in scenarios where there is no global knowledge or there is no previous information about users' privacy policies or information flows. Effectiveness offers a powerful advantage to provide real-time personalized solutions to users when they post or share information through ONS.

4.6 Conclusions

In this paper, we have presented a new model of privacy risk based on friendship layers. The concept of friendship layers allows us to provide information about user's privacy risk for different levels of risk perception. Based on this model, we propose two privacy risk metrics *Reachability* and *Audience*. *Reachability* provides information to the user about the probability that a message that he publishes reaches a specific friendship layer or a specific number of users in that layer. *Audience* provides information to the user about the percentage of users in a specific layer that is probable that see a message he published.

We evaluated the proposed *Reachability* and *Audience* through simulations in different social network topologies and considering different layers. The results show that network topology has a direct effect on the outreach of the information published when agents' privacy policy is "friends". In the scenario analyzed, if an agent publishes a message, there is a high probability (close to 0.9) that reaches a layer $l = 3$ and the percentage of agents that could see the publication will be close to 30% of the network. The results of the simulations provide a real vision of the privacy risk that is higher than the users risk initially might think, which reinforces the theories of invisible audiences.

Finally, we consider a different approximation of *Reachability* and *Audience* for scenarios where there is no previous information about users activity or the information about the traces of the messages cannot be obtained. The proposed approximations are based on structural centrality metrics. We analyzed the relation between *Reachability* and *Audience* and centrality metrics. We considered global centrality metrics that have a complete overview of the structure of the network and the local centrality metrics that only consider local information. Regarding the global centrality metrics, the results show that, to estimate the *Reachability* metric the best results are obtained by the random-walk betweenness centrality. To estimate the *Audience* metric the best results are obtained by the closeness centrality. Regarding local centrality metrics, effectiveness is the most suitable property to approximate *Reachability*. In the case of the relation between *Reachability* and centrality metrics, there are no relevant differences between the degree of correlation values obtained with global or local metrics. To estimate the *Audience* using local centrality metrics, in small-world and random networks, the best results are obtained with effectiveness centrality. For scale-free networks, effectiveness provides good results for the estimation of *Audience* in layers that are not close to the network diameter. Based on these results, we propose a common regression model based on the effectiveness centrality values of agents to approximate *Reachability* and *Audience* values in different network models.

As future work, we plan to validate *Reachability* and *Audience* metrics in a real scenario that allows us to obtain users' feedback to evaluate the suitability of the proposed metrics. We also plan the analysis of the effects of different informative methods to show the users' privacy risk in an online social network. Finally, we will extend the proposed metrics with the inclusion of new factors about the users (such as personality and trust) and about the publication (such as sensitivity and virality). These factors may have a great influence on the diffusion of a message in the social network and provide a more precise approximation about the publications' scope.

## CHAPTER 5

EMPOWERING OSN USERS ABOUT THE SENSITIVITY OF THEIR DATA THROUGH NUDGE MECHANISMS

*— Published by **Jose Alemany, Elena del Val,** and **Ana García-Fornes**
in the Hawaii International Conference on System Sciences [13]*

5.1	Introduction	106
5.2	Literature review	107
5.3	Proposal	113
5.4	Experiment	117
5.5	Discussion	120
5.6	Conclusions	121

5.1 Introduction

Online social networks have become a popular tool, being one of the main Internet activities among users [245]. OSN users[1] interact and socialize with each other by sharing their opinions and comments, supporting their friends and favorite groups, and posting their information, activities, etc. As a result, a huge amount of traffic of personal data is produced daily. The way to control the access and use of the data is via privacy policies. However, privacy is a very complex concept for users due to its diffuse nature and the number of factors that must be taken into account [231] (e.g., the sensitivity of the message, the properties/context of the receiver, the scope of the action, etc.). Even so, users are constantly confronted with the privacy decision-making process for each piece of data they share, which may produce privacy issues. These occur not only due to the users' lack of knowledge about privacy or the service provider's data usage but also because other users may have access to user data [213]. As a consequence, some users may be exposed to situations such as losing their reputations, experiences that make them feel uncomfortable, or publications that unintentionally become available to a broader audience than the audience initially expected [11]. For these reasons, users' concerns regarding the vulnerability of their personal data have been raised.

Although users state that they are concerned about their privacy [5, 125], there are works that highlight the difference between users' attitude and their actual behavior towards privacy [148, 24]. This phenomenon is known as the Privacy Paradox. A way to explain this phenomenon is the users' perception at the moment of privacy decision making [109]. When they are going to share personal data, users assess the benefits and risks of sharing personal data. If users perceive the benefits to be higher than the risks, they will share. However, privacy risks are perceived as being abstract and psychologically distant, and more related to the distant future, while the social rewards are perceived to be psychologically near and more concrete, and related to the short term. If users had informative and personalized metrics available about the risks, they could better assess their privacy decisions. The nudge mechanisms are a great solution since it may minimize regret and align the behavior with the stated preferences [7].

The information shared by users, especially personal data, has different levels of sensitivity ranging from totally trivial to extremely intimate data. Legislation such as the

---

[1]Over the course of this paper, when we use user and network concepts, we refer to OSN users and OSNs respectively.

GDPR[2], NIST[3], or UKAN[4] (which emerged from the need to protect users' data) distinguishes different levels of data sensitivity. Companies that buy, sell, and exchange users' data as an economic resource also consider different values of data based on the kind of information provided and whether they can link it to other data [172]. Companies have included the data as part of their business model in a data-driven economy. However, users are not completely aware of the value or sensitivity of their data. Moreover, we have different perceptions of sensitivity for our personal data depending on socio-cultural factors [221]. Therefore, if we empower users by making them aware of the value and/or sensitivity of their personal data through nudge mechanisms, they will be able to choose more suitable privacy policies [7].

In this work, our main contributions are the following: (i) a literature review about the different approaches to estimate the sensitivity of personal data (law, market, individuals, linguistic, and social networks); (ii) a proposal for a ranking/metric of sensitivity as the combination of all of the approaches that adapts them to the OSN domain; and (iii) a validation experiment that tests the effect of sensitivity nudges (based on our metric proposal) on real users' behavior. The paper is organized as follows. Section 5.2 analyzes and reviews previous works on establishing a sensitivity value for data. Section 5.3 presents our proposal for calculating the sensitivity value of social network publications. Section 5.4 includes the results of the experiment carried out to assess the effect of informing the user (via a nudge message) about the sensitivity of their publications before sharing them. We discuss our findings in Section 5.5 and provide our final conclusions in Section 5.6.

5.2   Literature review

5.2.1   Definition of personal data

First, we define what we mean when we speak about data, information, or personal data. Data is the raw material that is processed and refined to generate information that provides meaning. Individually, a single piece of data is rarely useful. For example a single date may be an appointment, a holiday, or an anniversary [217]. However, data is often used to specifically mean digitally stored quantified information. In this paper, we use the terms data and information to refer to the same concept. Personal

---

[2]European General Data Protection Regulation
[3]National Institute of Standards and Technology
[4]UK Anonymisation Network

data is information that can be linked directly or indirectly to an individual and can specifically identify him/her.

At the same time, the sensitivity of information is the potential loss that is associated with the disclosure of that information. This definition allows for the fact that sensitive information is perceived as being riskier and more uncomfortable to divulge [184]. Generally, by definition, personal data is more sensitive than data.

5.2.2 Quantifying the value of personal data

According to Acquisiti et al. [6], there is not just one method for properly establishing the value of privacy and personal data. Different references could be considered to establish this value, such as the money users would be willing to accept for their data, the money they would be willing to pay to protect their data, the cost of making their data public, etc. For this purpose, we reviewed the relevant research studies that proposed rankings and metrics. We have detected four different approaches for sensitivity that are based on (i) laws and regulations; (ii) market valuation; (iii) individuals' valuation; and (iv) linguistics. Below, we present and discuss the solutions provided by each one.

Law & regulation. In this approach, countries have been forced to regulate company activities that collect, store, and manage personal data. These regulations distinguish between different levels of sensitivity of the data that requires more protection than other data. The starting point for defining sensitive data under EU law is the list of "special categories of data" in the GDPR, which is based on the concept of privacy as a fundamental right. According to Article 9 of this regulation, sensitive data includes personal data revealing racial origin, political opinions, or religious or other beliefs as well as personal data on health, sex life, or criminal convictions [102]. Personal data that does not match these categories is also protected but is considered to be less sensitive, so companies do not have so many controls. In the UK, the UK Anonymization Network (UKAN) classifies data following two criteria: whether or not data is personal, and whether data may or may not be identifiable. It is interesting to consider the data that is not personal but that may be used to identify an individual such as vehicle registration or a dynamic IP address, since it may be strongly associated with an individual [79]. In US law, there is no comprehensive data protection regulation and no clear starting point for defining sensitive data that is analogous to the "special categories" of personal data found in the EU Data Protection Directive [140]. Agencies such as the National Institute of Standards and Technology (NIST) and the Department of Homeland Security have struggled to provide a precise definition of personally

identifiable information, but they have not completed the next step of defining different categories of sensitivity or developing a topology of personal data that quantifies
personal data. Current US laws and regulations cover only the use of certain types of
personal data, such as financial and medical information.

Based on laws that are related to the protection of individual privacy in personal information record-keeping systems, Turn proposes a sensitivity scale and classification for
personal information [256]. This scale consists of six levels that are based on the potential adverse effects on the individual, which may range from a mild annoyance to physical harm. The levels are: AS, public (by statute); A, public; B, limited; C, restricted; D,
confidential (by statute); E, sensitive (by statute); and F, secret (by statute). The work
also provides a simplified classification on three levels merging the ones above: basic
(AS, A, B); medium (C, D); and high (E, F). The main problem with the law and regulations approach is that it groups information into broad, abstract categories without
providing a scale or a ranking that indicates sensitivity in a fine-grained way.

Market valuation.   This approach focuses on the information value for companies.
Companies generate economic benefits from users' data and have decided to include
users' data in their business models. User data and knowledge derived from it are sold
and bought by companies for different purposes such as developing new features, offering new services, customizing an advertising campaign, etc. A report elaborated by
the OECD[5] [196] analyzes different methodologies for measuring and estimating the
value of personal data from a purely monetary perspective (i.e., without taking into
account the indirect impacts of the use of personal data on the economy or society).
This report analyzes approaches from two perspectives based on the market's valuation and individual's valuation. From the market perspective, the report assesses the
value of data from indicators such as the market revenues obtained per data record,
the market prices for data, the cost of a data breach, and data prices in illegal markets.
From the individual perspective, the report assesses the value of data from indicators
such as an individual's willingness to pay to protect data. The result is several rankings
based on different indicators. An example of ranking based on the indicator of the
market prices for data is made up of the following types of data that are ordered from
highest to lowest cost: bankruptcy information, felony, employment history, sex of-
fender, education background, unpublished phone number, business ownership, credit
history, marriage/divorce, past address, social security number, address, voter registration. Another example of ranking based on the prices that individuals are willing
to pay to protect their information is made up of the following criteria: the top tier

includes social security numbers (national identity numbers) and credit card information, which most people value highly (USD 150–240 per entry); the middle tier contains digital communication history, such as web browsing history as well as location and health information (around USD 50); the last tier of information contains facts about users, including online purchasing history and online advertising click history, to which individuals attach little value (USD 3–6).

The Financial Times newspaper developed a calculator app based on the analysis of industry pricing data from a range of sources in the US [236]. Malgieri et al. [172] distinguish the following categories according to their economic value (from lower to higher): general (mainly demographic) information about a person; shopping, financial, or vacation intentions; personal data of people going through certain important life events (such as getting married, having a baby, etc.); and personal data containing specific health conditions or information on taking certain prescription (the highest value). In their work, they found that all of the data of a single person is not much valuable economically (approximately less than one dollar). The authors emphasize that the price of personal data has followed a declining trend in recent years. Conversely, companies collect the personal data of more and more people and this data can be resold several times, increasing the profits generated. Another important factor that is highlighted is that there is a positive relationship between the sensitivity of data and its economic value (i.e., the more sensitive the personal data, the higher its economic value).

Individuals' valuation.   Another interesting approach is the individuals' perception of the data. After the analysis of the responses of 310 adults in a national survey, Milne et al. [180] detected six groups of personal information and established a ranking based on the consumers' perceived sensitivity. The groups detected (ordered from lowest to highest sensitivity) were: basic demographics, personal preferences, contact information, community interaction, financial information, secure identifiers. In addition, the authors detected that the perception of risk is multidimensional. They considered that there is not just one type of risk. They differentiated four types of risk where the six information groups could be classified: physical risk (secure identifiers); monetary risk (financial information and secure identifiers); social risk (community interaction); and psychological risk (community interaction and secure identifiers). Schomakers et al. [221] established a sensitivity ranking of 40 different data types. The authors compared their results with Brazilian, EEUU [174], and German individuals. Based on the ranking, they grouped data into three categories (high, medium, and low) using a linear clustering based on the sensitive value of data. Rumbold et al. [217] propose six categories of data (based on the UKAN): non-personal data; human-machine interactions; human demographics, behavior, thoughts and opinions; human characteristics (unprotected); human characteristics (protected); and medical or healthcare data. The authors propose a spectrum of sensitivity for these six categories and subcategories inside them, where the relative frequency with which data would occur is given by individuals.

Although these previous works highlight that the perceived sensitivity of a specific type of data varies depending on socio-cultural factors (i.e., religion is highly sensitive in areas where there is a high degree of sectarian conflict), the ranking of data based on sensitivity is similar among individuals [221, 217].

Linguistics. The last approach considered is centered on linguistics and the use of words. According to Viejo et al. [263], the terms that provide/disclose a large amount of information are also likely to be sensitive. In this respect, several privacy-protection methods for textual data and empirical studies have shown the close relationship between the informativeness of textual terms and their sensitivity [4, 219]. Therefore, Viejo et al. [263] measure the informativeness of a term according to its Information Content (IC), which is computed as the inverse of the term's probability of appearance in a corpus. To that end, they use the largest and most up-to-date electronic repository available: the Web. Other works such as Imran et al. [120] also consider the same idea of linguistics properties to quantify the sensitivity of data, but they use the ontological properties of DBPedia[6] resources to create taxonomic generalizations of words. To do this, they use SPARQL as a query language and the Semantic Web API. Thus, the deeper a word is in the taxonomic tree of generalization, the higher the sensitivity of the word.

5.2.3   Sensitivity in the OSN domain

Some of the categories and information types analyzed in the previous approaches may make no sense in the social network domain (e.g., DNA profiles or bankruptcy information). Conversely, other categories that were not included in the above approaches could appropriately be considered as sensitive due to the risks or consequences for the post's owner, such as personal attacks (which are very common in Twitter) [293].

An important aspect in the OSN domain is identification. Depending on the network platform, users need to provide a minimum amount of information about themselves

Information types from regrets in OSNs	Source
Location data	[50]
Personal and Family issues	[270, 293, 268, 50]
Work and Company data	[270, 293, 50]
Religious issues	[270, 230, 293, 268]
Political issues	[270, 230, 293, 268]
Health and Medical	[293, 268, 50]
Alcohol consumption	[270, 293, 268, 50]
Illegal drug use	[270, 293, 268, 50]
Sexual content	[270, 293, 268]
Negative emotions	[270, 230, 293, 50]
Positive emotions	[230, 50]
Attacks on individuals	[270, 230, 293, 268]
Attacks on collectives	[270, 230, 293, 268]
Lies and Secrets	[270, 230]

Table 5.1: Summary of the most common information types that cause regrets in social networks

in order to have a profile. Even when this information is not required, users upload information about themselves to be identifiable to others (e.g., their real name, birthday, a photo of themselves, etc.) [283]. This effect emerges from the nature of OSNs for communicating and socializing with others. When users are identifiable, they are easily included in the social network structure as friends or followers, and, in addition, they increase their social rewards with the interactions [59]. Therefore, information that users share could be personal by default.

As a consequence, there are a lot of works in the literature that collect and group different kinds of content based on users' regrets caused by sharing data on social networks [270, 230, 293, 268] (see Table 5.1). Most of them consider the most common regret as revealing too much information. Based on this regret, users usually highlight posting about categories like personal and family issues, religion, politics, health, work and company issues, and location data. These categories fully match the categories of personal data from the previous approaches analyzed. As an example, although it is not a common practice, posting lists of defaulters involves a high risk for the publisher and the defaulters due to other users' reactions. On the other hand, network usage has generated regrets that are related to self-presentation and reputation. The information types that could cause these regrets such as publications about alcohol or illegal drug use, obscenity, personal attacks, complaints, and curses were not considered in the approaches analyzed. Since these information types can change the other's perceptions towards the user that publishes, they are also sensitive for the users' privacy. Extreme emotions are also included in this same group. Most of them are negative emotions, but there are some cases of extreme happiness that can cause regrets by the reactions of others (in this case, moved by jealousy). Finally, this research also highlights regrets caused by posting lies and secrets, but no one (to the best of our knowledge) has enough information to detect them.

In fact, some works such as [50] have tried to identify some of these categories, but the only thing they did was to reveal the habits of users. They did not extend their work to enhance the users' awareness of the sensitivity of this type of information or privacy-seeking behavior. Our goal is to propose a quantification value for users' posts and to use it to improve users' privacy.

5.3   Proposal

In the proposal of this work, we address three issues: (i) providing a sensitivity value for each information type that might be present in the OSN domain; (ii) providing and justifying the sensitivity value for the regret-based information types; and (iii) the representation of the total value of sensitivity for a publication, taking into consideration that multiple information types could appear in the same publication.

For the first issue, we propose a ranking that combines the sensitivity values and the information types that appear in the works reviewed (see Figure 5.1). The value for each information type was normalized on a scale of 0 to 1, where 0 means no sensitive data and 1 means the maximum sensitive value of data. We added new information types based on users' regrets (see Table 5.1). For each of these information types, we proposed a potential sensitivity value considering the nature of the regret and its proximity to other information types. For the *Illegal drug use* information type, we propose positioning this information type between *Medication* and *Law enforcement files* (immediately next to *Medication*) since it could be considered as medication, but, depending on the kind of drug, it may lead to legal consequences. For the *Alcohol consumption* information type, we propose positioning this information type as individuals' behaviors, especially since it represents health-damaging behaviors [85] (below *Religion* and close to *Lifestyle*). For strong sentiments, works about regrets concurred that negative emotions are more regrettable than positive ones [270, 230]. Therefore, we propose positioning the positive emotions in the same place as demographic data, and the negative emotions over the *Opinions* information type. Finally, the information type related to attacks, curses, offensive comments, or profanity depends on the kind of target. On the one hand, if

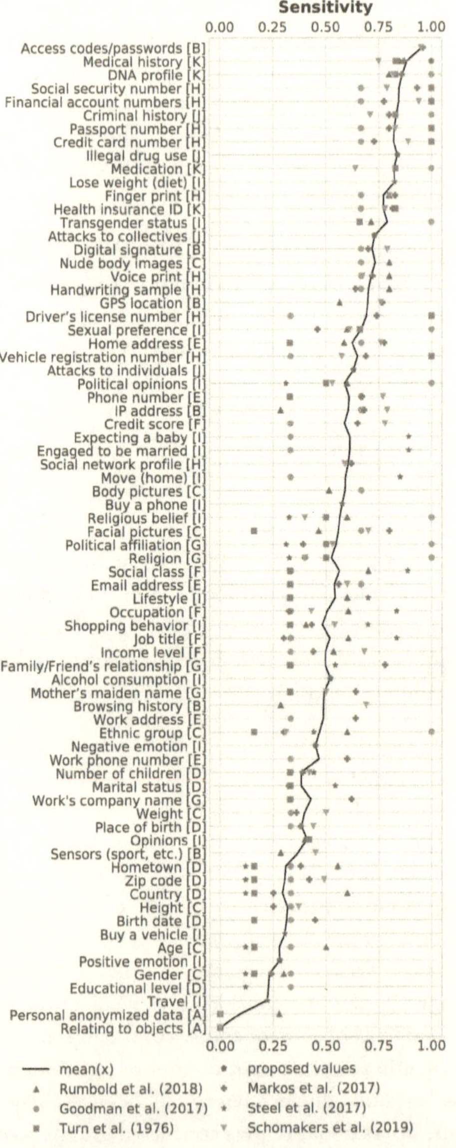

Figure 5.1: Sensitivity for information types. Categories are A=Non-personal, B=Human-machine, C=Human characteristics, D=Demographics, E=Contact info., F=Status/Financial, G=Association, H=Identifiable info., I=Behaviors/Intentions, J=Law-related, and K=Medical. The color of each point corresponds to the research paper that considered the data.

the target is an individual (i.e., *Attacks on individuals*), we propose positioning the information type between *Negative emotion* and types related to laws due to its possible legal consequences. On the other hand, if the target is a group or association (i.e., *Attacks on collectives*), the sensitivity is greater than the sensitivity of *Attacks on individuals*, and, in some countries, it could be considered as a hate crime against a collective.

Finally, using the sensitivity information types from previous works and the proposed sensitivity values for regrets, we created a ranking (see Figure 5.1) of 74 information types (y-axis). We grouped the information types into the following categories: (A) Non-personal, related to anonymized data or object data; (B) Human-machine, data generated from technology interactions; (C) Human characteristics, related to physical aspects; (D) Demographics, related to common features that are not identifiable; (E) Contact info., any information that allows others to contact you; (F) Status/Financial, related to monetary status; (G) Association, data able to link users with other individuals or collectives; (H) Identifiable info., data that can directly identify an individual; (I) Behaviors/Intentions, related to past and future actions; (J) Law-related, that can or have caused legal consequences; and (K) Medical, related to health data. Once we quantified and normalized the value for each information type, we placed them in order from the most sensitive types to the least sensitive types. The sort criterion was the mean value of the information type and the number of research works that assessed that information type. From the resultant ranking, we observed that there is a consensus in most cases for the information types at the extremes of sensitivity (the lowest and highest value). We also observe that information with low values of sensitivity is mainly demographic, anonymized, or related to objects, while information with the maximum values of sensitivity is mainly passwords/access codes (because they can give access to other sensitive information), health information, and identifiable and unique data of an individual. In contrast, the rest of the information types have less consensus with a huge sensitivity variability among the works. We highlight the information types of facial pictures, ethnic/race, and behavior/intentions as being of greatest variance. Furthermore, we also observe that behaviors/intentions of individuals (such as losing weight, expecting a baby, engaging to be married, etc.) are especially valuable for companies, while other approaches give them values that are significantly lower. For this reason, it is so important to consider all of the approaches involved.

In order to provide an estimated value by category, we selected the mean as the representative value for the category. Figure 5.2 depicts the distribution values per category, which includes a Box-plot to enhance visual comprehension. The mean values are included in the legend, which reflects the conclusions extracted in the ranking. Thus, if

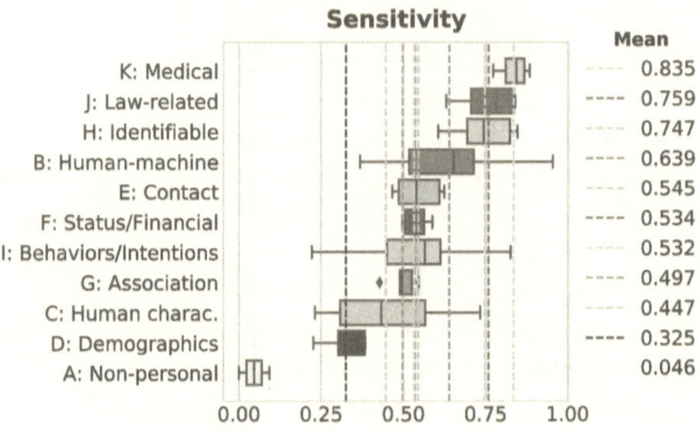

Figure 5.2: Distribution of sensitivity values for the identified categories of information types.

a relevant information type was not included in our proposal, other researchers could derive an approximate sensitivity value by classifying the new information type in a category and/or comparing it with the other information types.

We illustrate a common scenario for proposing a value of sensitivity for a publication. A user posts on a social network. The post (e.g., W) may consist of a media item (e.g., a photo), a textual message, or both [270]. The question that may arise is: What value of sensitivity s should the publication W have (i.e., $s(W)$)? In fact, the combination of information types ($t_i \in W$) actually creates value. When the attribute name is provided as "John" or the attribute gender is provided as "male", these are meaningless. Single attributes without any further context have no monetary value. Only when they are combined (i.e., when John is male) do these attributes create value [172]. In OSN, the profile provides a linkable space for new attributes. Therefore, assessing personal data sensitivity is not about assessing individual information types, but rather assessing combinations of personal data. Using the approach of the market pricing valuation of personal data [236], where data is bought and sold in a combined way, we propose using the same system (i.e., summing their values) to assess combinations of information types.

$$s(W) = \sum_{t_i \in W} s(t_i) \tag{5.1}$$

Thus, the more information types the post has and the more sensitive they are, the riskier it is to share the post.

Age [years]	mean(SD)	13.03 (0.70)
	12 years	22.45%
	13 years	51.53%
	14 years	26.02%
Gender	male	53.57%
	female	46.43%

Table 5.2: Demographics of participants (N=196).

5.4   Experiment

We ran an experiment to test the effect of informing the user (via a message) about
the sensitivity of their publications before sharing them. The message acts as a nudge
for users. Nudges attempt to influence decision making in order to improve individual
well-being without actually limiting users' ability to choose freely, thus, preserving
freedom of choice [7]. For this reason, we consider that nudges could reduce users'
regrets.

5.4.1   Methodology

The experiment consisted of a questionnaire that was distributed online within the context of a one-month workshop about social networks for teenagers. The questionnaire
was embedded in the social network platform that they used in the workshop. A total
of 196 Spanish participants (from the Valencia area) ranging in age from 12-14 years
old completed the experiment. The sample shows heterogeneous distributions regarding age (M = 13.05, SD = 0.71), and gender (53.57% male teenagers) (see Table 5.2). The
questionnaire consisted of asking participants to choose an audience (i.e., the privacy
policy) for real publications (selected previously from Twitter) as if they had written
them. The privacy options available were based on the social circles defined by [78].
We removed the social circles that made no sense for teenagers (such as coworkers), and
we combined the first and second level of family into a single social circle. The final
options were: *No one, Family, Friends, Acquaintances,* and *All*. We collected 53 tweets that
were classified by raters taking into account the information types that the tweets had
(Figure 5.1). We finally chose the 30 tweets with the highest level of agreement with
the information types identified to be included in the questionnaire. From the manual
classification, we calculated the sensitivity value of the tweet using our proposal (i.e.,
accumulating the sensitivity of the different information types, Eq. 5.1).

The questionnaire had two stages, which took place in different weeks, with 15 ques-

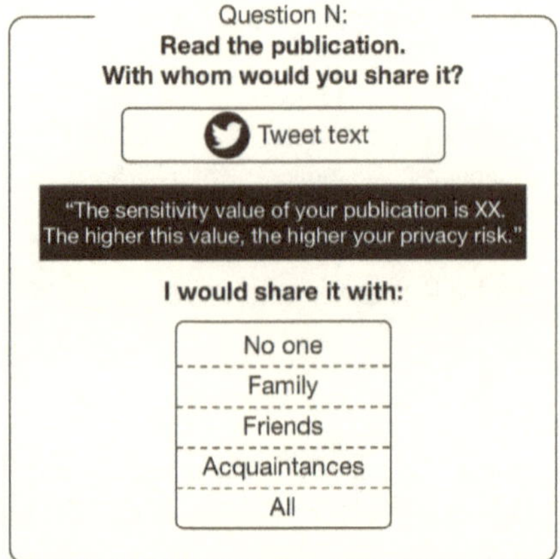

Figure 5.3: Template of the survey questions.

tions per stage. The questions were designed following the structure depicted in Figure 5.3. The difference in the questions between stages was the nudging message that was hidden during the first 15 questions. In the first stage, the nudges were not activated, so the participants did not receive any kind of advice concerning the privacy decision. In contrast, in the second stage, the nudges were activated, assisting the participants with the privacy decision. Thus, we observed and assessed whether meaningful changes in their behaviors were produced with nudges about the sensitivity of the publication.

5.4.2 Results

Once the experiment had ended, a total of 5880 privacy decisions (196 participants x 30 questions) were collected. Each entry consisted of the participant identifier, the tweet identifier, whether the sensitivity nudge was enabled, the sensitivity value, and the privacy policy choice. We codified the data following the next criteria: the sensitivity nudge variable as a binary value (representing whether it was enabled); the sensitivity value was discretized into four grades (*none*, *low*, *medium*, and *high* sensitivity); and the privacy policy choice was normalized taking into account how restrictive the choice was, considering *No one* as the minimum value (0), and *All* as the maximum value (4). Since participants did not repeat their choices for the same tweet, we considered running an independent sample test to assess the effect of the nudge messages on the participants' decisions. Moreover, we also wanted to evaluate the effect taking into

Source	df	Mean Squares	F	p	Effect Size
(A) Nudge	1	10.55	4.84	.028*	.001
(B) Sensitivity	3	165.26	75.87	.00**	.038
A × B	3	13.68	6.28	.00**	.003
Error	5873	2.17			

Table 5.3: ANOVA analysis for the privacy policy chosen ($\alpha = .05$). *$p < .05$, **$p < .01$.

account the information sensitivity value of the tweet. Therefore, we used an ANOVA
test ($\alpha = .05$) using the *privacy policy* value as the dependent variable and using the
sensitivity value and whether the *nudge* was activated as the fixed factors (see Table 5.3).

The results of the statistical tests reveal a significant difference in users' behavior regarding privacy policy choices. On the one hand, the presence of nudge messages was
significant to the privacy decision made (p-value = .028). On the other hand, the test
results also showed a significant difference in the privacy decision made by participants regarding the sensitivity value shown in the nudge message (p-value = .00). Finally, the combination of both variables (nudge and sensitivity) also revealed a significant difference in their decisions (p-value = .00). Table 5.4 depicts the comparison
of the mean value of the privacy policy decisions organized by sensitivity and nudge
variables. The table shows the differences in the mean of privacy policy choices, that
the ANOVA statistical test confirms that are significant. From the privacy decisions
made by the participants, we can extract some remarkable facts. First, the participants were able to slightly identify the sensitivity of the information contained in the
tweet. They showed more restrictive behavior for the information with higher sensitivity (see the *Mean* column for rows where the *nudge* variable is 0), except at the low
sensitivity level. We explored the information types identified in those tweets. Most
were from the Intentions category, which was one of the categories with the lowest
level of agreement. Therefore, we believe that that may have had some effect on their
initial decision-making. Second, the participants were less restrictive in their privacy
policy choices when the nudge message confirmed that the message was not sensitive
(see the *Mean* column for rows with non-sensitivity), while they were more restrictive
with sensitive content. Finally, the difference in the mean of the privacy policy choices
of the participants was higher when the sensitivity value of the message was higher.

Sensitivity	Nudge	N	Mean	Std. Error
none	0	784	1.858	.061
	1	784	2.042	.061
low	0	784	1.166	.048
	1	784	1.130	.047
medium	0	686	1.507	.056
	1	686	1.302	.058
high	0	686	1.408	.057
	1	686	1.117	.057

Table 5.4: Comparison of privacy policy mean values by sensitivity grade and nudges (0: the most restrictive policy; 4: the less restrictive policy).

5.5 Discussion

Depending on the information type, data is more or less sensitive/valuable due to: the cost of storing it [196]; the willingness of users to provide it [180]; the monetary benefits derived from extracting knowledge from it [236]; the loss of users' privacy [221]; the amount of information it provides [102]; etc. After the analysis and review of previous works that deal with the assignment of a sensitivity value to information types, we identified that some information types have small variability of value among the different works (especially in the case of information types that are located at the extremes of the sensitivity values). In this work, we have identified that categories such as demographics and human characteristics have a high degree of agreement among works that evaluate this data as being of low sensitivity. We have also identified that medical, legal and personally identifiable data categories also have a high degree of agreement, evaluating this data as being highly sensitive. For information types with less agreement among approaches, we highlight user behaviors and intentions. These may be valuable to companies, but the other approaches (laws & regulations and individuals' valuation) give them low sensitive value or they do not even assess the value of these types.

Regarding the proposal presented in this work, for estimating a sensitivity value for each information type, we decided to accumulate the values of all the works and calculate the mean value for each information type. Based on these values, we create a ranking. This ranking could be extended considering new values for a certain information type and including new information types. We included new information types from OSNs regrets positioning them by proximity to others types. However, this order could be also validated through questionnaires to users and companies about their perception of sensitivity/value of these new information types in comparison with the existing ones. Moreover, the value of estimated sensitivity introduced to users could be provided to users in different ways (e.g., as a monetary value, as a color scale, etc.) for testing which representation has a greater effect. Another aspect to assess other alternatives to estimate the aggregated value of data. Only few works calculate the sensitivity value of the information and, to the best of our knowledge, there is a lack of proposals that consider the combined value of information.

As some works point out [7, 172], empowering users during complex decisions with valuable information has two direct effects on them: (i) it raises their awareness; and (ii) it nudges their behaviors toward controlled decisions (i.e., with expected consequences). Wang et al. [272] proved that identifying the imagined audience before making decisions about posting changed the users' privacy decisions. Schöning et al. [222] tested significant differences by personalizing the styles of the nudges shown. Alemany et al. [12] tested personalized nudges based on an estimation of the final audience before posting. In that work, the authors reported that teenagers used more restrictive policies when they were aware of the potential audience. In this work, we empower users with nudges that contain information about the sensitivity value of the information they would share in OSNs. We assess how teenage users choose the privacy policy for a given publication when we nudge about its sensitivity. Through the experiment, we found out that the teenagers of the experiment had some previous knowledge about the sensitivity of information, because they chose restrictive privacy policies for the most sensitive posts when nudges were not activated. We also figured out that nudge messages about sensitivity had a significant effect on their behavior as well as the sensitivity level shown on the nudge message. The effect on teenagers' privacy behavior was more significant the greater the sensitivity value included in the nudge message (i.e., the privacy policy mean value decreased more for *high* sensitive posts than for *low* sensitive posts). From the results, we conclude that the teenagers were able to understand the nudge message that contained information about the sensitivity of their publications and they used them to have less risky behaviors on social networks.

5.6 Conclusions

This paper proposes a combined ranking using sensitive information types collected from an extensive literature review as well as a set of newly proposed information types for the OSN domain based on the most common regrets. The ranking provides the quantification of the sensitivity value of the different information types and could also be used to approximate the value of new information types that are not included in this work. Our proposal for assessing the sensitivity of a publication uses the ranking to estimate its value by accumulating the values of the different information types identified in the publication. The sensitivity value associated with a publication was used in nudges that were tested in an experiment with 196 teenagers. In this experiment, the teenagers had to choose a privacy policy for a set of publications with different degrees of sensitivity. The information provided by the nudges made them more aware of the privacy risk before choosing a privacy policy. The results of the experiment showed the relevance of empowering users with information about the sensitivity of their publications in order to make informed decisions that protect their privacy.

As future work, we plan to include our proposal in a real social network; thus, we could apply the nudges to the users' generated content in their daily usage. We also think that it would be interesting to match the topics of the publication with the sensitive categories developed in our proposal in order to improve its performance.

## CHAPTER 6

"Who should I grant access to my post?": Identifying the most Suitable Privacy Decisions on OSNs

*— (Under review status) by **Jose Alemany**, **Elena del Val**, and **Ana García-Fornes** in the **Internet Research***

6.1	Introduction	124
6.2	Literature review	126
6.3	Research model and hypothesis development	129
6.4	Methodology	135
6.5	Analysis and results	138
6.6	Discussions	144
6.7	Conclusion	148
6.A	Appendix	149

benefit and the disclosure of sensitive information with different receiver types. Disclosing personal information with trusted receivers, influencer receivers, and receivers from the circle of coworkers had a positive significant effect on social capital building. Conversely, disclosing personal information with receivers from the circle of family or unknown receivers had a significant negative effect on social capital building and even a significant positive effect on privacy concerns. Recent literature has documented the increasing interest of the research community in understanding users' concerns and interests in making the most suitable privacy decisions. However, most researchers have worked on understanding the disclosure action from a user-centered perspective and have not considered all of the elements of online communication. This study puts the focus on all of the elements of communication during disclosure actions, taking into account the properties of the message and receivers and the impact on users' cost-benefit value.

6.1 Introduction

As social network users, we are constantly faced with decisions that are the product of interaction and socialization with others that have a direct impact on our privacy. Research studies have shown that when we are faced with these decisions in online communication, we always assess the cost-benefit of the decision [210]. This process is well-known as the *Privacy Calculus theory*[1]. However, the privacy concept is very complex, and the number of factors to assess in online communication is higher than in traditional communication (e.g., the number of friends, the relationship types, the persistence of the information, etc.). Moreover, these decisions have tremendous importance because they may negatively affect our privacy and reputation [270]. Because of this, we often have difficulty in assessing the cost-benefit of disclosure decisions, which leads us to regret our decisions. In order to avoid regrets, decisions need to be made with information that is as perfect as possible, even though research experiments have demonstrated that we seldom have perfect information for deciding [5].

Research on online communication and users' behavior has studied a wide range of factors and relationships to explain information disclosure decisions in OSNs [211, 200, 161]. Most of these factors are related to the user transmitting the information through the following: personal characteristics, such as personality traits, gender, motivation for using the social network (self-presentation, enjoyment, building

---

[1]Privacy Calculus theory states that individuals always rationally weigh the potential benefits and potential risks of data disclosure decisions.

relationships, etc.); network usage characteristics, such as time of use, the number of friends, etc.; and users perceptions about information control, subjective norms, benefits, risks, etc. However, factors that are external to the transmitter (e.g., the sensitivity of the information, confidence in the channel, types of receivers, etc.) have been less studied. The study of communication elements study has been in decreasing order, the transmitter, the channel, the message, and, ultimately, the receiver. In traditional communication, the combination of the factors of the elements of communication favors effective communication similarly, the factors of the elements (channel, message, and receiver) in online communication must also be considered in order to favor communication that is free of regrets. The main objective of these studies is to understand the self-disclosure action of the users and which factors favor it and which do not. They do not, however, analyze in detail which factors are considered by a user for granting or denying access to a specific contact for a post (i.e., fine-grained privacy decisions). Thus, there is a gap in explaining which factors of communication elements and their combinations produce benefits and which produce privacy risks.

The main objective of this work is to understand the privacy decision-making process in social networks by making sense of each decision choice of the communication elements. We analyze the impact of communication element factors on privacy risks and social benefits in order to make suitable privacy decisions. To do this, we have developed a research model for individually granting/denying receivers access to information published in OSNs. We test our research model with real users to obtain feedback about how these factors influence the privacy decision-making process. The resulting model could be used to improve current privacy mechanisms, automatizing the assessment of the cost-benefit trade-off for each potential receiver, leading to suitable privacy policy decisions.

The paper is organized as follows. Section 6.2 includes a literature review about the social benefits and privacy for the disclosure process in OSNs. Section 6.3 presents our research model and the relevant factors regarding communication elements. Section 6.4 describes the research methodology. Section 6.5 presents the results obtained. Section 6.6 discusses the main findings. Finally, Section 6.7 presents some concluding remarks and future work.

6.2 Literature review

6.2.1 Privacy calculus theory and privacy decisions

The assessment of social benefits and privacy cost (well-known as Privacy Calculus theory) is a complex task that users should complete for effective communication in social networks [29]. This theoretical privacy calculus framework has been proven in the OSN domain by a large number of research works [151, 220, 54, 138]. However, these research works have mostly assessed the users' perceptions and preferences towards the privacy risks and socials benefits of information disclosure in a general way. When users face an OSN privacy decision, this decision has several sub-decisions that are directly linked to the elements of the communication. A clear example is when a user is going to share his/her holiday experience, he/she has to choose a social network on which to share it (the channel). The user then creates the publication (the message), and finally selects the social circles or audience that will have access to it (the receivers). This is when the receivers generate positive or negative responses (the feedback), which is related to social benefit building and loss of privacy (and possibly bad reputation), respectively. Therefore, there is a gap in the individual factors of those sub-decisions that may contribute or stand in the way of disclosing a specific message with a specific receiver.

Finally, privacy calculus is a short-term assessment that users make before making decisions. Literature reviews in human behavior show that online social well-being is usually tested as a long-term assessment of users' satisfaction for all decisions made [118]. The online social well-being of users can be seen as the individual's consciousness and feelings about their whole social lives, which consists of perceptions of pleasure, positive emotions, and greater satisfaction. Previous studies have tested well-being with respect to users' benefits [118, 144]; however, very little research has been done to test social well-being with respect to users' privacy cost.

6.2.2 Information disclosure and benefit

Disclosure actions can be defined as communicating personal information to other people [75]. The degree of disclosure is often based on trust and tries to reinforce the closeness of people. In OSNs, information disclosure actions can be carried out either using texts (status updates, commenting, location sharing, or private messages) or through other non-verbal means (sharing photos, videos, or links). Users generally tend to disclose different forms and types of information in order to achieve different gratifications. For instance, maintaining social relationships, seeking attention, feedback, and communications are some of the major gratifications that users seek by self-disclosing in OSNs [211, 200]. Furthermore, unlike traditional communication, in online communication (social networks), disclosure actions require the selection and configuration of more elements than just the message. It also involves the choice of the channel and the receivers, which in traditional communication is inherent by the context.

[251] found that people tend to disclose more information in OSNs compared to traditional communication. In addition, according to [192], the information disclosed is more sensitive. Some researchers such as [264] defend the ease of sharing information as a cause, while others relate this to the maintenance of users' contacts with weak ties. Another factor that they consider is the number of Facebook friends a user has. This could influence the user's self-disclosure since many of the social connections on Facebook require a certain degree of self-disclosure. Moreover, it has been shown that trust in contacts and in the social network platform influences the self-disclosure of information by users, which increases it [247]. These studies test the factors that influence the users' self-disclosure, but not how these factors provide them benefit. Other studies on the social benefit of self-disclosure, such as [144] and [161], have been done. However, those studies did not analyze the benefit obtained by information disclosure with certain factors of communication elements, with the exception of the study by [118] where several dimensions of self-disclosure (that included sensitive information) were tested. By extending the factors with respect to the channel, the message, and the receiver, the understanding of users' perceived benefit and efficient online communication could be advanced.

Focusing on the benefits of disclosing information, previous studies have used several theories to measure benefits such as social capital theory [144, 161, 62], social support [54, 118], motivation-based theory [151, 150], and other less popular theories such as [284]. However, these theories have not been sufficiently supported by the community of behavioral science studies, except for social capital theory. Therefore, we apply the well-known social capital theory to online communication to investigate the motivations behind users' behaviors of self-disclosure. Social capital is a theoretical framework that considers the benefits that individuals accrue from interactions with members of their social network [40]. Social capital is typically divided into two categories: bonding social capital and bridging social capital. Bonding social capital consists of the physical, emotional, and social support that an individual can provide to another member within the network. It is often associated with homogeneous dense networks and close intimate relationships since they are more likely to provide emotional aid and companionship than acquaintances [275]. Bridging social capital consists of information resources and influence among members of heterogeneous networks. According to [103], this kind of social capital is more likely among users with "weak ties" because they can provide more novel information and new perspectives than close relationships. Usually, bridging social capital provides the benefit of feeling connected to a larger group and having contact with a broad range of people. In OSNs environment, users can assess the social capital for both categories by taking into account the closeness of the relationship that supports them (bonding social capital), and the number of people reached (bridging social capital) [264].

6.2.3 Privacy cost and overexposure

The flip side of disclosing information on social networks is the loss of privacy and the potential consequences of it. In the literature, a rich discussion of the nature, definition, and conceptualization of privacy is offered. As [109] claim, privacy can be defined as a right, a commodity, and a state. This representation of privacy as a commodity matches the privacy calculus theory where users' privacy (the cost) is exchanged for social rewards (the benefits).

To measure the cost in privacy decisions, prior research used perceived privacy risks and/or privacy concerns to reflect the cost dimension of the privacy calculus equation. For instance, to measure the cost of self-disclosure decisions, [109] defined information privacy in four taxonomic dimensions: collection, unauthorized secondary use, improper access, and errors. Conversely, [138] consider that risk appraisal emerges from the vulnerability and the severity perceived in OSN decisions. These privacy concerns generally reflect a personal predisposition to worry about privacy and are therefore antecedent to risk beliefs, which are defined as the expectation of losses related to self-disclosure [151]. For the purpose of our study, we measure the privacy risk through users' privacy concerns about their information privacy on a website.

Similarly to the research on perceived benefits by disclosure actions, most research focuses on the influence of factors on self-disclosure (e.g., [264, 161]) and on understanding how perceived cost influences self-disclosure (e.g., [151, 109]). For this reason, very little is understood about how different kinds of factors related to communication impact users' cost during self-disclosure decisions. A few researchers have tested the users' cost perception of sharing sensitive information [284] and of sharing different types of personal information [138], but no one has tested factors related to the receiver.

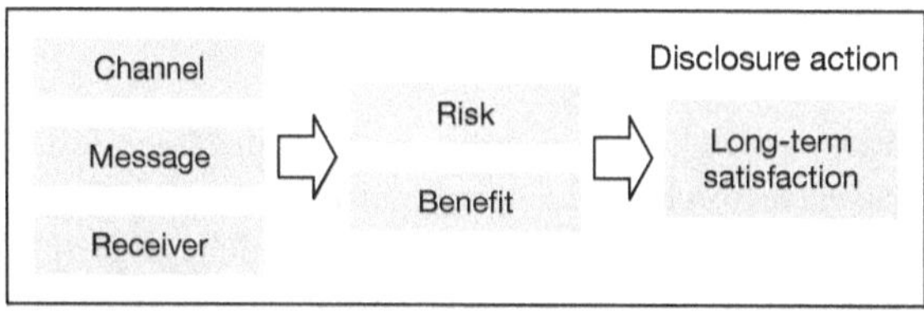

Figure 6.1: Conceptual model.

6.3 Research model and hypothesis development

The research model of this study is designed to explain the impact of the element properties of online communication (channel, message, and receiver) on users' assessment of social capital building and privacy concerns during information disclosure. In addition, it also includes the assessment of those perceptions (benefit and cost) regarding the users' final online social well-being, which can be interpreted as a long-term assessment of the benefits-costs of disclosure actions. All of the factors considered in our study are framed as dimensions of the disclosure action. Figure 6.1 provides the conceptual model used for the current study. Figure 6.2 presents the developed research model after the development of the hypotheses.

6.3.1 Channel factors

In online communications, the users' decision regarding the channel may be done at the OSN environment level (i.e., choosing the social network), or it may be done in a social network level (i.e., choosing the disclosure mechanism such as stories, wall-publications, etc.). The channel choice sheds light on the way users choose their preference for disclosing information on one social network platform and not on another; the mechanism choice sheds light on the properties that the disclosing mechanism offers to users. In this study, we focus on the properties of the privacy decision-making process of the channel from the first approach (the social network choice). Therefore, we assess how users' perceptions either support or do not support the users' privacy calculus evaluation. To do this, we consider two well-known factors: trust in the OSN provider, and the users' perceived capacity to control their actions.

Trust in the OSN provider

In previous literature, researchers describe trust as a multidimensional factor with different meanings. Some researchers consider *trust as a belief*, which may produce benefits, while other researchers interpret *trust as an intention*, which is linked to assuming risks [151]. In our work, we assess trust in both senses in order to link it with both sides of the privacy calculus (benefit vs. cost). Most of the time, trust in providers has positive impacts (e.g., on the willingness to participate in transactions in E-commerce [137, 208] and on self-disclosure in social networks [243]). Hence, trust in the OSN provider may positively empower the users' perceived benefits regarding disclosure actions, increasing their bonding and bridging social capital. However, with the new social network reports and scandals about the usage of user data [122], we want to confirm that trust in the OSN provider is still a cost-mitigating factor and contributes to social capital building. Therefore, we hypothesize the following:

Hypothesis 6.1: *Users' trust in the OSN provider is negatively related to their perceived privacy risk.*

Hypothesis 6.2: *Users' trust in the OSN provider is positively related to the building of (a) bonding social capital and (b) bridging social capital.*

Perceived Control

Information control refers to the capacity that people have to control information released online. Factors that determine the perception that people have of information control are related to the way in which web sites collect, store, and utilize users' personal information. Social networks offer users different privacy mechanisms and privacy settings to control the scope of their information. Some mechanisms provide more granularity, allowing users to choose the desired audience for each publication individually or based on social groups, while others use always the same social group (followers or friends). [285] empirically demonstrate the importance of providing self-controlling mechanisms in order to impact the perception of privacy calculus on OSNs. [151] considered perceived control as a cost-mitigating factor, and they validated this hypothesis in their study. In addition, by allowing users to control their information, [154] state that better choices can be made about the audience (specialized receivers), which finally contributes to improving the users' benefits. Hence, we hypothesize the following:

Hypothesis 6.3: *Users' perceived control is negatively related to their perceived privacy risk.*

Hypothesis 6.4: *Users' perceived control is positively related to the building of (a) bonding social capital and (b) bridging social capital.*

6.3.2 Sensitivity of the message

The information contained in a publication has great relevance in privacy calculus. Many works have reported regrets on social networks because of the information that users shared, mainly due to disclosing too much personal information or inappropriate information [270, 242]. In social networks, most users are identifiable so that their actions bring them social benefits [264]. As a consequence, the users' data becomes personal, but how does the sensitivity value of data in disclosure actions contribute to the users' cost-benefit? [138] assessed different types of personal data and how it impacts benefits and risks in video recommendation systems. They found a significant impact on all of the personal types regarding risk appraisal. According to the definition by [118], self-disclosure has five dimensions: amount, depth, honesty, intent, and valence. In our study, we assess self-disclosure on OSNs taking into account the sensitivity dimension that corresponds to depth, which is defined as *"the degree of intimacy of the information topic revealed"*. [197] observed an empowering effect on users' benefit regarding the benefits of information-sharing activity. Hence, we hypothesize the following:

Hypothesis 6.5: *Users' depth-disclosure action is positively related to their perceived privacy risk.*

Hypothesis 6.6: *Users' depth-disclosure action is positively related to the building of (a) bonding social capital and (b) bridging social capital.*

6.3.3 Differences between types of receivers

The privacy policy choice in social networks is essentially about deciding the receiver for a specific message (the publication). In this environment, the user interacts with user types that have different properties that could affect the privacy risks and social benefits of the user. Features such as the visibility/influence of users on the network and trust in other users have been used by [233] to assess user risks and calculate a privacy score for specific users. Many other works such as [288] have recently used these same features to calculate privacy policy recommendations for users. The influencer user's role, which is growing in popularity on social networks, is able to enhance the visibility of the user's information while the trusted user's role can ensure more secure communication of information. In addition to these types, users interact with other types based on social circles, even with unknown users [288]. The types represented by social circles often contain their own rules and information routines that can affect cost and benefit in different ways. [116] analyzed the influence of different social circles on image sharing and showed that information sharing with different types of relationships has a significant effect on the quality of the relationship. Furthermore, [270] who studied the most common regrets of social network users have stressed the relationship between regrets and disclosing information with some social circles such as family, friends, and coworkers. Therefore, we analyzed the types based on the primary social circles defined by [78]. Some of these types of receivers may overlap in a real user; however, for simplicity we consider them separately in this study. Therefore, in our research model, we analyzed the dissemination action with different types of receivers and how they compute for privacy.

In all of these decisions, since users always share personal information because it is linked with the OSN profile that usually identifies them, both decisions (message and receiver) are made together. Therefore, we have reformulated the previous hypotheses (H6.5 and H6.6) to include a specific receiver in the depth-disclosure action for each of the following types of receivers considered.

Trusted receivers

The strength of a relationship is a (probably linear) combination of the amount of time, the emotional intensity, the intimacy (mutual confiding), and the reciprocal services that characterize the relationship [103]. Previous evidence has shown a significant relationship between information disclosure with trusted members and social benefits [54]. [187] suggested that when trust exists between the parties, they are more willing to engage in cooperative interaction. [195] indicated that interpersonal trust is important in teams and organizations for creating an atmosphere for knowledge sharing. [151] have studied the relationship between trust in members (as a cost mitigating factor) and privacy risks but with no conclusive results. Therefore, we hypothesize the following:

Hypothesis 6.5.1: *Users' depth-disclosure action with trusted users is negatively related to their perceived privacy risk.*

Hypothesis 6.6.1: *Users' depth-disclosure action with trusted users is positively related to the building of (a) bonding social capital and (b) bridging social capital.*

Influencer receivers

The influencer role is a combination of desirable attributes (be they personal attributes like credibility, expertise, enthusiasm, or be they network-related attributes such as connectivity or centrality) that allows someone to influence (produce an effect on) others [20]. There are many research papers that analyze the users' characteristics to influence other users [186, 56]. Interacting with those users may potentially promote the visibility of a regular-user. This technique is commonly used in the design of optimal marketing strategies [100]. Social capital definition includes this aspect of border openness for obtaining social benefit by users; however, it might turn out to be a double-edged sword when unintended audiences access personal information [270]. This risk could be measurable for users [280]. Therefore, we hypothesize the following:

Hypothesis 6.5.2: *Users' depth-disclosure action with influencer users is positively related to their perceived privacy risk.*

Hypothesis 6.6.2: *Users' depth-disclosure action with influencer users is positively related to the building of (a) bonding social capital and (b) bridging social capital.*

Social circle-based receivers

Generally, each social circle contains its own rules and information routines. When we disclose information with one of them, depending on how sensitive the information is, it can affect users' cost and benefit in different ways. Reports of regret on social networks such as those of [270] and [242] have provided evidence of regret by divulging too much personal information with specific social circles. Differences between the most common social circles and their properties may have a common impact on users' cost-benefit. For our study, we have analyzed four different social circles, three of which are based on a simplification of Dunbar's relationship theory [78] (friends, family, and coworkers) and a new one based on the OSN domain to represent unknown users. These social circles also match the reasons for the disclosure decisions regretted by users in [270].

The reports about regrets on social networks [270, 242] indicate that most of regrets were related to disclosing too much personal information with close users like friends, family, and coworkers. It seems users are more concerned about their information when receivers are in a social circle that is closer to them (family, then friends, then coworkers). In contrast, there is also concern about unknown (or distant acquaintance) users accessing personal information [173]. Therefore, we hypothesize the following:

Hypothesis 6.5.3: *Users' depth-disclosure action with friends is positively related to their perceived privacy risk.*

Hypothesis 6.5.4: *Users' depth-disclosure action with family members is positively related to their perceived privacy risk.*

Hypothesis 6.5.5: *Users' depth-disclosure action with coworkers is positively related to their perceived privacy risk.*

Hypothesis 6.5.6: *Users' depth-disclosure action with unknown users is positively related to their perceived privacy risk*

With regard to the social benefits of disclosing personal information with each of these social circles, the context of these relationships may change the perceived benefits by users. [246] showed that, generally, friends and family members provide emotional support (which is related to bonding social capital) when disclosing information about personal issues, and coworkers provide informational support (which is related to bridging social capital). Also, professional networks encourage information exchange, promote interpersonal relationships, and lead to improvements in productivity and loyalty, which contributes to informational support [133]. Thus, friends and family members have less propensity to contribute to bridging social capital, and, conversely, coworkers have less propensity to contribute to bonding social capital. For users with no relationship with the user (i.e., unknown receivers), even though the interaction may provide informational support (like the coworker social circle), by sharing intimate information with them negative reactions may be elicited for a more public social circle [27]. Therefore, we expect a positive impact on social bonding by providing emotional or substantive support for friends and family circles, and we expect a negative impact on social bonding for coworkers and unknown users. In contrast, disclosing information with social circles that are not close may positively impact social bridging building. Thus, we hypothesize the following:

Hypothesis 6.6.3: *Users' depth-disclosure action with friends is (a) positively related to the building of bonding social capital and (b) negatively related to the building of bridging social capital.*

Hypothesis 6.6.4: *Users' depth-disclosure action with family members is (a) positively related to the building of bonding social capital and (b) negatively related to the building of bridging social capital.*

Hypothesis 6.6.5: *Users' depth-disclosure action with coworkers is (a) negatively related to the building of bonding social capital and (b) positively related to the building of bridging social capital.*

Hypothesis 6.6.6: *Users' depth-disclosure action with unknown users is (a) negatively related to the building of bonding social capital and (b) positively related to the building of bridging social capital.*

6.3.4   Online Social Well-being

According to [193], self-disclosure can improve an individual's physical and mental health from a positive psychology perspective. Moreover, it has been shown that positive reactions collected from social capital building contributes to improving the users' well-being [220]. In contrast, the users' concern regarding OSN risks is related to negative experiences resulting in a heightened awareness of privacy-related issues and increased privacy concerns. Those negative experiences could hinder the psychological state of users, impacting on their social well-being [286]. Thus, we hypothesize the following:

Hypothesis 6.7: *Users' perceived privacy risk is negatively related to their online social well-being.*

Hypothesis 6.8: *Users' building of (a) bonding social capital and (b) bridging social capital is positively related to their online social well-being.*

The overall research model is described in Figure 6.2.

6.4   Methodology

This study presents an initial attempt to investigate the role of receivers' properties and message sensitivity in the users' assessment of potential benefits and risks of data disclosure decisions in social networks. We also investigate how messages and receivers contribute indirectly to users' online social well-being. The research setting, data collection method, measurement, and demographics of the respondents are reported below.

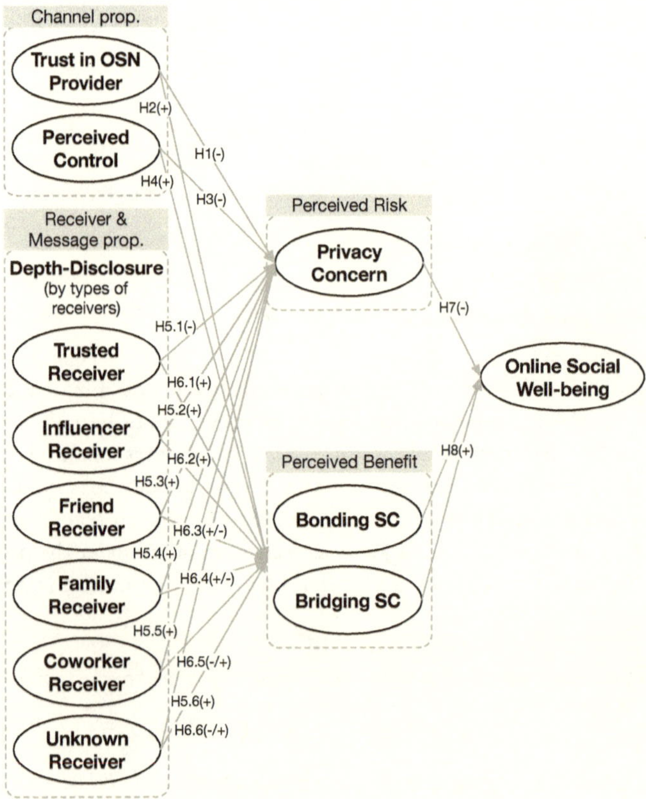

Figure 6.2: Research model.

6.4.1 Research settings

For this study, we chose the users of Facebook as the main object of discussion since it is one of the most popular and widely used online social networks. Launched on February 2004, Facebook allows its users to define different kinds of connections/relationships with each other (e.g., friends, acquaintances, followers, etc.) and to create social elements (e.g., groups, posts, albums, preferences, etc.) for interacting with others in a whole variety of ways (e.g., comments, tags, mentions, direct messages, etc.). More importantly, unlike other online social networks, Facebook offers users many mechanisms to decide all of the elements of online communication for users' disclosing actions in a fine-grained way. Users have complete and free capability to choose the channel, message, and receivers (by selecting a specific privacy policy) in a disclosure action. Therefore, we believe Facebook users are perfect for investigating the influence of these elements on users' cost-benefit perceptions (Privacy Calculus) and on the disclosure action.

6.4.2 Data collection

The data used in this study were collected through a survey created on Google Forms and shared through Prolific Academy [204], which is an online participant recruitment platform for surveys and market studies. The questionnaire that was developed for the survey was pre-tested by six researchers, three of whom are experienced in surveys and quantitative research. Their remarks and suggestions were used to make improvements and to clarify some questions, which led to the final version of the questionnaire. We also made a very small-sample experiment with colleagues to avoid potential errors (such as technical blips, etc.) and to measure the average time required for completing the questionnaire. Then, we linked the questionnaire to a study in Prolific. Before publishing the study, we made a custom pre-screening of the target audience of the study using the menus of Prolific. As required features for participating in the study, we selected the following: ($r1$) fluent English language comprehension so that the questionnaire was understood completely; ($r2$) being a regular Facebook user in order to fit our target population; ($r3$) a minimum of 50 completed studies on Prolific; and ($r4$) an approval rate greater than 90% for quality control. For quality control, we also included some attention check questions in the questionnaire asking participants to select a specific answer. The participants that answered at least one attention question incorrectly were excluded from the study. Finally, we published the study, and, after the participants completed it, we managed to collect completed questionnaires from 400 participants. The resulting files (demographic data from Prolific, and the questionnaire responses from Google Forms) were collected and joined for their later analysis.

6.4.3 Measurement

All of the measures in this study have been used and validated in prior studies (see Appendix 6.A.1). Minor changes in the wording were made in order to fit the current research context. Social bonding and social bridging were measured with items adapted from [280]. Privacy concern was measured with items adapted from [284]. Perceived control and trust in Facebook were measured by items adapted from [151]. Online social well-being was measured by items adapted from [62] and [80]. In addition, we took the dimension of depth (related to sensitivity of information) in information disclosure measured by items adapted from [279] as a reference in order to customize them for different types of receivers. Instruments for all of the constructs were presented on a five-point Likert scale, anchored from "1 = never" and "5 = always". We used a unipolar scale because, in comparison with a bipolar scale (such as "1 = strongly disagree" and "5 = strongly agree"), it allows users to focus on a single item's absence or presence, which may generate more accurate answers[2]. For each statement, the participants were asked to indicate how often participants agreed with the statement.

6.4.4 Sample characteristics

The demographic statistics of the respondents are reported in Table 6.1. Of the 400 respondents, 45.5% of them were male and 54.5% were female. The respondents' ages ranged from 18 to 76 years old with a positive skewness distribution (0.879), which means their ages had a major concentration in younger ages (below 35.3 years, average). Approximately 75.5% of the respondents were not students, and the majority of them were employed (around 70%). In addition, the respondents were mainly from Europe (87%), North-America (8%), and Australia (3%). Among European respondents, there was a high concentration of UK respondents (47%), followed by Portuguese (9.5%), Poles (7.5%), Italians (4.2%), and Spaniards (3.2%). We split the nationalities into sub-regions following the Eurovoc thesaurus to facilitate the reading of Table 6.1.

6.5 Analysis and results

The proposed research model was tested using partial least squares (PLS) analysis using Smart PLS 3.2.9 because PLS employs a component-based approach for estimation that minimizes residual distributions [58] and is best suited for testing complex relationships by avoiding inadmissible solutions and factor indeterminacy [55]. Moreover, PLS has less stringent sample size and indicator distribution requirements, as compared to the covariance-based structural equation modeling (SEM) approaches. Following the two-step data analytical procedures [108], the measurement model was first examined to evaluate the reliability and validity of measures, and then the structural model was tested to estimate the hypothesized relationships.

Measure	Items	Value	
Age	Range	18-76	years old
	Average	35.3	years old
Gender	Male:	45.5%	182 (400)
	Female:	54.5%	218 (400)
Nationality	Western EU:	54.0%	216 (400)
	Southern EU:	19.3%	77 (400)
	Central/Eastern EU:	11.7%	47 (400)
	Northern EU:	2.0%	8 (400)
	North-America:	8.0%	32 (400)
	Australia:	3.0%	12 (400)
	Others:	2.0%	8 (400)
Student status	Yes:	24.5%	98 (400)
	No:	75.5%	302 (400)
Employment status	Full-Time:	48.7%	194 (400)
	Part-Time:	19.8%	80 (400)
	Unemployed:	12.0%	48 (400)
	Other:	15.5%	78 (400)

Table 6.1: Demographic information.

6.5.1 Measurement model assessment

We evaluate the measurement model by examining the convergent validity and discriminant validity of measurement items. Convergent validity can be assessed by examining the factor loadings, the composite reliability, and the average variance extracted (AVE). Specifically, composite reliability refers to the internal consistency of the indicators measuring a given factor, and average variance extracted indicates the amount of variance captured by a construct as compared to the variance caused by the measurement error. Table 6.2 presents some descriptive statistics, composite reliability values, Cronbach's alpha values, and the average variance extracted of the principal constructs. A composite reliability of 0.70 or above and an average variance extracted of more than 0.50 are deemed acceptable. Cronbach's alpha scores of 0.70 or greater are also considered acceptable, while scores between 0.8 and 0.9 are considered satisfactory [95]. All of the values of composite reliabilities and Cronbach's alpha exceed 0.70, verifying the reliability of measurement items. From these facts, we conclude that convergent validity is fulfilled (i.e., constructs that theoretically should be related are in fact related). Appendix 6.A.2 extends Table 6.2 information including more statistic data and the factor loadings for each of the measured items.

Discriminant validity is established by initially ensuring that an indicator's outer loading on a construct is greater than cross-loadings with other constructs and the by ensuring that the square root of AVE is higher than the outer correlations for each construct [95]. Table 6.2 also presents the correlation matrix of the constructs and the square root of the average variance extracted for each construct. The results show that all outer loadings are greater than cross-loadings for each construct and that squared root of AVEs are higher than outer correlations. The results affirm discriminant validity (i.e., constructs that are not supposed to be related are actually unrelated). Overall, the results show the high reliability and validity of the posited measurement model.

Furthermore, variance inflation factors (VIF) were used to assess the degree of multicollinearity in the measures of our study. This test assesses how much the variance of an estimated regression coefficient increases if your predictors are correlated. The VIFs ranged from 1.030 to 2.351, which are all below the suggested threshold of 3.3 [145]. Therefore, we did not find a significant multicollinearity problem in this study.

6.5.2 Structural model assessment

The results of the analysis are provided in Table 6.3 and Figure 6.3. Table 6.3 presents the overall explanatory power with the hypotheses, the estimated path coefficients (β), and the associated t-value of the paths (all significant paths are indicated with asterisks). Figure 6.3 visually summarizes the results of the conceptual model with r-squared (R^2), path coefficients, and p-values. A test of significance of all paths was performed using the bootstrap resampling procedure. The research model of this study explains 25.1% of the variance in users' perceived privacy concern, 31.5% in users' perceived bonding social capital, and 26.6% in users' perceived bridging social capital for the intention of disclosing personal information with different types of receivers. Moreover, the model explains 19.1% of the variance in online social well-being as the product of all decisions made. In order to ensure that the findings of the analysis are not confounded by other variables, we controlled the possible effect of users' demographic information (age, gender, nationality, and student status) on perceived risk, perceived benefit, and online social well-being. All of the control variables were excluded from the final model due their insignificance. Therefore, the research model demonstrates satisfactory explanatory power to capture the effect of privacy trade-off between the different communication elements and users' self-disclosure decisions, and, in consequence, with their online social well-being.

The findings demonstrate that users' trust perception in the OSN provider (the channel), which in our case is Facebook, has great relevance in the privacy trade-off: de-

	Mean	SD	AVE	CR	CA	Construct											
						PC	TF	CN	BO	BR	DT	DI	DF	DA	DC	DU	SW
PC	3.69	1.14	.689	.917	.887	**.830**											
TF	2.16	1.05	.759	.904	.841	-.473	**.871**										
CN	3.04	1.08	.698	.874	.785	.318	.506	**.835**									
BO	2.83	1.28	.515	.889	.859	-.156	.299	.180	**.718**								
BR	2.86	1.15	.542	.922	.906	-.131	.353	.283	.483	**.736**							
DT	2.27	1.09	.733	.916	.877	-.111	.202	.077	.493	.353	**.856**						
DI	1.59	0.87	.667	.889	.832	-.046	.177	.038	.296	.317	.475	**.817**					
DF	2.38	1.09	.727	.914	.874	-.120	.176	.015	.336	.300	.670	.389	**.853**				
DA	2.48	1.25	.786	.936	.908	-.049	.219	.091	.265	.281	.579	.388	.636	**.887**			
DC	1.56	0.84	.777	.933	.904	-.120	.200	.056	.342	.268	.468	.558	.546	.526	**.882**		
DU	1.24	0.65	.705	.905	.840	-.021	.076	.070	.169	.234	.339	.594	.284	.206	.562	**.840**	
SW	3.07	1.01	.705	.905	.857	-.279	.435	.362	.317	.332	.175	.096	.152	.168	.187	.103	**.815**

Table 6.2: Results of convergent validity and discriminant validity analyses. Squared root of Average Variance Extracted (diagonal elements in bold) and correlation between constructs (off-diagonal elements). Note: SD=standard deviation; AVE=average variance extracted; CR=composite reliability; CA=Cronbach's Alpha; PC=privacy concern; TF=trust in Facebook; CN=perceived control; BO=bonding social capital; BR=bridging social capital; DT=depth-disclosure action with trusted receivers; DI=depth-disclosure action with influencer receivers; DF=depth-disclosure action with friends; DA=depth-disclosure action with family members; DC=depth-disclosure action with coworkers; DU=depth-disclosure action with unknown users; SW=online social well-being.

Hypotheses	Relations	β	t
H6.1	trust in facebook $\rightarrow$ privacy risk	-.416	7.44[***]
H6.2a	trust in facebook $\rightarrow$ social bonding	.159	3.06[**]
H6.2b	trust in facebook $\rightarrow$ social bridging	.193	3.83[***]
H6.3	perceived control $\rightarrow$ privacy risk	-.117	2.13[*]
H6.4a	perceived control $\rightarrow$ bonding sc	.073	1.42
H6.4b	perceived control $\rightarrow$ bridging sc	.158	2.99[**]
H6.5.1	DD: trusted receiver $\rightarrow$ privacy risk	-.038	0.58
H6.6.1a	DD: trusted receiver $\rightarrow$ bonding sc	.463	7.12[***]
H6.6.1b	DD: trusted receiver $\rightarrow$ bridging sc	.229	3.29[**]
H6.5.2	DD: influencer receiver $\rightarrow$ privacy risk	.053	0.85
H6.6.2a	DD: influencer receiver $\rightarrow$ bonding sc	.067	1.12
H6.6.2b	DD: influencer receiver $\rightarrow$ bridging sc	.124	2.01[*]
H6.5.3	DD: friend receiver $\rightarrow$ privacy risk	-.104	1.43
H6.6.3a	DD: friend receiver $\rightarrow$ bonding sc	-.014	0.19
H6.6.3b	DD: friend receiver $\rightarrow$ bridging sc	.051	0.70
H6.5.4	DD: family receiver $\rightarrow$ privacy risk	.163	2.48[*]
H6.6.4a	DD: family receiver $\rightarrow$ bonding sc	-.145	2.21[*]
H6.6.4b	DD: family receiver $\rightarrow$ bridging sc	.010	0.15
H6.5.5	DD: coworker receiver $\rightarrow$ privacy risk	-.100	1.37
H6.6.5a	DD: coworker receiver $\rightarrow$ bonding sc	.209	3.25[**]
H6.6.5b	DD: coworker receiver $\rightarrow$ bridging sc	-.018	0.24
H6.5.6	DD: unknown receiver $\rightarrow$ privacy risk	.052	0.82
H6.6.6a	DD: unknown receiver $\rightarrow$ bonding sc	-.129	2.27[*]
H6.6.6b	DD: unknown receiver $\rightarrow$ bridging sc	.050	0.75
H6.7	privacy risk $\rightarrow$ online social well-being	-.223	5.00[***]
H6.8a	bonding sc $\rightarrow$ online social well-being	.177	3.58[***]
H6.8b	bridging sc $\rightarrow$ online social well-being	.218	3.96[***]

Table 6.3: Partial least squares path estimators for the research model. Note: [*]$p < 0.05$, [**]$p < 0.01$, [***]$p < 0.001$.

creasing the users' privacy concern ($\beta = -0.416$, $p < 0.001$), which supports H6.1; and increasing the users' perception of bonding social capital ($\beta = 0.159$, $p < 0.01$) and bridging social capital ($\beta = 0.193$, $p < 0.001$), which supports H6.2a and H6.2b. The relationships between perceived control and benefits-risks are also significant, which supports H6.3 ($\beta = -0.117$, $p < 0.05$) and H6.4b ($\beta = 0.158$, $p < 0.01$), except for bonding capital building (H6.4a) which was not supported.

The findings further indicated interesting results between the depth dimension of self-disclosure and the different types of receivers. For the disclosure with trusted receivers,

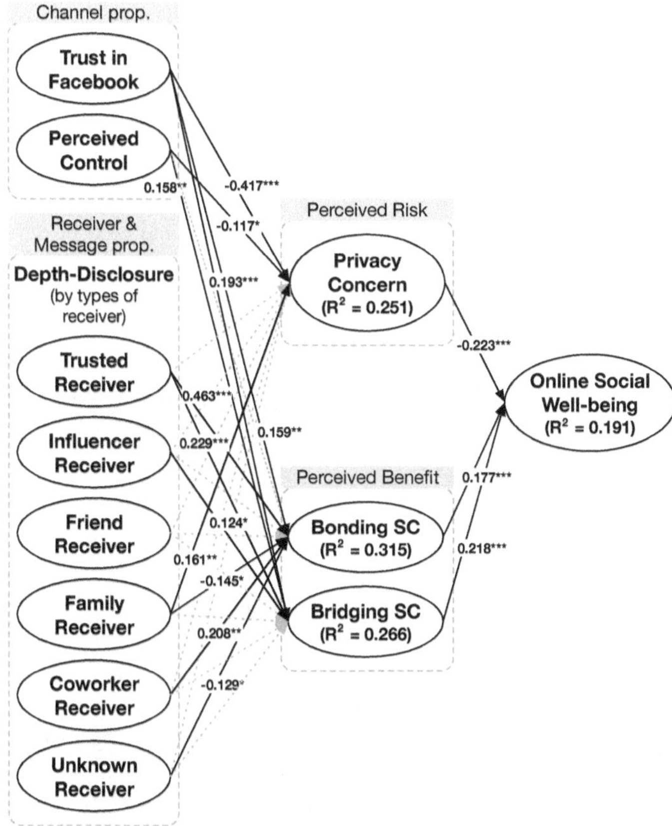

Figure 6.3: Results of the research model.

there was a significant increasing relationship with both dimensions of social capital, which supports H6.6.1a (β = 0.463, $p < 0.001$) and H6.6.1b (β = 0.229, $p < 0.01$), while no significant relationship was found with privacy concern (H6.5.1). For the disclosure with influencer receivers, there was only a significant increasing relationship with bridging capital (H6.6.2b), while H6.5.2 and H6.6.2a were not supported. For the disclosure with friend receivers, there was not a significant relationship with privacy concern (H6.5.3) or with social capital (H6.6.3a and H6.6.3b). For the disclosure with family members, we found a significant increasing relationship with users' privacy concern (β = 0.163, $p < 0.05$) and a significant decreasing relationship with social capital (β = -0.145, $p < 0.05$), which supports H6.5.4 and H6.6.4a and does not support H6.6.4b. Finally, for the disclosure with coworkers and unknown receivers, there was only a strong relationship between coworkers and bonding social capital (β = 0.209, $p < 0.01$) and a strong relationship between unknown receivers and bonding social capital (β = -0.129, $p < 0.05$), which supports H6.6.5a and H6.6.6a, respectively. Therefore, the rest of the hypotheses that link the depth dimension of self-disclosure with receivers were not supported (H6.5.5, H6.6.5b, H6.5.6, and H6.6.6b).

Finally, as we expected, the users' perceptions of benefits and risks of self-disclosure with their online social well-being had strong significance, which supports H6.7, H6.8a, and H6.8b. The relationship between privacy concern and their online social well-being had a significantly decreasing impact (β = -0.223, $p < 0.001$). The relationships between the two social capital dimensions (bonding capital (β = 0.117, $p < 0.001$) and bridging capital (β = 0.218, $p < 0.001$)) and their online social well-being had a significantly increasing impact.

6.6 Discussions

The current study has evaluated users' privacy trade-offs (cost-benefit) in the privacy decision-making process in social networks taking into account the different element properties of communication. The relationship between the theory of privacy calculus (PCT) and users' trade-off perceptions of the properties of the receiver, message, and channel was conceptualized and empirically tested, performing a study about the participants' online social network usage. While there was a mix of supported and unsupported hypotheses in the results, the change in significance between constructs of depth-disclosure actions by receiver types and the perceived benefit-risk was the most interesting.

There was a striking significance between the trust factors (trust in the OSN provider, and trust in other users) and the users' perceptions of benefits. As previous research works state [137, 208] and our study confirms, trust in the OSN provider helped to reduce the users' privacy concerns (H6.1) and increase the users' perception of both dimensions of social capital building (H6.2a and H6.2b) to the same extent. Trust in other users significantly increased both dimensions of social capital building (H6.6.1a and H6.6.1b), but there was a stronger impact on bonding capital. However, there was no relation between trust in members and privacy concerns. For the control perceived by users, there was a less significant effect than trust factors on users' perceived benefits-risks. This also helped to reduce the privacy concerns (H6.3) and partially increase the social capital building of users (only for the bridging capital, H6.4b).

There was a striking significance between the trust factors (trust in the OSN provider, and trust in other users) and the users' perceptions of benefits. As previous research works state [137, 208] and our study confirms, trust in the OSN provider helped to reduce the users' privacy concerns (H6.1) and increase the users' perception of both social capital building (H6.2a and H6.2b) to the same extent. In the case of trust in other users, it increased significantly both social capital building (H6.6.1a and H6.6.1b), but with a stronger impact on bonding capital. However, there was no relation between trust in members and privacy concerns. Regarding the control perceived by users, it had a less significant effect than trust factors on users' perceived benefits-risks, helping also to reduce the privacy concerns (H6.3) and increasing partially the capital building of users (just the bridging capital, H6.4b).

When disclosing personal information to different kinds of users, there was a significant difference in users' privacy calculus perception. As we predicted, based on OSN users' regrets [270], the social circle of family members had a significantly positive impact on users' privacy concerns (H6.5.4) and a partially negative impact on social capital building (H6.6.4a). Although the social circle of coworkers also showed some limited evidence of regrets as in the family case, our study did not find a significant effect on users' privacy concerns but we found a significant positive effect on bonding social capital (H6.6.5a). This behavior might be explained by a desire for strengthening ties with coworkers with whom we spend an important amount of time daily and for the seeking of job satisfaction [119]. Curiously, the social circle of friends had no significant effect on users' perceptions of benefit or risk. It could be that the friend social circle has become the most open to interpretation for the users. For instance, social networks like Facebook collapse other context relationships within friends [68], so this social circle blends in with a lot of other types of receivers. As we predicted, disclosing personal information with influencer receivers had a significantly positive effect on bridging capital building (H6.6.2b), while there was not a significant impact on users' privacy concerns. Users do not perceive disclosing their information with influencer users to be risky. However, if they do not know them (unknown receivers) and they disclose their personal information, it has been shown that there is a significantly negative effect on their bonding capital (H6.6.6a). Taken together, these findings reveal that relationships that are too close (family) or, the flip side, unknown relationships are perceived by users as not being beneficial. Conversely, disclosing users' personal information with highly trusted receivers and influencer receivers improves their social capital building. Generally, most of the relations between depth-disclosure with different receivers and user privacy concerns did not have a significant relationship. As [151] state, this could be due to the fact that user privacy concerns mainly center on organizational risks such as the collection and secondary use of their information. Users may believe companies have more incentive to abuse their information compared to other network members (except for family members who are a conflicting audience). Also, many of the relations between depth-disclosure with different receivers and bridging social capital did not have a significant relationship. This could be due to the fact that not all of the members of a specific social circle contribute in the same way to this factor and that the features (trust and influence) of an individual are those that produce a significant effect on bridging social capital.

Finally, the findings confirm that the benefit and risk constructs that we tested contributed to the online social well-being of users, inversely relating users' privacy concerns with online social well-being (H6.7) and directly relating social capital with online social well-being (H6.8a and H6.8b).

6.6.1 Theoretical implications

This study contributes to the existing literature in the following three important ways. First of all, we have examined in detail the OSN users' decisions in the information disclosing context with insights from the elements of online communication (channel, message, and receiver) and how they contribute to the users' benefit-risk perception. Previous research was mainly focused on exploring self-disclosure as a single decision. They just modeled users' perceptions of the social network properties (the channel) and users' interests and how these constructs impacted their social benefits and privacy risks. Those research works took an approach that is closer to OSN business features in order to increase the number of users' self-disclosing actions instead of an approach that focuses on users' privacy and their understanding of online communication. In contrast, the research presented in our work takes into account the users' perspective focusing on privacy decision-making.

Second, we have tested the impact of the elements of online communication on the users' perceptions of privacy risk and social benefit. It is important to note that people disclose their personal information as a continuous trade-off between relinquishing some privacy in exchange for some social benefits. Academic attention to potential receiver types and the sensitivity of the message to be disclosed will generate a more comprehensive picture of information disclosure on social networks and will further improve our current understanding of which features contribute to users' benefit and risk and to what extent they contribute.

Third, we have investigated the disclosure of personal information with types of receivers based on social circles, which is a mechanism that is commonly offered by social networks to users for privacy policy selection. Similarly to the research work by [138] where different types of personal information were investigated, we found differences in significance towards social circles. In contrast to the findings of [138] for different types of personal information, our study found more relationships between depth-disclosure actions (by types of receivers) and users' perceived benefit than between deep disclosure actions and risk perceptions. These findings could also improve the understanding of users' regrets on social networks and online communication.

6.6.2 Practical implications

The current research also has several implications for practitioners in the context of social networking apps. It has been shown that privacy decisions are a burdensome task because users have too many connections (also known as friends), and they are required to assess the disclosure decision for each one. These research results shed light on the relevance of each factor in privacy decision-making and its relationship with others. A better classification of users' relationship types, trust estimation, and the visibility properties of a user on the network could provide improvements in current privacy mechanisms. Those mechanisms combined with our results could help to recommend suitable privacy policies, automatizing the individual process of privacy calculus and maximizing the users' social benefits obtained by disclosing their information. Therefore, recommending audiences that are highly trusted, influential, or belong to the coworkers circle will be prioritized over other audiences such as family members or unknown users that might reduce the benefit of the user or even increase his/her risk. For example, a user belonging to a social circle of coworkers with a high level of trust and influence on others will be recommended as an audience for a social network post, while family members will not be recommended (unless there is an extremely high level of trust with the user).

6.6.3 Limitations and future research

While the current research provides several implications for theory and practice, there are limitations that must be acknowledged and opportunities to be considered for future research. Even though the sample size of our study is sufficient, it could be unbalanced or biased for some external and uncontrollable factors. The reiterative confirmation of the presented findings should be performed to validate that our samples are not biased. In our findings, we observed a few more significant relationships for perceived benefit than for perceived risk. According to [109], users easily perceive benefits as being closer, while privacy risks are perceived as being abstract and psychologically distant. Thus, a limitation of our work is that we do not know how our proposed research model could fit a population that is only composed of participants that have had negatives experiences when disclosing personal information on social networks. Another limitation was the constructs used. We mainly checked the self-disclosure decision and the influence of properties of other elements of online communication. However, individually analyzing the decisions for those elements could shed light on their suitability for users' self-disclosure. Our future research will be directed towards the application and validation of our research model in a social network (e.g., in our prototype of a social network called Pesedia[3]). The research model will be used to automatically compute privacy policies during disclosure decisions in social networks. We will test our privacy mechanisms based on the validated model versus other privacy mechanisms considered in the literature. For future research, it would also be interesting to test our research model with OSN users that have already had negative experiences when disclosing personal information on social networks. This would include analyzing a target population with more experience with privacy risks in order to confirm whether or not our hypotheses are also supported. In addition, future studies can extend the current study by including additional constructs that have not been evaluated in the current research, such as risk aversion, general risk, ease of use, and an expansion of message and receiver properties.

6.7 Conclusion

The goal of the current research was to evaluate the relationship between the elements of online communication (especially channel, message, and receiver), personal information disclosure, and privacy trade-off in the social network context. Based on the literature, a research model was derived and tested using the responses of a study that assesses the constructs of that model. The results revealed a change in privacy trade-off perceptions and their influence on disclosure behaviors with different properties/factors of the elements of communications such as the social circles of receivers, the sensitivity of the message, and the trust in the OSN provider or in other users. While most of the users' perceptions mainly influenced social capital building, there were some significant relationships between family members and unknown relationships that had negative effects on social capital building. In the case of family members there were also repercussions on their privacy concerns. As we predicted, there was no relationship between the message or receivers; however, there was a decrease in users' perceived risk in the case of channel trust and control perception. Last, we confirm that users' perceptions of benefit and risk were properly aligned with their online social well-being. With the extension of privacy trade-off in users' privacy decision-making in social networks, the current research established varying effects of the relationships to different elements of online communication, creating a strong foundation for future studies in privacy decision-making research.

6.A Appendix

6.A.1 Measurement instrument

Construct	Code	Items
Privacy	PC1	I am concerned that Facebook is collecting too much personal information about me.
Concern	PC2	I am concerned that unauthorized people may access my personal information.
[284]	PC3	I am concerned that Facebook may keep my personal information in an inaccurate manner.
	PC4	I am concerned about submitting personal information to Facebook.
	PC5	It bothers me when Facebook asks me for this much personal information.
Trust in	TF1	I believe that privacy of my personal information is well protected by Facebook.
Facebook	TF2	I believe that Facebook will not use my personal information for any other purpose.
[151, 173]	TF3	I believe that Facebook is a secure platform for sharing my personal information.
Perceived	CN1	I feel in control over the information I provide on Facebook.
Control	CN2	I feel in control over who can view my information on Facebook.
[151, 57]	CN3	Privacy settings allow me to have full control over the personal information I provide on Facebook.
Bonding	BO1	There are people on Facebook I trust to help solve my problems.
Social	BO2	There are people on Facebook I can turn to for advice about making very important decisions.
Capital	BO3	There are people on Facebook I can talk to when I feel lonely.
[280, 80, 62]	BO4	The people I interact with on Facebook would put their reputation on the line for me.
	BO5	The people I interact with on Facebook would be good job references for me.
	BO6	The people I interact with on Facebook would help me fight an injustice.
	BO7	There is no one on Facebook that I feel comfortable talking to about intimate personal problems. (reversed)
	BO8	There is no one on Facebook I know well enough to get them to do anything important. (reversed)
Bridging	BR1	Interacting with people on Facebook makes me interested in things that happen outside of my close contacts.
Social	BR2	Interacting with people on Facebook makes me want to try new things.
Capital	BR3	Interacting with people on Facebook makes me interested in what people unlike me are thinking.
[280, 80, 62]		

(Table continued)

Construct	Code	Items
	BR4	Interacting with people on Facebook makes me curious about other places in the world.
	BR5	Interacting with people on Facebook makes me feel like part of a larger community.
	BR6	Interacting with people on Facebook makes me feel connected to the bigger picture.
	BR7	Interacting with people on Facebook reminds me that everyone in the world is connected.
	BR8	On Facebook, I am willing to spend time to support general community activities.
	BR9	Interacting with people on Facebook gives me new people to talk to.
	BR10	On Facebook, I come in contact with new people all the time.
Depth-Disclosure (by receiver type), adapted from [279, 127, 118]	DR1	With <u>receiver</u> on Facebook, I intimately disclose who I really am, openly and fully in my conversations.
	DR2	With <u>receiver</u> on Facebook, once I get started, my self-disclosures last a long time.
	DR3	With <u>receiver</u> on Facebook, I typically reveal information about myself without intending to.
	DR4	With <u>receiver</u> on Facebook, once I get started, I intimately and fully reveal myself in my self-disclosures.
Online Social Well-being [118]	SW1	In my Facebook social life, in most respects, I am close to my ideal.
	SW2	In my Facebook social life, the conditions are excellent.
	SW3	In my Facebook social life, I am satisfied.
	SW4	In my Facebook social life, so far, I have obtained the important things I want.
	SW5	In my Facebook social life, if I could live it over, I would change almost nothing.

6.A.2 Descriptive statistics, reliability and validity results

Construct	Item	Mean	SD	Skew	Kurt	FL	AVE	CR	CA
Privacy Concern	PC1	3.87	1.14	-0.65	-0.61	.820	.689	.917	.887
	PC2	3.62	1.12	-0.42	-0.59	.801			
	PC3	3.36	1.21	-0.25	-0.84	.782			
	PC4	3.75	1.09	-0.59	-0.45	.810			
	PC5	3.88	1.09	-0.74	-0.33	.812			
Trust in Facebook	TF1	2.27	1.03	0.37	-0.77	.775	.759	.904	.841
	TF2	2.05	1.09	0.74	-0.42	.831			
	TF3	2.15	1.04	0.47	-0.80	.758			
Perceived Control	CN1	3.02	1.15	-0.11	-0.93	.834	.698	.874	.785
	CN2	3.03	1.07	-0.16	-0.79	.801			
	CN3	3.07	1.05	-0.17	-0.71	.738			
Bonding Social Capital	BO1	2.56	1.17	0.30	-0.84	.809	.515	.889	.859
	BO2	2.52	1.21	0.30	-0.97	.819			
	BO3	2.92	1.31	-0.06	-1.22	.746			
	BO4	2.20	1.06	0.58	-0.46	.681			
	BO5	2.42	1.16	0.42	-0.79	.589			
	BO6	2.72	1.08	0.18	-0.67	.681			

| | | | | (Table continued) | | | | |
Construct	Item	Mean	SD	Skew	Kurt	FL	AVE	CR	CA
	BO7[*]	3.56	1.27	-0.54	-0.78	.600			
	BO8[*]	3.73	1.14	-0.62	-0.44	.532			
Bridging Social Capital	BR1	3.16	1.06	-0.19	-0.61	.784	.542	.922	.906
	BR2	2.93	1.09	0.08	-0.69	.723			
	BR3	2.88	1.09	0.07	-0.63	.714			
	BR4	3.37	1.08	-0.27	-0.60	.693			
	BR5	2.87	1.20	0.11	-0.97	.786			
	BR6	2.88	1.14	0.08	-0.81	.791			
	BR7	3.29	1.14	-0.25	-0.71	.652			
	BR8	2.32	0.99	0.36	-0.55	.655			
	BR9	2.60	1.18	0.22	-1.05	.728			
	BR10	2.30	1.07	0.74	-0.08	.636			
Dept-Disclosure:	DT1	2.43	1.15	0.41	-0.76	.870	.733	.916	.877
Trusted Receiver	DT2	2.27	1.08	0.57	-0.44	.859			
	DT3	2.11	1.02	0.70	-0.19	.766			
	DT4	2.27	1.09	0.51	-0.66	.922			
Dept-Disclosure:	DI1	1.65	0.93	1.32	0.95	.859	.667	.889	.832
Influencing Receiver	DI2	1.65	0.92	1.36	1.14	.772			
	DI3	1.56	0.79	1.41	1.80	.742			
	DI4	1.49	0.86	1.87	2.96	.885			
Dept-Disclosure:	DF1	2.57	1.16	0.30	-0.82	.872	.727	.914	.874
Friends Receiver	DF2	2.37	1.06	0.36	-0.60	.865			
	DF3	2.21	1.03	0.58	-0.26	.762			
	DF4	2.38	1.10	0.37	-0.77	.906			
Dept-Disclosure:	DA1	2.72	1.32	0.12	-1.20	.906	.786	.936	.908
Family Receiver	DA2	2.43	1.21	0.42	-0.89	.897			
	DA3	2.25	1.16	0.61	-0.59	.810			
	DA4	2.54	1.28	0.26	-1.14	.931			
Dept-Disclosure:	DC1	1.60	0.87	1.51	2.02	.905	.777	.933	.904
Coworkers Receiver	DC2	1.64	0.94	1.46	1.45	.833			
	DC3	1.49	0.75	1.43	1.27	.850			
	DC4	1.53	0.80	1.49	1.77	.934			
Dept-Disclosure:	DU1	1.20	0.58	3.58	14.1	.918	.705	.905	.857
Unknowns Receiver	DU2	1.33	0.82	3.04	9.45	.734			
	DU3	1.24	0.57	2.68	7.45	.791			
	DU4	1.21	0.60	3.38	12.1	.902			
Online Social	SW1	3.01	1.03	-0.39	-0.47	.813	.663	.907	.874
Well-being	SW2	2.96	0.90	-0.27	-0.08	.779			
	SW3	3.34	0.99	-0.75	-0.01	.815			
	SW4	3.11	1.00	-0.52	-0.40	.802			
	SW5	2.96	1.07	-0.20	-0.91	.750			

Note: SD=standard deviation; FL=factor loadings; AVE=average variance extracted; CR=composite reliability; CA=Cronbach's Alpha. [*]responses reversed prior to evaluation.

ENHANCING THE PRIVACY RISK AWARENESS OF TEENAGERS IN ONLINE SOCIAL NETWORKS THROUGH SOFT-PATERNALISM MECHANISMS

*— Published by **Jose Alemany, Elena del Val, Juanmi Alberola,** and **Ana García-Fornes** in the **International Journal of Human-Computer Studies** [12]*

7.1	Introduction	154
7.2	Related work	156
7.3	Nudging Mechanisms	159
7.4	Experiment	166
7.5	Results	170
7.6	Discussion	181
7.7	Conclusions	184

7.1 Introduction

Teenagers constitute one of the main user groups of Online Social Networks [258]. The use of social networks is part of children's daily living routine. According to Livingstone et al. [166], 93% of 9-16-year-old users go online at least weekly (60% go online every day or almost every day). Although teenagers obtain a benefit from sharing and consuming information on OSN (i.e., instant messaging, watching videos, or playing games), they are also exposed to privacy risks (i.e., cyberbullying or experiences that make them feel uncomfortable) [155, 223]. Recent surveys have shown that users' privacy concerns regarding social networks have increased in the last few years [5, 125].

There are clear differences in behavior between teenagers and adults on social networks. The comparison carried out by Christofides e t. al [61] reveals that teenagers spend significantly longer on SNS per day, and they have more contact with strangers [87] (17 percent of teens have become "friends" with people who they have never personally met, and 43 percent of teens have been contacted online by strangers). They can be easily convinced to share their personal information with the promise of a small prize or gift. Since children and teenagers tend to be trusting, naïve, curious, adventuresome, and eager for attention and affection, potential offenders and strangers have found that children and teenagers are perfect targets for criminal acts in cyberspace [52]. The combination of both factors (i.e., the number of friends and their vulnerability), makes the risk (i.e., the probability of reaching a broader audience) of a teenager's publication higher than an adult's publication. Therefore, the privacy risk of teenagers actions increases. The need of mechanisms oriented to increase privacy awareness when teenagers share information in social networks or applications becomes more relevant. Despite the importance and vulnerability of this demographic group, this subset of the community has hardly been researched in the context of privacy in social networks.

In this research, we focus on teenage users' behavior regarding online privacy. In this context, three processes are considered to be important [235]: risk assessment (i.e., calculating risk probability and magnitude); risk evaluation (i.e., determining the acceptability of a given risk); and risk management (i.e., the process of reducing risk to an acceptable level). When users are going to publish a message on an OSN, they should evaluate the benefits and risks of performing that action. The privacy decision-making process is complex and users often do not have full knowledge of the audience that will see the publication or how other users are going to use the disclosed information. In addition, the evaluation of all the possible scenarios of a disclosure could be overwhelming for a user, especially for teenagers [10].

Several approaches have been proposed to facilitate the decision-making process of users in OSN that may affect their privacy. For instance, some social network applications offer privacy-settings controls. However, in some cases, these controls are complex for non-expert users that are unable to fully understand the implications of their own settings. In other cases, the configuration of privacy settings is considered by users to be a tedious task, so they prefer to maintain the default settings [164]. In addition, privacy controls in OSN are more focused on protecting the information related to the user profile than on protecting the privacy of the user's publications [164, 189, 225]. There are other approaches that address the problem of users' privacy with the automation of privacy settings configuration [86, 262, 34, 244]. However, these proposals usually require an initial user intervention. Other approaches try to improve user awareness about the misalignment of users' expected audience with the actual audience to reduce the negative effects of performing an action in an OSN [49, 129, 178]. Several works also propose privacy risk metrics to asses users in the management of their privacy just before performing a sharing action [11]. However, to facilitate the decision-making process of users, it is not only important to measure the privacy risk (i.e., risk assessment), but also the way the metric will be shown to users. The way the information is shown can influence the users' decision-making process (i.e., risk evaluation and management).

According to Staksrud and Livingstone [235], it is relevant to assist teenagers to cope with risk without restricting their freedom of online exploration that society promotes for children in other contexts. In recent years, there has been growing interest in the use of mechanisms from behavioral economics to improve decision-making processes where lack of information or cognitive overload may unfavorably affect user privacy [21]. These mechanisms are known as soft paternalistic interventions (i.e., nudges). They attempt to influence decision making to improve individual well-being, without actually limiting users' ability to choose freely, thus, preserving freedom of choice [7].

In this paper, we present two soft-paternalism mechanisms to assist users (especially teenagers) to make better decisions about actions in social networks that may increase their privacy risks. The aim is to increase their privacy awareness. In this paper, privacy awareness refers to the users' knowledge about the potential audience that might see a user's publication disclosure. The proposed mechanisms "nudge" users to reconsider the disclosure actions before performing them. The proposed mechanisms use information from a Privacy Risk Score (PRS) metric that considers different levels of friendship and the potential audience that may have access to the disclosed message [11]. The first mechanism shows the profile images of users that are part of the potential audience that may have access to the message and a risk-level alert. The second mechanism shows the number of users that are part of the audience that may have access to the message and a risk-level alert. We tested the mechanisms in a four-week experiment with 42 teenagers in an online social network called PESEDIA. The results obtained through the analysis of the social network logs suggest that the use of soft-paternalism mechanisms could be a suitable option to assess in the decision-making process and prevent teenagers from privacy risk publications that could have negative consequences.

The rest of the paper is structured as follows. Section 7.2 presents previous works that are related to privacy protection and awareness. Section 7.3 describes in detail the nudging mechanisms proposed. Section 7.4 describes the methodology followed for the experiment (i.e., their study subjects, protocols, and types of evaluations). Section 7.5 presents the evaluations and results derived from the teenagers' activities and interactions during the study. Section 7.6 presents our discussions about how the results obtained should be interpreted and what was learned from the research. Finally, Section 7.7 presents conclusions and future work.

7.2 Related work

As the number of activities in online social networks increases, teenagers have to deal with an increasing number of privacy decisions. These decisions are made with incomplete and asymmetric information (i.e., limited knowledge about the reachability of a publication) and with bounded rationality (i.e., limited resources to evaluate all possible options and their consequences). Previous studies [229] state that the limited attentional capability of humans results in their bounded capacity to be rational.

Several educational strategies have been carried out by education centers and public administrations to leverage teenage users' awareness of privacy risks and to reduce their exposure to associated negative experiences [258, 1, 260]. There are also some studies that evaluate the impact of educational initiatives which suggest that they are successful in increasing awareness about online risks [67, 232]. However, the research community considers that awareness and confidence do not necessarily promote less risky behavior among young people [166]. This result is in the line of the number of young people that report negative online experiences despite the initiatives carried out

As an alternative to educational materials, mechanisms from the field of behavioral research have been considered to be appropriate for designing systems that nudge users towards better decisions concerning privacy [7]. Specifically, soft-paternalism interventions have been considered as a suitable method to influence teenagers' privacy behaviors without losing freedom of choice or liberty.

In the context of privacy in mobile applications, Almuhimedi et al. [16] propose the creation of an application that includes soft-paternalism mechanisms with the aim of raising the awareness of data collected by other applications. The authors carried out an 8-day experiment where the participants installed the proposed application. The application alerts consist of messages describing the number of apps accessing one information type and the total number of accesses in a given period. The alerts triggered changes of 58% in the data access permissions of other applications. The results suggest the positive effect of the soft-paternalism on the awareness of users' data that is being used by third-parties. This work monitorizes and informs once a third-party application has already accessed to user's data. However, our proposal is oriented to the creation of preventive action messages that would avoid future regrets about the sharing action.

Other works have used soft-paternalism mechanisms to deal with privacy in instant messaging applications. Patil et al. [202] carried out an experiment with 50 participants to evaluate whether privacy preferences of the social circles influence privacy setting configuration. When the participants were configuring their preferences for six privacy-relevant settings, they also had information about the privacy choices made by the majority of their contacts. The results of the experiment show that the primary driver in establishing a certain setting value is the privacy aspect. The privacy choice of user's social circle is a secondary source of guidance to establish privacy settings. The results also show that one's personal perception of privacy is an influential characteristic. Therefore, it could be considered appropriate provide information about the user's situation regarding privacy when he is going to perform an action in order to influence in his behaviour.

Soft-paternalism mechanisms have also been applied to online social networks. Konings et al. [149] present an approach that controls the access to information published on social networks and for how long it would be available. This proposal combines a policy-based cryptographic enforcement system with social signaling. Social signaling is used to label sensitive information. The authors propose a set of privacy icons to label the information shared on a social network. When users publish a message, they can select the users that will have access to the message, how long they will have

(i.e., private, keep information internal, not print, etc.). However, users do not have information about the potential audience that might see the message. Users only have the option to express their personal preferences about the audience.

Wang et al. [273] present the results of a 6-week experiment with 28 Facebook users. In the experiment, the authors introduced three types of nudges: audience nudge (contains textual and visual information of the audience), timer nudge (introduces a visual delay of 20 seconds after a user clicked the "post" button before publishing the submitted post), and the combination of the two. The results conclude that participants that use Facebook to post personal opinions perceive the nudges as being more beneficial than those who use it to broadcast news articles or for commercial purposes. Moreover, the users that have experience in the configuration of privacy settings considered that the nudges could be more useful for people without experience in social networks. However, in the case of the audience mechanism the privacy risk that a user could have if the expected audience re-share the user's publication is not considered. This information could provide him a broader view of the potential reachability of his publication. The results of the experiment suggest that these mechanisms can be useful for people who are starting to use social networks (e.g. children and adolescents).

A similar 12-day experiment with 21 participants was carried out in [271]. The authors propose different nudging mechanisms to be integrated into Facebook. The first mechanism "audience nudge" provides images of the audience that could see the post. Similarly to the audience mechanism proposed in [273], this mechanism also does not take into account the potential audience in the case of user with permissions re-shares the publication. The second mechanism "timer nudge" includes a time delay before a user posts a message on the social network. The third mechanism "sentiment nudge" consists of an estimation of the sentiment associated to the post that the user is going to publish. The authors analyzed the data collected from the experiment (i.e., number of changes in online privacy settings, number of canceled or edited posts, post frequency, and topic sensitivity) and the data of a questionnaire after the experiment. They found clear evidence of changes in posting behavior for some of the participants. The participants mentioned that the "audience nudge" was useful for thinking about customized groups. For the "timer nudge", the users mentioned that the mechanism provided them the opportunity to stop and think about the publication. In general, the "sentiment nudge" was perceived as being a less useful nudge than the others. The authors mention that the reasons could be associated with the sentiment algorithm that was used.

It is important to provide mechanisms that facilitate the increase of privacy aware-ness. The concept of privacy awareness varies depending on the research work. Some

derstanding of privacy controls and settings [30]. Others define privacy awareness as the perception of the elements in an environment, threats, and implications from personal information disclosure [228]. In this work, we consider a more specific concept of privacy awareness to be the knowledge of the users about the potential audience that might see a user's publication disclosure. Specifically, we propose a nudge approach similar to the one proposed by Wang et al. [271, 273] to increase users' privacy awareness. However, the work presented here differs from the previous ones in several ways (see Table 7.1). First, we integrate a privacy risk metric in the nudges, which considers the potential audience of a publication (i.e., if a user of the intended audience re-shares the information). The current approaches consider the audience based only on the privacy policy defined by the user, without considering the potential re-sharing actions. Second, we introduce a new quantitative nudge that shows the number of potential users that may see the publication instead of showing the users' profile images. We also evaluate whether there are differences in the influence on users' behaviors between the visual nudge or the numeric nudge. Third, we evaluate the nudges in a population of teenagers between 12 and 14 years old.

7.3   Nudging Mechanisms

Recent research works state that social media users underestimate their audience size, guessing that their audience is just 27% of its true size [31, 43]. Users usually do not remember which users are part of their direct audience in social networks, and, therefore, it is highly complicated to determine those users that can be reached from their direct audience. Therefore, users do not usually apply privacy tools (e.g., audience selectors or access lists) to define who has access to their information. As a consequence, users post information that may reach undesired audiences without being conscious of it. This information can even reach other communities that were not in their intended audience.

The idea of nudging was popularized by Thaler and Sunstein [250] as a form of soft-paternalism to guide individuals toward certain behaviors. A nudge can be viewed as an intervention that can modify people's behavior without forcing them. Hansen [112] stated that users are not usually aware of biases that may result in choices that have potentially adverse outcomes. Therefore, nudges can be viewed as mechanisms oriented to mitigate human biases to provide more beneficial outcomes for users. In decision-making scenarios that are involved in social networks, nudge mechanisms can

	Nudges	Nudges for privacy	Media
Almuhimedi et al. [16]	• application message alerts (number of apps accessing one information type and the total number of accesses in a given period)	✓ Considers AppOps logs shown for each app-permission	Mobile app
Patil et al. [202]	• user's social circle	✓ Considers the actions performed by the user's social circle	Instant messaging app
Konings et al. [149]	• privacy icons for social signaling	✓ Considers the user's preferences	
Wang et al. [271] (2013)	• audience (profile images of the publication audience) • time (visual delay) • audience + time	✓ Considers the privacy policy of the publication ✓ Considers the privacy policy of the publication	Social network
Wang et al. [273] (2014)	• audience (profile images of the publication audience) • time (visual delay) • sentiment	✓ Considers the privacy policy of the publication	Social network
Our work	• visual audience + text message with a degree of privacy risk • numerical audience + text message with a degree of privacy risk	✓ Considers a privacy risk metric that estimates the potential audience of a publication ✓ Considers a privacy risk metric that estimates the potential audience of a publication	Social network

Table 7.1: Overview of approaches related to soft-paternalism mechanisms. We considered three main features: (i) the type of nudges used; (ii) if the nudges are applied to prevent privacy risk scenarios and what information was considered to establish the privacy risk; and (iii) the environment where the nudges are applied.

According to this, we propose informing the users about the potential audience of their publications using soft-paternalism mechanisms based on a privacy risk metric. The metric used in this work to support the nudges is the Privacy Risk Score [11].

7.3.1 Privacy Risk Score (PRS)

We assume that there is a social network G that consists of N nodes, where every node

bidirectional links that represent friendship relationships and correspond to the edges $E \subseteq N \times N$ of $\mathcal{G}$. We define the Privacy Risk Score (PRS) [11] for a user a_i that publishes a message as an indicator of the potential risk of this message to be diffused over the social network (i.e., potential visibility). The higher the PRS value, the higher the threat to user a_i's privacy.

To estimate the PRS, two important factors are considered: (i) the user's position in the network. Those users located in paths where messages follow frequently, have a higher privacy risk than others; and (ii) the newness of a message. As stated in [69], the diffusion of a message in a social network is dependent on the lifetime since this message was created. In our case, the message diffusion process of a message m is based on other models [139, 106], in which users are initially represented as deactivated nodes, since they did not received the message. Users become activated as they receive this message and the diffusion process finishes when no activations occur from time step s to $s + 1$. The estimation of the PRS is described in more depth in [11].

According to this process, the privacy risk of a user by performing a message's diffusion is related to the amount of users that this user can activate. Figure 7.1a shows a social network in which user a_1 is publishing a new message. Blue nodes represent users that have not seen this message and can potentially see it (are deactivated nodes), while red nodes represent users that have already seen the message (are activated). The privacy risk associated with user a_1 for the diffusion of this message is high, since the probability to reach deactivated nodes (i.e., the rest of the users apart from a_1) is high too. Figure 7.1b shows a social network in which user a_1 is publishing a message that was forwarded by user a_2. However, this message has already been seen by a large number of users of the social network. In this case, the privacy risk associated with user a_1 for the diffusion of this message is low, since there are only 3 remaining deactivated users that can potentially be activated. Therefore, we say that the privacy risk associated with a user for a message diffusion process is high when a user publishes a new message since no other users have viewed it yet (i.e., they are deactivated). In contrast, the privacy risk is low when a user publishes a message that has already been viewed by others (i.e., they have become activated).

To represent this, we define $S = \{1, 2, \ldots, n\}$ to indicate the number of steps that a message has taken from its creation. Considering these two factors, we define a $S \times N$ reachability matrix γ_i associated to each user a_i to represent the number of messages that a_i has published at a certain step s and have been seen by other users. As an example, the value $\gamma_{i,\ldots}$ represents the messages published by a_i in step s that were

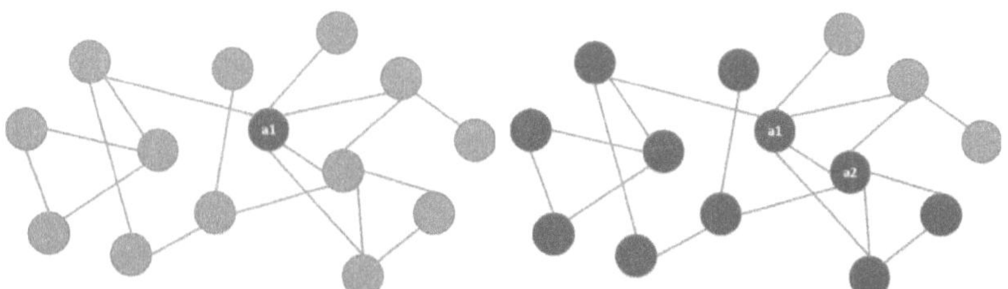

(a) High privacy risk of user a_1 for sharing a message non-seen yet.

(b) Low privacy risk of user a_1 for sharing a message seen by the majority.

Figure 7.1: Representation of user's privacy risk for different diffusion times of a message.

In a general view, the PRS value for a user a_i can be calculated as the percentage of agents of the social network that potentially see a message published by a_i at any stage (Equation 7.1).

$$PRS(a_i) = \frac{1}{S} \sum_{s=1}^{S} \left(\frac{\sum\limits_{a_j \in N} \gamma_{i_s, a_j}}{\gamma_{i_s, a_i} \cdot |N|} \right) \tag{7.1}$$

The PRS takes a value in the interval $[0..1]$. If this value is close to 0 when a user is about to publish a message, it indicates that this message is expected to be seen by a small number of users. In contrast, if this value is close to 1, it indicates that the potential audience of the message is the majority of the social network. It is possible to define PRS value intervals. Each interval is associated with informative labels (i.e., none, low, medium, high) that will appear in the nudging mechanisms. The definition of the intervals depends on the domain.

This metric provides an estimation of the potential audience that could have access to a publication in terms of the users of the social network that potentially see a message published by another user. The goal of the PRS is oriented to helping users to manage their sensitive and non-sensitive information, thereby improving their experiences in the social network.

Figure 7.2 shows a scenario where the privacy risk score is calculated for users a_1 and a_2 in a social network. We assume for simplicity that all of the users in $\mathcal{G}$ have the privacy policy that only their direct friends can see their walls. The maximum value for parameter S cannot exceed the network diameter (i.e., the longest of all of the

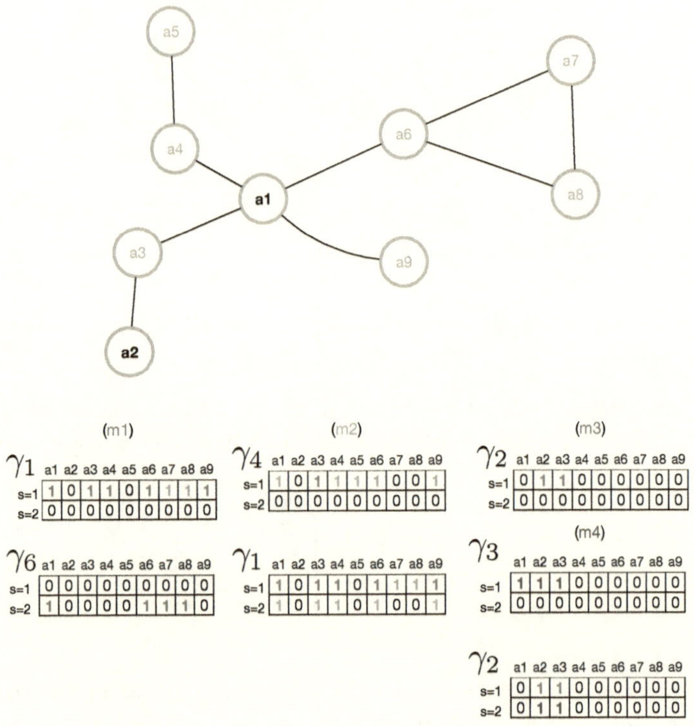

Figure 7.2: Example of social network activity and the PRS calculation process.

use the value 2 for parameter S.

Following, we define a diffusion process of four messages (m1, m2, m3, m4):

m1) User a_1 publishes a message m_1 on its wall. Since a_1 sends this message at $s = 1$, γ_1 is updated at $s = 1$, adding a value of 1 to a_3, a_4, a_6, and a_9, which are the agents that can see the message. Then, a_6 decides to share m_1 on its wall. Users a_1, a_7, and a_8 can see m_1. The information about the users that can see m_1 is updated in γ_6. The interaction of user a_6 with m_1 occurs after user a_1 shares it (i.e., the interaction is produced in the step $s = 2$). Note that the values of γ_1 are updated at $s = 1$ because γ_1 measures the reachability of the messages when user a_1 has interacted with them. Therefore, in row $s = 1$, columns a_7 and a_8

m2) Then, user a_4 publishes m_2. This message is seen by a_1 and a_5. This information is updated in γ_4 at $s = 1$. After that, user a_1 decides to share m_2, and agents a_3, a_4, a_6, and a_9 can see m_2. Therefore, γ_1 is updated with this new information. However, in this case, the row $s = 2$ is updated since the sharing action of a_1 implies the second step of m_2.

m3) User a_2 decides to publish m_3 and only user a_3 can see it. The γ_2 matrix is updated accordingly.

m4) The message m_4 is generated by user a_3. This message is viewed by its direct neighbors a_2 and a_1, and the γ_3 matrix is updated with this information. Finally, user a_2 decides to share m_4, and only a_3 can see it. Its γ_2 its updated at $s = 2$ with this new information.

Considering these four messages, the PRS for a_1 and a_2 can be calculated as:

$$PRS(a_1) = \frac{1}{2}\left(\frac{6}{9} + \frac{4}{9}\right) = 0.6$$

$$PRS(a_2) = \frac{1}{2}\left(\frac{2}{9} + \frac{2}{9}\right) = 0.2$$

As can be observed, the PRS for a_1 is 0.6, indicating that messages published by a_1 are expected to be seen by a high number of users. In contrast, the PRS for a_2 is 0.2, indicating that messages published by this user are not expected to reach a lot of users. If we consider intervals for PRS values of size 0.25 (i.e., None [0, 0.25]; Low [0.25, 0.5]; Medium [0.5, 0.75]; High [0.75, 1]), the PRS(a_1) indicates that the risk is medium and the PRS(a_2) indicates that the risk is none.

7.3.2 Nudges

Considering the PRS, nudges are shown to users by means of two soft-paternalism mechanisms in order to propose more beneficial choices regarding the privacy of this publication. These mechanisms are *Picture Nudge*, which is based on profile images of the potential audience, and *Number Nudge*, which provides numerical information about the potential audience of a publication. These nudge mechanisms try to increase the users' awareness about the reachability of their publications. Then, users can reconsider the privacy policy of a publication more carefully or can even decide not to

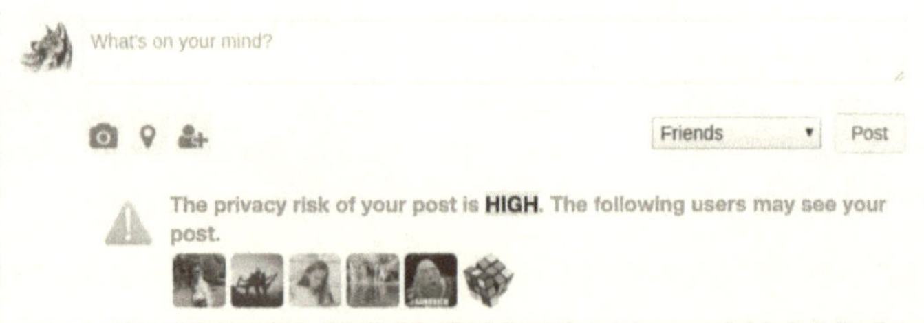

Figure 7.3: Picture Nudge. A notice indicates the privacy risk estimation associated with the action that the user is going to perform. The risk is categorized as high. The nudge shows the profile pictures of part of the audience that potentially could see the publication.

Picture Nudge The Picture Nudge is a mechanism that is triggered when a user is about to submit a publication (Figure 7.3). This mechanism consists of showing profile images of some users that are part of the audience that will have access to this publication. Users to be displayed are selected based on the PRS values of the post's audience and the probability of reaching new users. The probability increases if a user can be reached in more than one way. The selection of profile images to be displayed in the nudge prioritizes users outside of the intended audience. Although only six users are explicitly shown, the size of the audience can be very large. In addition, a warning is also shown according to the privacy risk estimation of this publication (high, medium, low, or none).

Unlike other proposals that provide mechanisms to detect and remove risky friends [28], the aim of the picture nudge proposed is to increase awareness about the potential audience that might see a user's publication. This does not imply that the users that appear in the images provided by the nudge are "risky" users. These users are part of the potential audience that may see the publication.

Number Nudge The Number Nudge is also triggered when a user is about to submit a publication (Figure 7.4). This mechanism consists of displaying the number of users that may have access to this publication. Similarly to the previous nudge, a warning

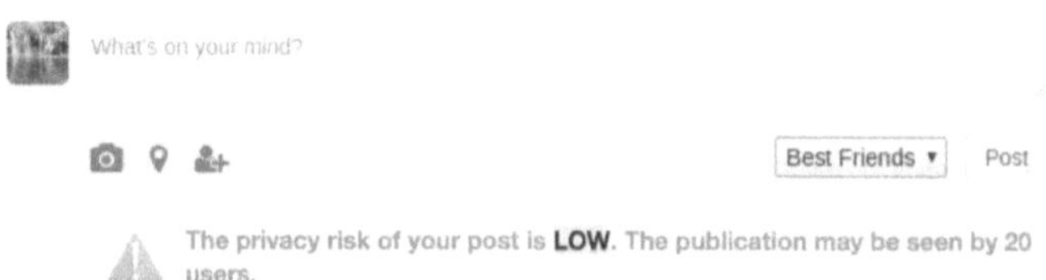

Figure 7.4: Number Nudge. A notice indicates the privacy risk estimation associated with the action that the user is going to perform. The risk is categorized as low. The nudge shows the number of users that eventually could see the publication.

7.4 Experiment

We propose two research questions and two hypotheses to test the effects of the proposed nudging mechanisms in users' behaviors regarding privacy. We focus on the privacy aspect related to the content publishing, specifically, the selected audiences. First, we should consider that a new social network (or app) has a "learning curve" (i.e., a period of learning and discovery, until users start to use it regularly). This may influence the participants' behavior regarding privacy during the experiment. Therefore, we investigate the following research question:

Research Question 7.1: *How does the private privacy policy rate differ between the learning/discovery period and later when users publish content regularly?*

In other words, the private privacy policy for published content includes all of the private audiences ("only me", collections[1], and "friends").

Second, regarding the designed nudge mechanisms, we want to know if the nudge before publishing content and the information provided in it (about the potential audience) produce an effect towards better privacy practices. Therefore, two hypotheses are proposed:

Hypothesis 7.1: *The private privacy policy rate changes when teenage users publish content using the Picture Nudge mechanism.*

Hypothesis 7.2: *The private privacy policy rate changes when teenage users publish content using the Number Nudge mechanism.*

---

[1] Collections are groups of "friends" that are specialized and customized by users (e.g., best friends

Finally, we investigate the differences between the effects of the designed nudge mechanisms in order to analyze which mechanism has a more powerful effect on users' behavior. Therefore, we investigate the following research question:

Research Question 7.2: *How does the private privacy policy rate differ between the Picture Nudge and the Number Nudge when teenage users publish content?*

To evaluate these effects, we performed an experiment in the context of the 2017 Summer School organized by the Universitat Politècnica de València. We focused the experiment on teenagers aged between 12 and 14 years old because they are starting with the use of social networking sites, and, at the same time, they are among the heaviest users of social networking [214]. Moreover, this particular group is developmentally vulnerable to privacy risks such as depression, sexting, and cyberbullying [171, 198, 166, 47]. Therefore, the effect of nudge mechanisms can be highly beneficial to them since these users may still not be aware of all of the consequences of their actions in social applications regarding their privacy. In the following sections, we describe the social network platform PESEDIA where the experiment was performed and the methodology used for measuring the effect of the proposed nudges on real users.

7.4.1   Platform

PESEDIA is an online social network for educational and research purposes that includes: (i) the design and development of new metrics to analyze and quantify privacy risks [11]; (ii) the application of methods to change users' behavior regarding their privacy concerns; (iii) the implementation of new features to improve the management of users' content; (iv) and the evaluation and testing of new proposals with real users.

The underlying implementation of PESEDIA uses Elgg [64], which is an open source engine that is used to build social environments. The environment provided by this engine is similar to other social networks (e.g. Facebook). Figure 7.5 shows the architecture of PESEDIA. The PESEDIA architecture has two main components: the *Platform Layer* and the *User Layer*. The *Platform Layer* is the core of the architecture. This layer contains the Social Network Services, which provides the main functionality of the social network, and the Storage System, which provides persistent storage of all of the information generated in the social network. Among other modules, the Social Network Services include the Privacy Risk Module, which is responsible for estimating the risk a user has when performing an action in the social network, and the Nudging Mechanism Module, which is responsible for providing a suitable visualization of the privacy risk

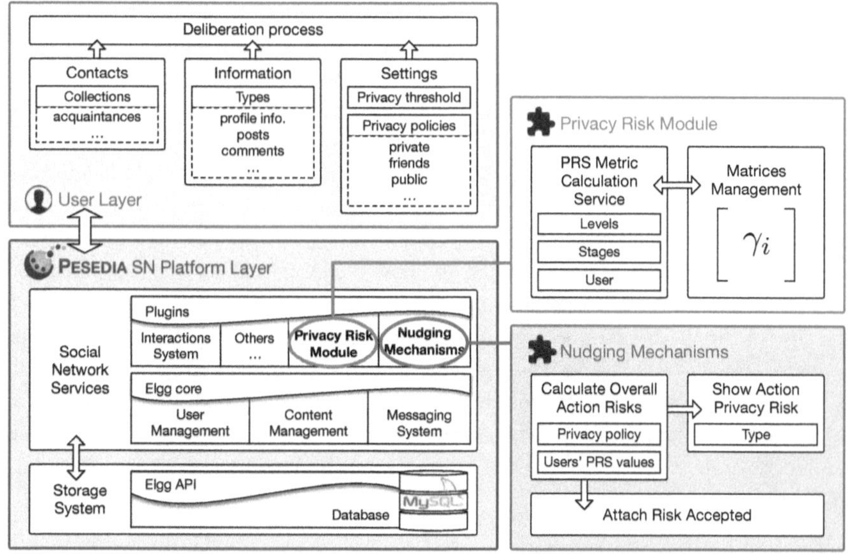

Figure 7.5: Block diagram that represents the architecture of Pesedia SN. Also represented are the relevant plugins for this work: the Privacy Risk Module, and the Nudging Mechanisms.

charge of managing information associated to each user. This information is divided in three categories: contacts (grouped or non-grouped); information (e.g., profile items, publications, etc.); and settings, which are mainly focused on privacy settings, such as privacy policies and privacy thresholds.

7.4.2 Setup

The experiment was carried out on the PESEDIA social network. Nudging Mechanisms and Privacy Risk Module plugins were included in PESEDIA. We activated a log system to record all of the users' actions in order to analyze them after the experiment. Moreover, we also included a registry controller (by a secret token) to avoid undesired registrations that could affect the security of the participants and the experiment.

The experiment period was 21 days. A total of 84 teenagers participated in it. During the period of the experiment, the participants had access to the PESEDIA social network to share their experiences and feelings about the Summer School. We organized three

of the experiment. These three on-site sessions were distributed at three points in time: session 1, at the beginning of the 21-day period; session 2, in the middle, and session 3, at the end. The aim of these sessions was to clarify any doubts that might arise among the participants about the social network functionality and new features introduced. In the first session, we introduced PESEDIA to the participants and they signed up on the social network. In the second session, the nudges were activated and introduced to the participants. During this session, we described how the Picture Nudge and Number Nudge mechanisms worked to all the participants. We provided details about the information that each nudge provided and how they worked. We also explained both nudges through a set of examples to clarify any doubt about their performance. In the case of the Picture Nudge, we clarified that the users that appeared in the images provided are not "risky" users, they are part of the potential audience that may see the publication. The participants should evaluate, based on the potential audience shown by the nudges, whether their publication may reach more users than the initial expected audience. In the third (and last) session, the participants answered the questionnaire about the experience.

In order to test the research questions and hypotheses proposed in this work, we split the participants into three groups and considered two stages in the experiment (see Figure 7.6). The splitting of all the participants into the three groups was done before the second session (i.e., after completing stage 1), and based on the private privacy policy rate of users' posted content on Pesedia to have the groups balanced. The groups are explained below:

- Group G_1 did not have any nudges activated during the entire experiment. This group was created to evaluate whether the "learning curve" influences the users' privacy behaviors (RQ7.1).

- Group G_2 did not have any nudges activated during stage 1, but the Picture Nudge mechanism was activated during stage 2. Group $G2$ was created to evaluate whether the Picture Nudge influences users' privacy behavior (H7.1).

- Group G_3 did not have any nudges activated during stage 1, but the Number Nudge mechanism was activated during stage 2. Group $G3$ was created to evaluate whether the Number Nudge influences users' privacy behavior (H7.2).

Moreover, in order to reinforce the data obtained from social network activity, the teenagers completed a survey questionnaire about the experiment. This questionnaire

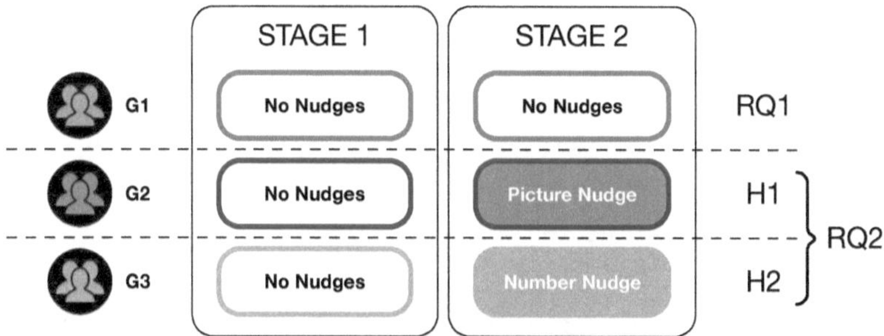

Figure 7.6: Structure of the experiment. Two stages and three groups of participants ($G1$, $G2$, and $G3$) were considered. In $G1$, the participants did not have any nudges activated during any stage. In $G2$, the participants did not have any nudges activated during stage 1, but the Picture Nudge was activated during stage 2. In $G3$, the participants did not have any nudges activated during stage 1, but the Number Nudge was activated during stage 2.

7.5 Results

In this section, we show the results obtained from the experiment. First, we introduce the participants' demographics and their initial attitude toward privacy as well as data related to posting behaviors. All of the information about participants was collected from the PESEDIA platform through their profiles, activity, and settings. Second, we analyze the participants' activity during stage 1 (where none of the groups had the nudging mechanisms activated) and during stage 2 (where G_1 and G_2 had the nudging mechanisms activated) in order to quantify the impact of the nudges on the participants. We applied statistical significance tests to answer the research questions and to validate the hypotheses about the nudge effects on participants' behaviors. Finally, we present the participants' perception of the benefits and drawbacks of the nudges based on the survey results.

7.5.1 Demographics and activity

In this subsection, we provide an accurate description of the participants of the experiment. We show the participants' descriptive data and their performance in PESEDIA. In addition, we focus on the privacy decisions made by the users during the experiment.

From the initial 84 participants that attended the experiment, we removed the participants who did not participate in both stages as well as participants who did not publish

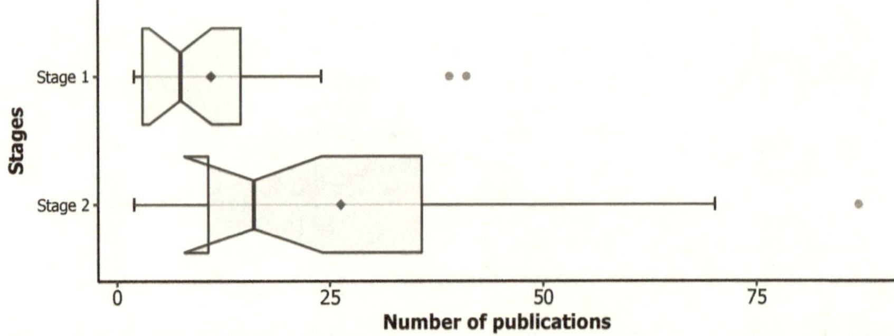

Figure 7.7: Distribution of the number of publications by the participants in Pesedia during the experiment by stages.

were removed). Also, there were participants that assisted to both sessions but they did not publish in both sessions any content with its corresponding privacy policy in the social network (e.g., they only performed "like" actions or comments). These users were also excluded from the experiment (23 participants were removed). In addition, we also performed a cleaning process of the data. This process consisted on removing those users who were extreme outliers from the data (8 participants were removed). "Outliers" are those points which stand out for not following a pattern which is generally visible in the data. To detect data outliers, we plotted the data points about users' activity. Figure 7.7 shows a boxplot representation of the distributions of the number of publications of participants in each stage. The activity of those users who lay far outside the general distribution (i.e., participants who fall more than 1.5 times the interquartile range above the third quartile) were analyzed in detail to detect if there was an anomalous behavior. In the context of the experiment, we considered users with an anomalous behavior those users whose activity was to repeat/create a message with nonsense content (i.e., random sequence of characters or empty messages) a disproportionate number of times. Once we had cleaned the data, the total number of participants included in the analysis was 42.

The following analysis is based on the behavior of the 42 participants. Table 7.2 includes information about the participants' age and gender and their behavior (previous to the experiment) on social networks, which is centered on the nature of the relationships and how active the participants are. That information was collected with an initial questionnaire during the first session to check the specific characteristics of teenagers that differentiates them from adults. The average age of the participants was 13.35

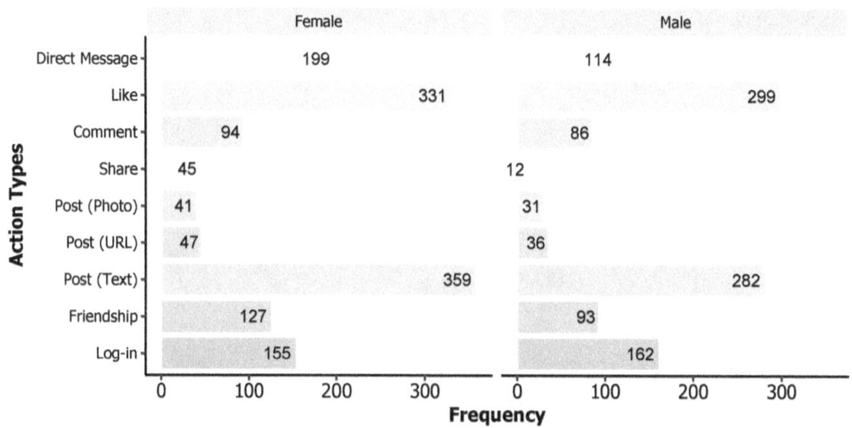

Figure 7.8: Information of participants' activity by gender in Pesedia.

network sites, and the proportion of unknown friends was high (see the acceptance threshold of friendship requests and the values of real friends).

Figure 7.8 shows quantitative information related to their activity by gender, including log-in actions, friendship relations, and interactions considering different types (posts, likes, comments, shares, and private messages). These data are the result of the 21 days of the experiment. During that period, the participants did 317 log-in actions, established 220 relationships, and created 1976 pieces of content. In general, the most frequent activities were posts (641), likes (630), and direct messages (313). Taking into account the experiment duration, they carried out an average of 15 log-in actions per day, and 2.25 interactions per day and participant. Moreover, they performed a mean of 10.49 friendship relations. With regard to gender differences in activity, we highlight that the female participants were slightly more active creating content, especially with textual posts, share actions, and direct messages. In contrast, the male participants were more passive and performed more log-in actions.

With regard to the participants' attitudes towards privacy, we analyzed: (i) the participants' privacy policies assigned to social network dimensions such as profile, settings, and posts; and (ii) the participants' privacy concern through privacy setting changes, post updates, and collection creations. Collections are customized lists made by users (e.g., best friends, family, etc.). Figure 7.9 displays the distribution of the participants' privacy policy decisions grouped by dimensions. The dimensions considered are: Pro-

CHAPTER 7. ENHANCING THE PRIVACY RISK AWARENESS OF TEENAGERS IN ONLINE SOCIAL NETWORKS THROUGH SOFT-PATERNALISM MECHANISMS

Demographic info.

Variables				Number (%)
Age	G_1	G_2	G_3	Total
12	2	2	1	5 (11.90%)
13	6	6	5	17 (40.48%)
14	6	8	6	22 (47.62%)
Gender	G_1	G_2	G_3	Total
Male	6	8	5	19 (47.62%)
Female	7	8	7	22 (52.38%)
Users of SNS	G_1	G_2	G_3	Total
Yes	13	15	11	39 (92.86%)
No	1	1	1	3 (7.14%)

Friendship info.

Variables				Number (%)
Friends	G_1	G_2	G_3	Total
0 − 20	2	3	2	7 (16.67%)
20 − 80	4	3	3	10 (23.81%)
80 − 150	3	4	1	8 (19.05%)
> 150	5	6	6	17 (40.47%)
Real Friends	G_1	G_2	G_3	Total
90 − 100%	3	5	1	9 (21.43%)
60 − 70%	9	7	7	23 (54.76%)
30 − 40%	2	3	3	8 (19.05%)
10 − 20%	0	1	1	2 (4.76%)
Acceptance threshold	G_1	G_2	G_3	Total
All	1	3	0	4 (9.52%)
Some unknown people	4	4	4	12 (28.58%)
Friends & Acquaintances	8	6	7	21 (50.00%)
Close Friends	1	3	1	5 (11.90%)

Activity info.

Variable	4-point likert scale* - Number (%)															
	4				3				2				1			
Activity rate	G_1	G_2	G_3	Total	G_1	G_2	G_3	Total	G_1	G_2	G_3	Total	G_1	G_2	G_3	Total
Using SNS	4	5	5	14 (33.33%)	6	5	3	14 (33.33%)	3	5	3	11 (26.19%)	1	1	1	3 (7.15%)
Text posting	1	1	1	3 (7.15%)	0	2	1	3 (7.15%)	11	10	8	29 (69.05%)	2	3	2	7 (16.67%)
Photo posting	0	1	0	1 (2.38%)	0	1	0	1 (2.38%)	12	11	9	32 (76.19%)	2	3	3	8 (19.05%)
Video posting	0	1	0	1 (2.38%)	0	0	0	0 (0.00%)	3	2	6	11 (26.19%)	11	13	6	30 (71.43%)
Share	1	1	1	3 (7.15%)	3	3	2	8 (19.05%)	7	8	6	22 (52.38%)	3	3	3	9 (21.43%)
Comment	2	3	2	7 (16.67%)	4	1	5	10 (23.81%)	4	8	3	15 (35.71%)	4	4	2	10 (23.81%)
Like	7	5	7	21 (50.00%)	4	7	3	12 (28.57%)	2	3	1	6 (14.29%)	1	1	1	3 (7.15%)

Table 7.2: Participants' information organized by demographic, friendship, and activity categories.
Likert scale: 4 = extremely frequent, 1 = not frequent at all

ticipants' profile information: age, gender, description, phone, location, school, and interests. In Settings, there are five general privacy setting options: default privacy option, tag visibility, friend list visibility, who can post on your wall, and the privacy policy for posts written on your wall. In Activity, we collected the privacy policy of all the posts published. The different privacy policies were: *Only me*, Collections, *Friends*, and Public; scored from 0 to 3, respectively. In Figure 7.9, the top red dashed line represents the mean privacy policy set as default in PESEDIA.

The privacy policy defined by default in PESEDIA for all of the participants was public to be completely permissive. In the case of the Profile dimension, the expected behavior

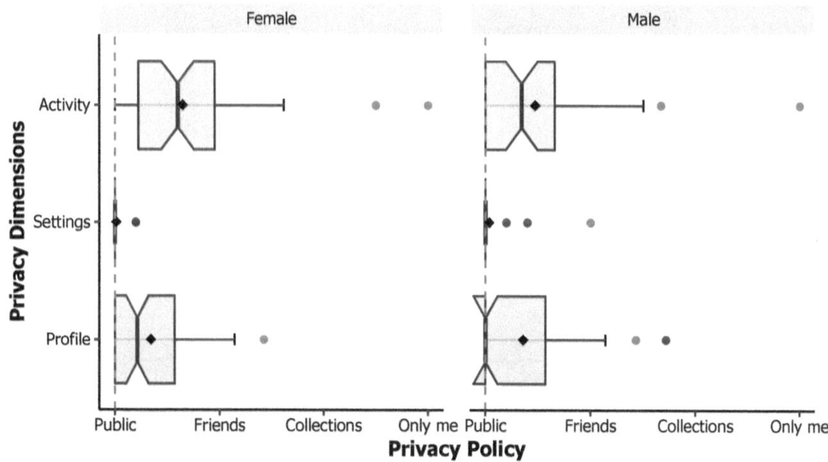

Figure 7.9: Distribution of privacy policies (represented as numbers: *Only me*, 0; Collections, 1; *Friends*, 2; and Public, 3) that were used by the participants in the different dimensions and disaggregated by gender.

ever, as shown in Figure 7.9, this behavior was weaker than the expected, especially for profile items that contain sensitive information. In the case of the Settings dimension, the participants showed very little concern about it. Only 11.72% of the participants changed their privacy settings. However, in the case of the Activity dimension, the privacy policies that participants used for their posts were more restrictive than in the other dimensions. Since we are considering all of the posts published during the study, these results may be a consequence of the nudging mechanisms. Another point to highlight is the differences between gender participants; the female participants, on average, chose more restrictive policies than the male participants (for Activity and Profile dimensions). In general, we have observed that, although the participants modified their privacy options, they maintained permissive policies except for postings. In the following sections, we analyze these behaviors in more detail and how the nudging mechanisms influenced them.

7.5.2 Participants' posting behavior

In this section, we analyze the behaviors of the participants when they publish content

Privacy Policies	Stage	G_1 Control Group	G_2 Picture Nudge	G_3 Number Nudge	All
Only me	S1	3.17% (4)	8.43% (7)	6.58% (5)	5.61% (16)
	S2	9.09% (14)	11.87% (33)	9.92% (13)	10.66% (60)
Collections	S1	0.00% (0)	0.00% (0)	0.00% (0)	0.00% (0)
	S2	0.00% (0)	3.24% (9)	4.58% (6)	2.66% (15)
Friends	S1	46.03% (58)	27.71% (23)	30.26% (23)	36.49% (104)
	S2	17.53% (27)	35.61% (99)	44.28% (58)	32.68% (184)
Public	S1	50.80% (64)	63.86% (53)	63.16% (48)	57.90% (165)
	S2	73.38% (113)	49.28% (137)	41.22% (54)	54.00% (304)
Total posts	S1	126	83	76	285
	S2	154	278	131	563

Table 7.3: Participants' posting behavior for the privacy aspect split into groups and stages. S1 and S2 denote stage 1 and stage 2, respectively.

levels of privacy risk accepted for content published) by the participants who had the nudges enabled.

To understand the privacy behavior of the participants during posting activities, we extracted the participants' privacy policy for each post from the social network PESEDIA. In Table 7.3, we show the privacy policies used for all of the participants. The participants are split into groups and stages to be able to compare behaviors with and without nudge mechanisms. We analyzed the total number of posts published and which percentage of these follow a specific privacy policy (i.e., *Only me*, Collections, *Friends*, or Public). Thus, we were be able to detect behavioral privacy changes between stage 1 and 2 and measure the effect of nudges.

In stage 1, the participants published and shared a total number of 285 posts on the PESEDIA social network. Considering all the participants (42) and the duration of this stage (10 days), one out of every two participants published or shared a post per day. This participation was low, but it can be considered normal because the participants were new to PESEDIA and they had to explore all of the functionality and services that our social network offers. From the privacy point of view, in general, the participants were not concerned about the privacy of postings. The majority of messages where published with public privacy policy (57.90%), followed by *friends* privacy policy (36.49%), then *only me* privacy policy (5.61%), and finally, no usage of collections by participants was done (0.0%). It is important to remember that the default privacy policy was public in the social network. Analyzing this information by groups, it can be observed that

Risk level	G_2 Picture Nudge	G_3 Number Nudge	All
NONE	1.90% (2)	0.00% (0)	2
LOW	27.62% (29)	42.59% (23)	59
MEDIUM	5.71% (6)	5.56% (3)	9
HIGH	64.76% (68)	51.85% (28)	96
Total	105	54	159

Table 7.4: The risk level of the posting action that participants took when nudges were activated.

other groups. For G_1, they used the friend policy more times than the other groups, with usage being close to that of public policy. In conclusion, during this stage of the study and with public policy as default, the participants were able to change the privacy of their posts to adapt it to their needs. However, the majority of the participants maintained the public policy.

In stage 2, the participants published and shared a total number of 563 posts. The participants' activity increased considerably as a consequence of popularity, with a daily activity of about 51.18 posts per day (563 posts divided by 11 days), and more than 2 posts per user and day (51.18 posts divided by 42 participants). From the privacy point of view, if we analyze the average behavior of all of the participants and we compare it with the behavior in stage 1, it can be observed that privacy behaviors change. The use of more restrictive privacy policies such as *Only me* and Collections increased, while *Friends* and Public policy usage was reduced. When focusing on the behavior of each group, we found important differences between participants with and without nudge mechanisms. The participants in the G_2 and G_3 groups evolved their behaviors into more protective privacy policies, while G_1 did the opposite and evolved to more relaxed privacy policies. G_2 had a conservative privacy behavior since they shared half of the posts as public and the other half with private circles such as *Friends*, Collections, or *Only me*. When observing their previous activity in stage 1, there is a progression towards more secure privacy habits for social network activity. G_3 had the most conservative privacy behavior with values close to 60% of posts shared with private circles, while the rest of posts were shared as public. For both nudges, the use of the Collections policy for sharing posts increased, but it was still too low. The privacy behaviors of G_1 were less restrictive since they shared the majority (73.38%) of their posts as public. When considering the participants' behavior in stages 1 and 2 as the reference behavior, the nudging mechanisms seem to have a positive effect on the

With regard to the posts published by nudged participants, Table 7.4 shows the proportion and quantity of posts labeled with different risk levels (calculated with the PRS metric and showed by the nudge mechanisms) that were accepted by participants when publishing posts on PESEDIA. Quantities were shown as complementary information to the participants' acceptance of risk since, as we mentioned in previous sections, the nudges were shown to them with a probability, thus avoiding upsetting the participants. The privacy risk accepted by participants was slightly higher in G_2 than G_3. That information is coherent with the data shown previously (Table 7.3), where the participants chose more protective privacy policies. Furthermore, the HIGH values of privacy risk (64.76% for Picture Nudge; 51.85% for Number Nudge) are greater than the public policies chosen. This reflects the risks of using friends policies for some users since these are not still enough to protect sensitive information.

7.5.3   Research questions and hypothesis testing

In this section, we test the research questions and the hypotheses proposed in this work in relation to the effects of nudges on users' privacy behavior. We use data collected from participants' posting activity to test whether there is a significant difference between the privacy behavior of participants between stages for the different conditions (G_1, G_2, and G_3 groups). In this way, we are able to measure the effect of nudges on participants' behavior.

Given the filtering of participants done by the conditions required to test the research questions and hypotheses (see subsection 7.5.1), we ran a samples equivalence test over the private privacy policy rate of users of the different groups at stage 1 to ensure that there were no existing differences between the samples. Kruskal-Wallis test of statistical significance to compare the mean of the three groups (over the 42 participants) revealed no significant differences were founded in the private privacy policies rate between groups in stage 1 (p-value > .05). The samples equivalence test provides more confidence that these samples were equivalent on related the participants' privacy behavior in stage 1.

In order to ensure whether or not there is a significant difference in privacy behaviors between groups during stages, some research questions and hypotheses for testing. We collected data from the privacy policies of the participants' publications during stage 1 and 2 (see Table 7.3), and we normalized this data by the number of publications for each participant. Due to the continuous nature of the variable and the number of samples (less than 30 per group), we used the paired-sample t-test ($\alpha = .05$). For this test,

		t-Test						ANOVA			
		Mean	Std. D	t		df	p	F	p	partial η^2	$1 - \beta$
RQ7.1	S1	.409	.395	−.348		13	.734	.111	.742	.004	.062
	S2	.457	.366								
H7.1	S1	.249	.350	−3.813		15	.002*	6.260	.002	.173**	.678
	S2	.557	.344								
H7.2	S1	.295	.385	−2.412		11	.035*	4.301	.044	.164**	.509
	S2	.613	.367								
RQ7.2	G_2	.557	.344	−.416		24	.681	.175	.679	.007	.069
	G_3	.613	.367								

Table 7.5: Tests for the differences in privacy behavior between nudged and non-nudged participants. $^*p < .05$ **partial $\eta^2 > .01 = $ small, $> .06 = $ medium, $> .14 = $ large effect [63]

In statistical hypothesis testing, a Type I error is the rejection of a true null hypothesis. Thus, we are able to reject the null hypothesis (H_0) to accept the alternative (H_1). We also measured the power test, which indicates the probability that the test correctly rejects the null hypothesis. And, thus, we obtain the Type II error, also referred to as the false negative rate (β) since the power is equal to $1 - \beta$. Therefore, we are able to accept the null hypothesis (H_0). Moreover, we measure the effect size to determine the magnitude of the phenomenon. To do this, we carried out a one-way MANOVA test. The sizes of effect can be classified as falling between small ($> .01$), medium ($> .06$) and large ($> .14$) [63]. Table 7.5 contains the results of the hypothesis testing methods carried out.

To answer the research question RQ7.1 about how the private privacy policy rate differs between the learning/discovery period and later when users publish content regularly (in the G_1 group), we tested mean differences between the two samples. In particular, we ran a paired-sample t-test ($\alpha = .05$) and the results ($t = −.348$, p-value= .734, partial $\eta^2 = .004$) revealed no significant differences between the samples. We also measured the power ($1 - \beta = .062$) and the effect size ($> .01$) using the one-way MANOVA test, which results also suggest no significant differences. Therefore, the results revealed that no significant differences were found in the privacy policies used by the participants in the G_1 group during stage 1 and 2.

H7.1 predicted that the Picture Nudge mechanism produces an effect on the participants' privacy behaviors (of the G_2 group), specifically in the private privacy policy rate of posting action. To address H7.1, we ran a paired-sample t-test ($\alpha = .05$) and

pothesis. Therefore, significant differences were found in the privacy policies used by participants in the G_2 group during stage 1 and 2, and also the effect size was large ($> .16$). H7.1 was supported.

H7.2 predicted that the Number Nudge mechanism produces an effect on the participants' privacy behaviors (of the G_3 group), specifically in the private privacy policy rate of posting action. To address H7.2, we ran a paired-sample t-test ($\alpha = .05$) and the results of the test ($t = -2.412$, p-value $= .035$, partial $\eta^2 = .167$) rejected the null hypothesis. Therefore, significant differences were found in the privacy policies used by participants in the G_3 group during stage 1 and 2, and also the effect size was large ($> .16$). Thus, H7.2 was supported.

To answer the research question RQ7.2 about how the private privacy policy rate differs between the Picture Nudge (G_2) and the Number Nudge (G_3) when teenage users publish content (in stage 2), we tested mean differences between the two samples. In particular, we ran an independent-sample t-test ($\alpha = .05$) and the results ($t = -.416$, p-value $= .681$, partial $\eta^2 = .007$) revealed no significant differences between the samples. We also measured the power ($1 - \beta = .069$) and the effect size ($> .01$) using the one-way MANOVA test, which results also suggest no significant differences. Therefore, the results revealed that no significant differences were found in the privacy policies used by the participants with the Picture Nudge mechanism enabled (G_2) and the Number Nudge mechanism enabled (G_3) in stage 2.

7.5.4 Participants' perception about nudges

We asked the participants directly about the privacy nudges using a survey embedded in PESEDIA. The results extracted from the survey represent the perceptions of the 31 participants who finally completed the survey. Of these participants, 11 participants were nudged with the Picture Nudge mechanism; 9 participants were nudged with the Number Nudge mechanism; and 11 participants were not nudged. The nudged participants were asked about the perceived benefits and drawbacks of the privacy nudges that they experienced. The non-nudged participants were asked about their desire to have tools (ours or similar ones) in social networks to inform them about privacy risks in order to improve their privacy awareness. Specifically, the following five questions were asked:

- Q1: Did you consider the nudges useful for preserving your privacy on the post-

		Picture Nudge	Number Nudge	Non-Nudge	Total
# participants		11	9	11	31
Q1: Did you consider the nudges useful for preserving your privacy on the posting action?	Y	8	7		15
	N	3	2		5
Q2: Did you consider the nudges irritating?	Y	4	3		7
	N	7	6		13
Q3: Did you use the nudges for setting/fitting the audiences?	Y	8	6		14
	N	3	3		6
Q4: Would you have liked to have a tool that informs you about privacy risks in order to improve your privacy (e.g., **showing the picture** of potential users that will have access to your publication)?	Y		5	8	13
	N		4	3	7
Q5: Would you have liked to have a tool that informs you about privacy risks in order to improve your privacy (e.g., **showing the number** of potential users that will have access to your publication)?	Y	6		7	13
	N	5		4	9

Table 7.6: Opinion from a subset of participants about the privacy nudges.

- Q2: Did you consider the nudges irritating?

- Q3: Did you use the nudges for setting/fitting the audiences?

- Q4: Would you have liked to have a tool that informs you about privacy risks in order to improve your privacy (e.g., **showing the picture** of potential users that will have access to your publication)?

- Q5: Would you have liked to have a tool that informs you about privacy risks in order to improve your privacy (e.g., **showing the number** of potential users that will have access to your publication)?

Table 7.6 shows the results of the participants' opinions about privacy nudges. The results are organized by the nudging mechanisms that the participants had during the study. The rows in the table represent the number of participants that responded (Yes or No) to a specific question. The empty values of the table are due to the fact that those participants were not asked the question (i.e., it made no sense to ask non-nudged participants about the inconveniences of the nudge). Questions Q1, Q2, and Q3, which targeted the nudged participants, evaluate whether the participants consider the nudges to be useful. Whereas questions Q4 and Q5, which targeted the non-nudged participants, evaluate whether the participants would like to have tools inform

According to the participants' responses, both nudges had a good level of acceptance. For question Q1, three out of four participants considered the nudges to be useful for preserving privacy. For question Q2, about 65% of the participants did not consider the nudges to be irritating. These responses make sense if we consider question Q2 as being the opposite of question Q1. Nevertheless, the percentage is slightly lower than for question Q1, this may be because some users considered the nudge, though useful, should have been more appealing or less intrusive. For question Q3, almost three out of four participants considered the nudges to be helpful for setting the audiences. For the remaining questions (Q4 and Q5), we observed that non-nudged participants positively accepted the need of tools to improve their privacy on social networks. Overall, the participants were satisfied with the nudging mechanisms that contain the PRS metric to improve their privacy awareness on social networks.

7.6   Discussion

This paper reports the results of a 21-day field experiment about the use of two types of nudging mechanisms to influence teenagers' posting privacy behavior in the social network platform PESEDIA. Nudge mechanisms proposed in this paper did not limit participants' ability to share information in the social network. Instead, they encouraged the participants to reflect on their potential audience that may have access to the information. In general, previous soft-paternalism approaches not only in the context of social networks state that these mechanisms make users reflect and become more aware of their decisions, avoiding risky behaviors [16, 202, 273].

Initially, we thought that the "learning curve" of a new social network platform such as PESEDIA would influence the users' privacy behaviors. However, after the analysis of the behavior of users without mechanisms during the period of the experiment, we found that there was not a significant difference in their posting privacy behavior between the initial days of the experiment and the last days.

There is significant evidence that users' privacy behavior for posting actions changed when the nudging mechanisms were activated. Independently of the mechanism used (i.e., picture or number nudge), when the nudging mechanisms were activated, the number of messages published with a private policy (i.e., *only me*, collections, or *friends*) was higher than the number of messages with a public policy. Therefore, this change could be driven by the nudges. Although users seem to publish with a more restrictive privacy policy, we noticed that most of them used friends or private policies without

use of this policy in PESEDIA requires the manual creation of the collection or because it is a concept that is not present in the social network platforms that they are used to, and, therefore, they do not initially consider it as a possible option. Previous studies already showed the importance of nudges for increasing users' awareness about privacy and, thus, modify their behaviors. In this paper, we focused our experiments on teenagers, who are usually less concerned about privacy risk [171]. Although the effect of nudging mechanisms was appreciated, it is expected that more visible behavioral changes can appear if the experiment was extended in time [258].

Previous works that proposed the use of different types of nudge mechanisms do not pay attention to the differences between them on users behavior [271]. In this experimental study, we analyzed whether there is a significant difference between the effects on the privacy posting behavior of teenagers that had the Picture Nudge or the Number Nudge activated. The results revealed that there are no significant differences between mechanisms. This could be because the teenagers were focused mainly on the highlighted text about the risk level than on other details such as the profile pictures of users that may see the publication or the number of users that may see the publication. In the literature, we cannot find studies that sharply measure the effect of some type of nudge to be more beneficial in terms of changing the posting behavior. However, some authors such as [143] and [281] state that the design of nudges that are more tailored to users would cause these nudges to be more effective. This would require aspects such as not receiving alerts about information that is already known or designing personalized nudges according to what is more effective for each specific user. This can be viewed as a limitation of our proposal that can be explored in future works.

With regard to the perception of users about the nudges, the majority of teenagers considered nudges to be useful mechanisms to preserve their privacy in posting. This follows the results obtained by Wang et. al. [273] where the users that were involved in a similar experiment with nudges in social networks mentioned that nudges could be more useful for people without experience in social networks (i.e., teenagers). Although the majority of the participants perceived nudges as beneficial, some of them considered them as irritating, and this is considered as a disadvantage towards the effective implementation of privacy nudges [124]. Wang et. al. [273] suggested that this behaviour can be associated to the profile of the publications (personal or not), but there is not any clear study that demonstrate this fact. In line with what is stated above, future research line should consider the design of more personalized nudges that really show information that is really valued by the specific user.

Regarding the ethical concerns of the mechanisms proposed, we would like to mention

that might see their publications. Previous research works detected that users often forget who are their friends in a social network or overwhelming the evaluation of all the possible scenarios when they share a message in the network [31]. The intended audience might be different to the final potential audience that could have access to the publication. The Picture nudge mechanism uses a list of public profile pictures of the users that may have access to a shared publication. The aim of this list is not to labeled or presented the members of the list as "risky" users. The final goal is to encourage users to be more aware of and more cautious about the privacy policy that they use when sharing information. Moreover, based on the conclusions provided by the research question RQ7.2, if the Profile Nudge mechanism were to be integrated into a social network platform where there was some concern about using a list of profile images of users, Numeric Nudge mechanism could be used, as the results suggest that there are no significant differences in the effects they produce on user behavior.

The main reason for eliminating those users considered outliers within the experiment was to keep the population of users who attended the different sessions of the experiments proposed and followed the guidelines in each session. This caused the analysis of the effect of privacy nudges during posting actions on users is limited to users with a behavior within the average population. Previous research works as [216, 42, 281] highlight different kind of users taking into account their posting behavior in social networks (e.g., influencers). It would be interesting to apply different privacy nudges on different kind of users for comparing the changes in their behaviors (this, of course, for large enough population). Thus, identifying which factors and nudges improve the effect of privacy nudges for each kind of users, we would be able to maximize the effect produced on them.

The results of the experiments suggest that the use of nudge mechanisms seemed promising for assisting users in social networks activity. We encourage the inclusion of this type of mechanisms to commercial social network platforms as part of their functionality. Nudge mechanisms might be included as an optional functionality that can be activated by the users. These mechanisms could help their users to avoid any regrettable experiences disclosing information. We consider that nudges could especially help to those teenagers that start using these social platforms.

Despite the valuable conclusions extracted, the study carried out has several limitations. First, the current research was conducted for 21 consecutive days, and the nudging mechanisms were enabled only in the last 11 days. That is why only a short-term impact on users' privacy behaviors could be measured. As we stated above, we do not know the consequences of long-term usage of nudging mechanisms and their impact

deactivate the nudge mechanisms. While the observed immediate effect of nudges was desirable, future research extending the period of usage could be interesting to analyze if the effect of the nudges is stronger or if it is mitigated, and in that case, think of new nudge alternatives to maintain the effects. Second, the modeling of the experiment to test our hypotheses and the different mechanisms designed forced us to split the participants into groups. The limited number of participants in the experiments has consequences for the interpretation of the results since these cannot be generalized for the entire population of teenagers. Third, it is possible that other approaches of nudging mechanisms that are focused on the sensitivity of the post could produce more effective changes in behaviors regarding privacy. However, according to the research work described in [271], providing sentiment information about the message that is going to be published was not perceived as useful. In addition, it is often difficult to measure the effect of a nudge; users may not react to them in a noticeable way or the reaction might be gradual. Finally, the participants considered for the experiments have a certain age distribution (approx. 12-14). Therefore, these results cannot be extrapolated to users that are in other age range.

7.7 Conclusions

Teenagers are considered to be one of the vulnerable groups to suffer privacy risks because of their limited capacity for self-regulation and susceptibility to peer pressure. Most privacy approaches proposed in the literature try to deal with privacy in social networks to facilitate the configuration of privacy. However, there is still an open problem of making teenagers aware of the extent of disclosing information on social networks, even if users have defined a specific audience. In this paper, we focus on providing soft-paternalism mechanisms that integrate a privacy risk estimation (PRS) of the action that users are going to perform. The proposed mechanisms (nudges) attempt to influence users' decision making to improve their privacy, without actually limiting users' ability to choose freely. One of the mechanisms consists of displaying profile images of those users that might have access to the user's publication. The other mechanism consists of displaying the number of users that might have access to the user's publication. The proposed mechanisms are displayed when the user starts to write a message to disclose.

To evaluate the effect of mechanisms in a real context, we did a 21-day experiment with 42 teenagers ranging in age between 12 and 14 years. We included the proposed nudge mechanisms in the social network PESEDIA. The experiment was divided into two

activated. We collected data about the teenagers' activity during the experiment and analyzed the privacy policy assigned to the publications. The results of the analysis show that there is a significant difference in teenagers' privacy behavior during stage 1 and stage 2. Therefore, the results suggest that the proposed nudges can be considered a useful tool for enhancing privacy awareness in social networks. The results of the analysis also show that there are no significant differences between the two nudges proposed. Finally, we analyzed the level of acceptance of the proposed nudges using a questionnaire. According to the participants' responses, nudges were not seen as irritating. The participants considered the proposed nudges to be useful for preserving their privacy.

As future work, we plan to propose new nudge mechanisms to increase privacy awareness. One of the extensions is the inclusion of an evaluation of the content of the message that users are going to disclose in order to provide a more accurate informative message about the privacy risk. Currently, we provide information about the reachability of the audience without considering the content. Another extension would be to design personalized nudges depending on what is more effective for each user. In addition, we expect to analyze the use of nudge mechanisms in two additional situations: (i) to assist users in the definition of the privacy policies associated to their profile items (i.e., profile photo, age, gender, city, etc.) and (ii) when users receive a friendship request. We also plan to do more experiments with a larger and more heterogeneous population to evaluate whether the mechanisms are appropriate for different user profiles. Moreover, we plan to introduce PESEDIA in the educational context for its continued use, so that, we can analyze the nudging effect on users' behavior regarding privacy in the long-term.

## CHAPTER 8

ASSESSING THE EFFECTIVENESS OF A GAMIFIED SOCIAL NETWORK FOR APPLYING PRIVACY CONCEPTS: AN EMPIRICAL STUDY WITH TEENS

*— (In press status) by **Jose Alemany**, **Elena del Val**, and **Ana García-Fornes***
*in the **IEEE** Transactions on Learning Technologies*

8.1   Introduction 188
8.2   Literature review 190
8.3   Experimental design 193
8.4   Results 201
8.5   Discussion 209
8.6   Conclusion 212

8.1 Introduction

Social networks are an important element in the daily lives of teenagers (ages from 13 to 17). According to the latest Pew Research Center report [18], most teenagers have a profile on an Online Social Network (OSN). This report also points out that there is no clear consensus among teenagers about the effect that OSNs have on their lives. OSNs make it easier for them to keep in touch and interact with others (i.e., friends and family or others with similar interests), but they also entertain them and provide a new way of learning things. However, as teenagers benefit from the use of social networks, they are also exposed to the risks [259, 223, 26, 168] when interacting, publishing, or sharing information in OSNs. This lack of knowledge about the opportunities and risks derived from the use of OSNs (as new consumers and users) may have negative consequences on their lives. Therefore, they need a proper education to enhance their current and future performance in social networks.

To promote a critical and safe use of OSNs, researchers and governments have empha-sized the role of school education to teach teenagers how to safely interact with others in OSNs [260]. Specifically, the European Union has developed initiatives to support safer online access and use of OSNs for children [82, 44]. An example is *The European Strategy for a Better Internet for Children* [44] that has as goals, among others, promotion of the production of creative and educational online content for children as well as to increase children's awareness of the Internet and to empower them to use it safely and responsibly. In addition, online safety has been formally included in school curricula in many European countries through media literacy to improve skills to avoid risks in OSNs [260, 167]. However, it is unclear if these mechanisms can effectively increase privacy awareness (i.e., the attention and understanding of an individual regarding privacy aspects) [296] and prevent unsafe behaviors in OSNs.

Recently, an approach that is rising in popularity is the use of game mechanics and game components in a non-game context (i.e., gamification) [123]. Gamification as an educational learning tool is a powerful approach for dealing with the teach-ing/ learning of tedious or complex tasks [73], such as the learning of safe privacy behaviors in social networks. This approach is powerful due to its ability to teach and reinforce not only knowledge but also important practical skills that might be useful for their daily lives. On the other hand, existing studies have highlighted the influence of OSNs for improving usage levels and perceived levels of learning in students [72]. The properties offered by social networks such as centrality, communication, and connectivity significantly influence learners' performance. Therefore, taking into account the context of the learning goal (social networks, opportunities, and risks), it could be interesting to use both approaches to improve users' learning performance. Moreover, the use of a real social network allows us to assess the users' behavior in real scenarios after the learning period.

The aim of this work is to analyze the effect of introducing gamification in a social network so that students could autonomously learn the functionality of the network and the options and consequences of the different privacy options. We assessed the application of what was learned by the students in the network and analyzed the influence that gamification had on this process. Therefore, this study contributes to the research field in the following ways: 1) by illustrating the value of social gamification for introducing the social network features to new users (reducing the "learning curve") and for learning and promoting the application of privacy behaviors that prevent users from performing actions that could have negative consequences; and 2) by exploring the effects of social network gamification on teenagers by gender and age. Moreover, the gamified social platform proposed in this work may be relevant and useful for educators who wish to develop and enhance teenagers' privacy skills, or for a broader base of aspects related to the development of digital competences and technology in education. The technical and design contributions that the paper makes to the development of learning technologies are: 1) the development of a social network for educating teenagers about safe privacy behaviors and social network features as a unique tool in the "learning by doing" approach; and 2) the design of the learning strategy integrated into the social network with the gamification system.

In the remainder of this article, we first highlight relevant research for education about privacy in social networks and the advantages of gamification (Section 8.2), which will lead to the postulation of four research questions. Then, we discuss the method of our study (Section 8.3) and report the results (Section 8.4). We end this article by discussing the implications of the findings, what we learned compared with current significant research, and the limitations of the study (Section 8.5). Finally, we conclude this article

8.2 Literature review

8.2.1 Educating teenagers about OSN privacy

Teenagers grow up surrounded by a wide range of social media platforms and most of them are both consumers and creators of content in them. However, they are not always aware or have a limited perception of the implications of their online actions and the risks that they can encounter. Several educational strategies have been carried out by education centers and public administrations to leverage teenage users' awareness of privacy risks and to reduce their exposure to cyberbullying or experiences that make them feel uncomfortable in OSNs [53, 258, 45, 260]. Previous studies that have evaluated the impact of educational initiatives suggest that these strategies are successful in increasing awareness about online risks [67, 232]. However, the research community considers that awareness and confidence do not necessarily promote less risky behavior among young people [166]. This result is aligned with the number of young people who report negative online experiences despite the initiatives carried out by education institutions [166].

As an alternative to educational materials, the use of technological tools [121, 267] has been proposed as a means of offering practical experience to learn appropriate attitudes and behaviors when using social network sites. Inoue et al. [121] presented an online and offline version of a tool that helps students to understand privacy risks in online social networks. They performed an experiment in a practical lesson in a school where the teacher interacted with the students using the tool, creating scenarios where the privacy of the students might be compromised. After each scenario, the teacher and students analyzed the effects and potential consequences of their performed actions. A survey conducted after the experiment concluded that the students retained the knowledge about how to handle personal information in OSNs. Wang et al. [267] proposed the development of education tools with high levels of usability and effectiveness to increase knowledge about privacy risk in online sites. The authors presented a prototype based on an educational game that incorporates ideas collected from online crowds to increase the awareness of online privacy. An extension of this proposal was presented in [269]. Along the same lines, Li et al. [157] proposed the development of labware for teaching location privacy in online services. This labware was the mechanism to provide a deeper knowledge about the topic of privacy and to increase the students' privacy awareness. Although the tools proposed in these previous works made it easier to learn safer behaviors on social networks, most were what-if web tools based on hypothetical scenarios that did not put the user into a real social network environment

8.2.2 Social networks and Gamification in education

Although the use of technological tools has a positive effect on the users' learning process of online privacy, these tools are isolated from the context of the educational goal. Therefore, they cannot determine whether the knowledge learned (reflected as awareness and concern about privacy) will promote privacy-seeking behavior in real scenarios (i.e., the actions that users get involved in to safeguard their information on the social network). Studies that focus on using technological tools for improving the teaching/learning process have highlighted the influence of social networks on improving usage levels and perceived levels of learning in students [72]. Research works such as [215] have tested the power of social networks to improve engagement and satisfaction with the course. Properties of social networks such as communication, interaction, and information are translated into support, motivation, and experience. These can reduce the anxiety levels of students [107] and turn the educational expectations into reality by applying a real social context in the teaching/learning process that requires real decisions.

The inclusion of gamification is of interest to the design of activities that are oriented to getting positive feedback (possibly in a competitive environment). Recent research in this field [123, 254, 110] has emphasized the gamification features in order to facilitate a user-centered, autonomous, and flexible learning environment that allows students to follow their own learning path and encourage users to pursue their own goals. The reviewed papers about the application of gamification are mainly focused on MOOCs and e-learning sites [73]. Moreover, according to Dicheva et al. [76], many works focus on the use of gamification in education, but the majority only describe some game mechanisms and dynamics without empirical research that validates the effectiveness of including game elements in learning contexts. Hanus et al. [113] also mention that although the benefits of gamification are mentioned in many works, there is still a need for deep empirical research on the effectiveness of gamification.

Social gamification aims to bring together gamification and social networking to combine the potential of the two approaches in order to create compelling socially-driven user experiences. From an educational perspective, social networks facilitate communication and interactions between students (and with teachers) and highlight relevant content elements. Their potential can also be harnessed to cooperate and create meaningful conversations in learning interactions. On the other hand, gamification stimulates motivational aspects such as participation and engagement with learning content and with other participants. In addition, different skills such as competition, collab-

used [123]. There is little previous research in social gamification [72, 252], and, to the best of our knowledge, none focus on the teenage population or the context of improving users' online privacy through the learning of privacy-seeking behaviors. Therefore, we set out to address the following research question:

Research Question 8.1: *Is there a significant impact on teenage users' learning and behavior about online privacy between social network configuration with gamification and configuration without gamification?*

Furthermore, we want to know if the gamification of the social network improves teenage users' engagement to the social network (i.e., breaking the barrier of joining a new social network site and consolidating them as regular users). Therefore, we set out to address the following research question:

Research Question 8.2: *Is there a significant impact on teenage users' engagement between social network configuration with gamification and configuration without gamification?*

8.2.3 Individual differences

Different authors have shown that personal characteristics play a role in the individual's behavior. Acquisti et. al. [7] analyze how different biases on information introduction and personal characteristics influence users' behaviors and decisions. Al-Rahmi et. al. [9] test how education impacts learning differently depending on students' gender. Koivisto and Hamari [146] study how individual learners interpret game elements differently in highly unique ways. Pedro et al. [203] perform a gender study in a virtual learning environment with gamification. The results indicate that gamification contributed to improving student performance in the case of male students and did not have any effect on motivation and performance in the female students. However, this work was a preliminary study with 16 students; hence, the results cannot be generalized. In this work, we aim to statistically validate conclusions regarding the influence of gender in gamified learning environments. We investigate the impact of gender and age on teenage users regarding their learning about privacy and social network features, safe privacy behaviors, and engagement in the gamified social network. Therefore, we set out to address the following research questions:

Research Question 8.3a: *Do female teenage users learn and have more privacy-seeking behavior in the gamified social network than their male counterparts?*

Research Question 8.3b: *Do female teenage users engage more in the gamified social network*

Research Question 8.4a: *Does the age of teenage users influence learning and privacy-seeking behavior in the gamified social network?*

Research Question 8.4b: *Does the age of teenage users influence engagement in the gamified social network?*

8.3   Experimental design

8.3.1   Study site

Introduction to Social Networks (ISNs) is a course that briefly covers the basics of social networking and provides students with basic competency for deciding which privacy policy is most appropriate when they share information in social networks. The course is aimed at teenagers who are starting with the use of social networks. They are among the heaviest users of social networking [214]. Moreover, this particular group is developmentally vulnerable to online risks such as depression, sexting, and cyberbullying [171, 198, 166, 47].

The course lasts one month and has a total workload of 4.5 hours that matches with on-site teaching lessons. We only have three on-site lessons and the course should be a fun learning experience. An ethics consent letter was obtained from each participant prior to the course. The participants knew that anonymized data would be collected about their activity on the social network. During the course, we provided teenagers with access to our social network, PESEDIA[1] (similar to Facebook), where only they could use it and practice the learned knowledge acquired during the course. PESEDIA was active and accessible 24/7. At the end of the course, we analyzed the behaviors of the teenagers in the social network to evaluate the success of the course, and we presented them with some conclusions. Previous course edition experiences had shown low motivation and participation rates in the proposed activities. Providing teenagers with tools to motivate participation may therefore be a sound approach to improve learning, safe privacy behaviors and engagement. For this reason, we added a gamification module in PESEDIA.

Instrument	Features	Approach & targeted benefit
Social networking	Posting, sharing, comments, liking, friends, activity river, user profiles, private messaging, surveys, external guidance (tutorials & activities)	- Cooperation and communication among participants - Boost participation, collaborative work, and community building - Promote student-driven discussion
Social networking with gamification	Posting, sharing, comments, liking, friends, activity river, user profiles, private messaging, surveys, points, badges, achievements, score, status, leaderboard	- Cooperation, communication, and competition among participants with gamification - Boost participation, collaborative work, and community building - Promote student-driven discussion - Motivate participation through public leaderboard comparison

Table 8.1: Summary of instruments remarking the main features of the different means and targeted benefits.

8.3.2 Instruments

In order to compare the performance as well as the attitude towards social gamification, we carried out an experiment using two configurations of our social network. One configuration consisted of using only the instruments provided by a social network similar to Facebook. The other configuration consisted of including a module in the social network to provide gamification instruments. The social network, called PESEDIA, was the same for both configurations of the experiment. A summary of the instruments used for each configuration is presented in Table 8.1.

PESEDIA is an online social network for educational and research purposes. PESEDIA was designed as a tool for the teaching/learning of OSN features and to increase concern, awareness, and seeking behavior on privacy, especially in the case of children and teenagers who are just beginning to use OSNs. The main goals of PESEDIA include: (i) the design and development of new metrics to analyze and quantify privacy risks [11, 13]; (ii) the application of methods to influence users' behavior towards safer actions regarding their privacy [12]; and (iii) the evaluation and testing of new proposals with real users [14]. The underlying implementation of PESEDIA uses Elgg [64], which is an open-source engine that is used to build social environments. The environment provided by this engine is similar to other social networks (e.g., Facebook). We devel-

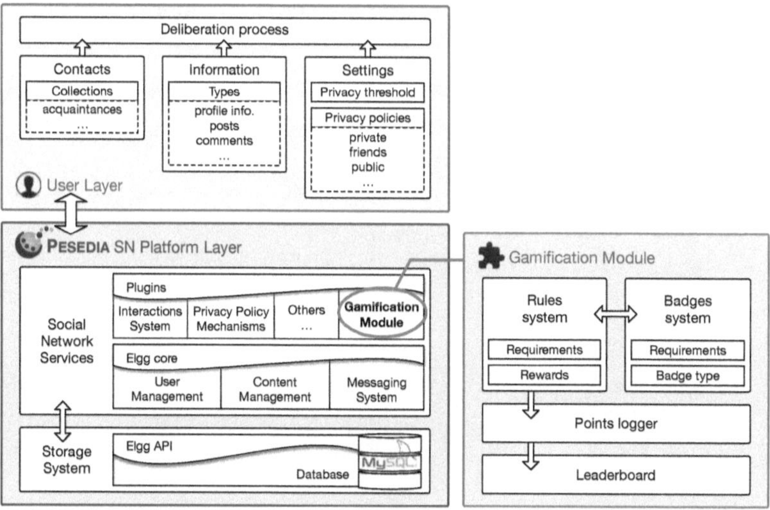

Figure 8.1: Block diagram that represents the architecture of Pesedia. Also represented is the relevant plugin for this work: the Gamification Module.

the Elgg engine (see Figure 8.1). The modules allow us to enable and disable online features of the social network at any time, adapting them to the needs of the experiment. Moreover, the use of our social network allowed users to interact with each other and to perform the course activities.

The first configuration was based on the last non-gamified course edition done. It was a non-gamified configuration of PESEDIA, which provided the environment to perform the activities planned in each lesson. Figure 8.2 depicts the different elements that the social network offered to users: a profile view with their profile elements presented (in the center of the figure); a wall, where users post their publications and comments (at the bottom of the figure, accessible via the "Activity" tab or the profile icon in the top bar); friendship management (group icon in the top bar); private messaging service (message icon in the top bar); and other instruments that are easily identifiable in the figure. The difference between the PESEDIA course editions is the gamification module, so the "Score" and "Badges-and-points" tab were not available in the non-gamified course. The other instruments used in this configuration were mainly tutorials and activities. The difference between these instruments was related to the grade of teaching assistance needed to complete them.

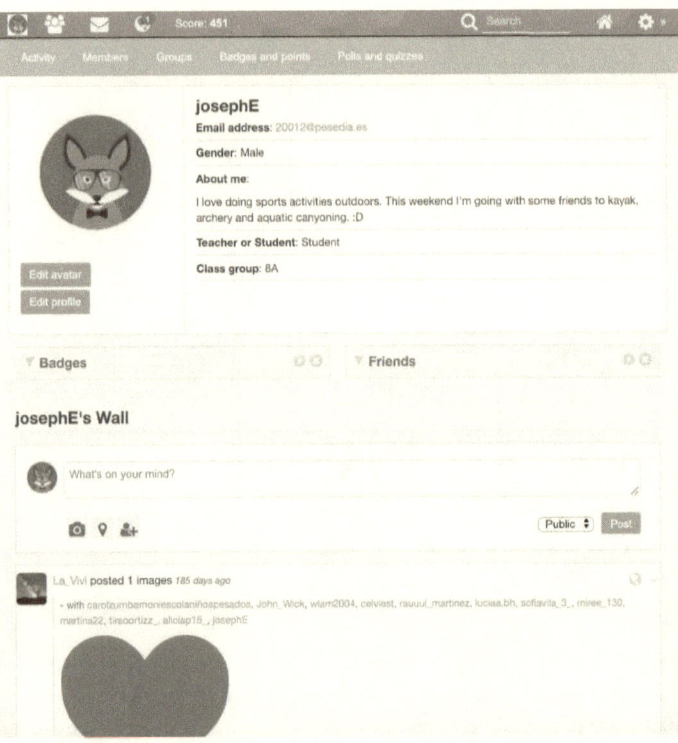

Figure 8.2: User wall of the social network Pesedia. This screenshot belongs to the gamified social network. The non-gamified configuration does not include the "Score" representation in the top bar or the "Badges-and-points" menu.

the activities planned in each lesson autonomously at their own pace without the intervention of teaching assistants. The gamification design included in PESEDIA offers users the possibility to choose what activities to complete and there are no penalties for poor activity performance. We have considered game design elements at two levels of abstraction: (i) educational gamification design principles, and (ii) game mechanics [76, 295]. The gamification design principles selected are based on the idea of progress. The intention was to present practical lessons in stages that scale by difficulty (i.e., scaffolded instruction), but that each user can accommodate to his/her own pace and needs [113]. We considered a set of stages of mastery following the stages established by Dreyfus when looking at how people engage with systems [77]. The stages of mastery

- Newcomer: The user who just arrived to the social network. He/she has created an account in the social network and has logged in.

- Rookie: Similar to a newcomer but with information already in hand about some privacy aspects. He/she is on his/her way toward figuring out how the social network works and what functionalities it offers.

- Trainee: Users have increased their practice in a wide variety of typical social network actions such as sharing and/or commenting on other publications, uploading photos, likes or labeling friends. Users also achieve a deeper knowledge about the options that the social network offers in order to restrict the visibility of their actions. The situations that they deal with in the social network are stored in order to provide a basis for future recognition of similar situations that could appear in the future.

- Expert: The user starts to think about the different configurations of privacy policies and which ones are the most suitable by considering different scenarios and types of information (i.e., profile items or posts). He/she learns how to create different personalized audience groups and how to use them to restrict the audience of a publication.

- Master: The expert performer in the social network has reached the final stage in the step-wise improvement of privacy awareness and good practices that we have been following. The user repertoire of experienced situations is now quite broad, and he/she can intuitively dictate an appropriate action for each specific situation.

The game mechanics proposed are based on the following three key elements:

- Points: These allow us to see how users are interacting within the social network, design for outcomes, and make appropriate adjustments. We have considered two types of points: experience points, which are used to track the user activity in the social network; and skills points, which are assigned to specific activities within the social network that reflect whether the user has acquired certain skills (see Figure 8.3).

- Badges: These offer a visual representation of progress and are given for special achievements. We have considered different kind of badges: Status and Expe-

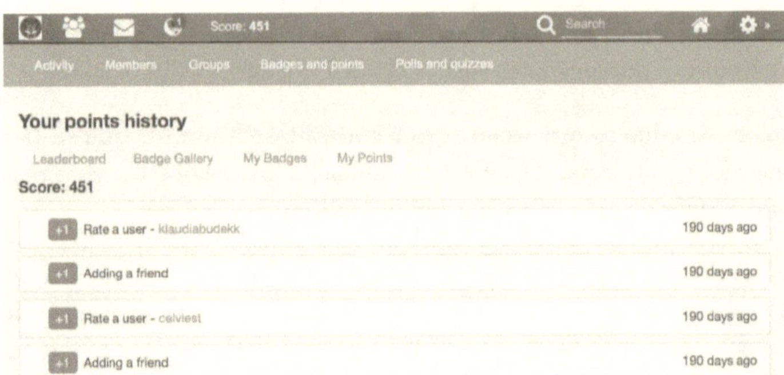

Figure 8.3: View of "My Points" with a registry of the latest points obtained for a specific user.

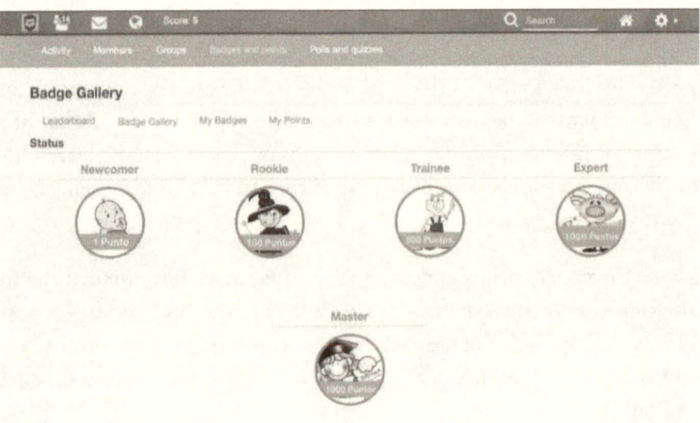

Figure 8.4: View of the "Badge Gallery" with all of the badges the user has not achieved yet.

Master) are represented as Status badges, while activities are represented as Experience badges. Each Status badge is composed of a set of Experience badges (see Figure 8.4).

- Leaderboard: The goal of the leaderboard is to make simple comparisons. Based on the points and badges, users are ranked on a leaderboard that encourages engagement through competition (see Figure 8.5).

All of these instruments included in the gamification module were used to complete

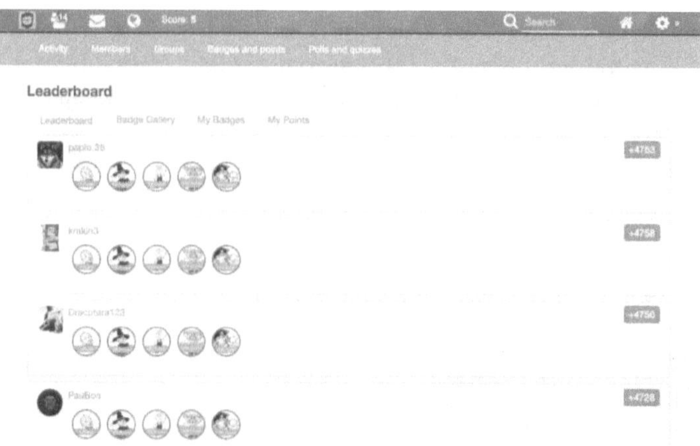

Figure 8.5: View of the "Leaderboard" with a top-ten ranking of the users with the most points.

experience points or skills points). Moreover, an activity was associated with the requirements to obtain a badge. To obtain a badge, the students had to complete several activities depending on the level of the badge (i.e., Newcomer, Rookie, Trainee, Expert, or Master), thus giving them a sense of progression towards mastery and also providing points on the achievement of each badge. The different activities/badges were gradually enabled during each lesson so that the participants could complete the activities/badges and have time to practice the learned knowledge acquired before continuing with the other activities/badges. In other words, a lesson had a set of activities/badges that were enabled at the beginning of the lesson, and once the participants completed them, they had time to practice them before the next lesson started. Based on the number of activities performed (represented as badges and points obtained), the leaderboard offered the possibility to see other students' positions in the ranking for competing and sharing their achievements. Once they achieved all of the badges (from a lesson, or from the whole course), the participants could still get some extra points for performing actions related to the activities. Therefore, they could continue practicing the knowledge acquired on the social network but without activity support.

8.3.3 Participants

A total of 405 teenagers participated in the experiment. Of these, we excluded the par-

participants who decided not to participate (5 participants did not log into PESEDIA). Finally, 387 participants completed the experiment (196 females, 191 males, 86 12-year-olds, 199 13-year-olds, and 102 14-years-olds, $M_{age} = 13.04$, range: 12-14 years old). We included the participants in the experiment taking into account their age in order to have a sample of the teenage population (participants older than 12 years old). All of the selected participants were attending high school in different school centers of the Valencia area at the time of the experiment. When the participants enroll, they were assigned to one of the two groups of the experiment based on when they sign up. The social network without gamification was administered to a group of 178 teenagers (97 females, 81 males, 38 12-year-olds, 93 13-year-olds, and 47 14-year-olds, $M_{age} = 13.05$). The social network with gamification was administered to a group of 209 teenagers (99 females, 110 males, 48 12-year-olds, 106 13-year-olds, and 55 14-year-olds, $M_{age} = 13.03$).

8.3.4 Procedure

Experimentation took place during the summer period. Both course editions had a duration of one month and had the same content and activities. The experiment was carried out on the PESEDIA social network where both configurations were applied: one configuration without the gamification module, and another with the gamification module enabled. To prevent interferences, we included a registry controller (using a secret token) to avoid undesired registrations that could affect the security of the participants and the experiment. The participants of the experimental group who used the social network without gamification took the course first. Then the course was taken by the participants of the experimental group who used the social network with gamification. During the period of the experiment, the participants had access to the PESEDIA social network to share their experiences and feelings.

We organized three on-site lessons of 90 minutes in equipped labs at the university to use as control points of the experiment. In these lessons, activities were delivered sequentially to be completed in the same session or from home. These three on-site lessons were distributed at three points in time: lesson 1, at the beginning of the one-month period; lesson 2, in the middle; and lesson 3, at the end. The aim of these lessons was to clarify any doubts that might arise among the participants about the functionality and features of the social network. Each lesson started with a brief explanation of the activities that they should try to complete during the lesson, and then participants had time to interact using the social network and complete the different activities. The

doubts that could arise during the performance of the activities. In the first lesson, we introduced PESEDIA to the participants and they signed up on the social network. Then, they had to complete some activities that focused on customizing their user profiles, setting up their general setting options, and building their friendship relations (low-medium difficulty). In the second lesson, they had to complete activities that focused on interacting and posting, choosing their audience (medium-high difficulty). In the third (and last) lesson, the participants had to complete an extra activity (challenge). Finally, to conclude the course, we also presented them with a course summary regarding their behaviors and answers to the survey.

8.3.5 Measures and data analysis

During the experimentation, a log system was activated to record all of the participants' actions in order to analyze them after the experiment. Information such as the privacy policies chosen for profile items, general setting options, and posts were used to assess the users' privacy-seeking behavior. The rate of private policies used over the total number of privacy decisions chosen was computed for each participant. Information such as the amount of content created, and the rate of activity and survey completions were used to calculate the users' engagement with the educational process. All of these values were normalized on a 0-1 scale, except for the content-created variable. The Shapiro-Wilk test was used to check the normality of the data distribution for the variables. That indicated to us that we had to use non-parametric tests since the data gathered did not follow a normal distribution. Therefore, Mann-Whitney and Kruskal-Wallis tests was used to analyze differences between groups.

8.4 Results

In this section, we present the participants' results regarding the behavior and activities performed on PESEDIA for both configurations (Non-Gamified and Gamified). We also test the research questions considered above about the participants' behaviors towards privacy concepts as a consequence of the privacy teaching/learning process, the participants' engagement with the social network, differences in gender and/or age behavior of the participants and their attitude towards the instruments used. Note that the Shapiro-Wilk normality test was run to analyze the distribution values of the private privacy policies rate and the participation rate of the participants (Tables 8.2, 8.3, and 8.4) collected from the social network PESEDIA for running the appropriate statistical

$\alpha = 0.05$). Therefore, non-parametric statistical tests were applied to investigate our research questions.

8.4.1 Privacy-seeking behavior

The participants' behavior regarding privacy was measured through the usage that participants made of PESEDIA. We specially analyzed the data collected from the privacy policies of the participants' profile items, general setting options, and publications. The data collection was done for the duration of the experiment, which was one month.

Figure 8.6 shows the participants' behavior regarding different privacy decisions on the social network, which are split into three dimensions: the privacy policy of profile items (e.g., name, phone number, etc.), the general privacy setting options (e.g., friend list visibility, "who is allowed to tag me", etc.), and the privacy policy of publications. The values represent the rate distribution of private privacy policies used by the participants (ranging from 0 to 1, where 0 means that no private privacy policies were used while 1 means that only private privacy policies were used). Private privacy policies include: *Friends*, personalized access lists (also known as *collections*), and *Only me*. An analysis of the results reveals three notable points for discussion. First, the profile items that contain the most sensitive information of participants such as name, email, or phone number had more permissive privacy policies in the Non-Gamified configuration than in the Gamified configuration. Although we explained to the participants how to change these privacy policies in both course editions, they figured out how to customize them better in the Gamified configuration. In contrast, in the Non-Gamified configuration, the vast majority of participants shared their personal profile data with public policies (all of the quartiles of the boxplot are in the 0 value) except for a few participants (representing the outliers). Second, the general setting options about privacy are an instrument that participants seldom take care of, regardless of whether there is gamification. Both scenarios have a median of value 0 for private privacy policies (represented as a line in the middle of the boxplot figure). The participants changed their privacy setting options towards more restrictive privacy policies only in a few cases, more in the Gamified configuration than in the Non-Gamified configuration (where all of the quartiles of the boxplot are in the 0 value). The most changed privacy setting options were "who is allowed to tag me", "who is allowed to publish on my wall", and the visibility of the friend list, in that order. Third, the posting action, which is the main action for interacting with others in a social network, also has a median value of 0 for the Non-Gamified configuration. However, there are no outlier

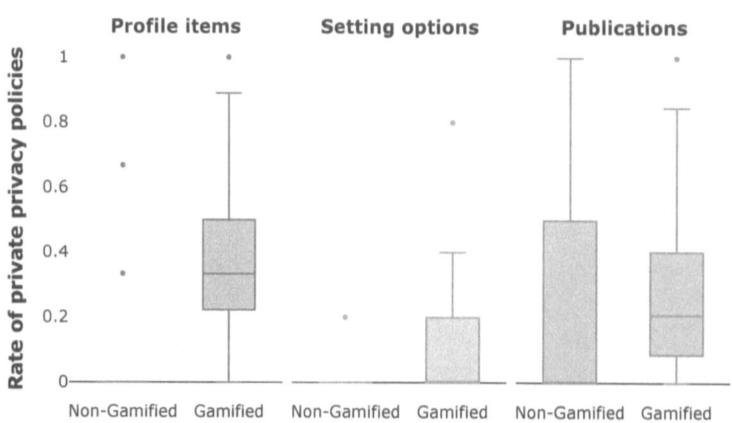

Figure 8.6: Participants' behaviors regarding privacy decisions on profile items, general setting options, and publications on Pesedia for Non-Gamified and Gamified configurations. Values (ranging from 0 to 1) represent the rate distribution of private privacy policies (e.g.,*Only me*, *Collections*, or *Friends*) used by the participants, where 0 means that no private privacy policies were used and 1 means that only private privacy policies were used.

means that a significant portion of participants also used private privacy policies. For the Gamified configuration, the participants followed more restrictive privacy policies for posting actions. Even so, we observed that, in this configuration, the privacy policies were slightly less restrictive than for the profile items. This is normal since the information sensitivity of the profile item dimension is probably higher than for the publication dimension. Finally, for all of the dimensions about privacy decisions in the Non-Gamified configuration, the participants used the social network without taking too much care about who could access their information. Research works such as [271] highlight OSN users' learning through regrets of their actions due to bad decisions as the most common practice. In contrast, the use of gamification to introduce and educate users about privacy aspects in social networks as shown in our experiments may help to improve these hurdles.

Research question RQ8.1 was tested in order to determine whether or not there is a significant difference in privacy behaviors between Gamified and Non-Gamified PESEDIA. We collected the data from the privacy policies of the participants' profile items, settings, and publications for the duration of the experiment, which was one month. The rate data of the private policies was normalized for each participant. Due to the non-normality of the variables and the number of samples, we used the Mann-Whitney test

Variable	Category	Descriptive statistics						Shapiro-Wilk test		Mann-Whitney test	
		N	M	SD	SE	Min	Max	W	p-value	U	p-value
Profile privacy	Non-Gamif.	178	.013	.096	.007	0	1	.120	< .001	3108	< .001
	Gamif.	209	.373	.246	.017			.939	< .001		
Settings privacy	Non-Gamif.	178	.001	.015	.001	0	1	.048	< .001	11314	< .001
	Gamif.	209	.090	.124	.008			.670	< .001		
Posting privacy	Non-Gamif.	126	.259	.368	.033	0	1	.706	< .001	9642	< .001
	Gamif.	201	.265	.235	.016			.902	< .001		

Table 8.2: Summary of descriptive statistics, the Shapiro-Wilk normality test, and the Mann-Whitney test for investigating research question RQ8.1.

closer to the nominal level. We investigated the research questions taking into account the theory of the null hypothesis as well as the Mann-Whitney test. In statistical hypothesis testing, a Type I error is the rejection of a true null hypothesis. Thus, we are able to reject the null hypothesis (H_0) to accept the alternative (H_1).

To answer research question RQ8.1 about how the gamification of the social network impacts the participants' behaviors towards privacy concepts and safe practices in social networks, we tested the mean differences between the Gamified and Non-Gamified social network, especially taking into account the behaviors regarding private privacy policies for the dimensions of the profile, settings, and posting (see Table 8.2). Specifically, we ran the Mann-Whitney test ($\alpha = .05$) and the results rejected the null hypothesis of similarity for profile, settings, and posting dimensions (p-value=$< .001$). Therefore, significant differences were found in the impact on the participants' behaviors towards privacy concepts and safe practices in the social network between the Gamified configuration and the Non-Gamified configuration of the social network. Thus, RQ8.1 was supported.

8.4.2 Social network engagement

The participants' engagement with the social network was measured through the actions they did publishing content and completing activities on PESEDIA. We specially analyzed the amount of content created (such as posts, comments, likes, private messages, etc.), the rate of completed activities, and the rate of completed surveys. The data collection was done for the duration of the experiment, which was one month.

Figure 8.7 shows the distributions of the engagement of the participants in the social network in the experiment taking into account the following three features: the amount

activities (i.e., the number of completed activities normalized by their total), and the rate of completed surveys. For the content creation column, the values represent the amount of content created by the participants. Both distributions have the same shape, both have a few participants that are very active and produce great amounts of content and a majority of participants who only publish a few publications. Even so, the rate of participation in the Gamified configuration (with a median of about 80 contents created by each participant) is clearly higher than the rate of participation in the Non-Gamified configuration (roughly 15 contents created by each participant). Moreover, the most active participants using the Non-Gamified configuration created the same amount of content as a regular participant using the Gamified configuration. For the activity and survey participation columns, the values represent the rate distribution of completed activities and surveys by each participant. The activities (for both the Non-Gamified and the Gamified configurations) were focused on improving the learning of the social network features, the privacy-seeking behavior, and the engagement to participate actively. However, in the Non-Gamified configuration, only a few users participated in the activities. The opposite occured in the Gamified configuration, where the median rate of completed activities was 95% (represented as a line in the middle of the boxplot figure). In the case of the surveys, the rate of completion was high in both configurations. Nevertheless, the number of completed surveys was slightly better in the Gamified configuration. We considered that the huge difference in activity participation for both configurations could be because gamification provides participants with the autonomy to complete the activities at their own pace, while the Non-Gamified configuration does not provide this advantage.

Research question RQ8.2 was tested in order to determine whether or not there was a significant difference in social network engagement between configurations. We analyzed the amount of content created by the participants, the activity participation, and the survey participation. The participation rate was normalized for each participant. Due to the non-normality of the variables and the number of samples, we used the Mann-Whitney test ($\alpha = .05$). For this test, we calculated the mid p-value since its Type I error rate is closer to the nominal level. We investigated the research questions taking into account the theory of the null hypothesis as well as the Mann-Whitney test. In statistical hypothesis testing, a Type I error is the rejection of a true null hypothesis. Thus, we are able to reject the null hypothesis (H_0) to accept the alternative (H_1).

To answer research question RQ8.2 about how the gamification of the social network impacts the participation rates of teenage users, we tested the mean differences between the Gamified and Non-Gamified social network, especially taking into account

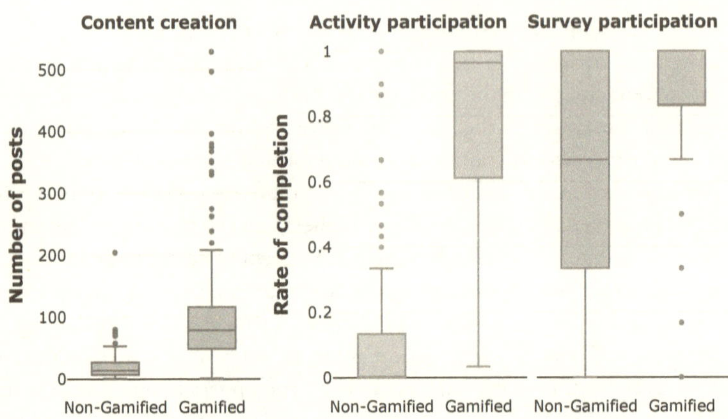

Figure 8.7: Participants' engagement based on the amount of content created, the rate of activities completed, and the rate of surveys completed on Pesedia with and without gamification.

Variable	Category	Descriptive statistics						Shapiro-Wilk test		Mann-Whitney test	
		N	M	SD	SE	Min	Max	W	p-value	U	p-value
Content creation	Non-Gamif.	178	20.2	21.8	1.6	0	-	.686	< .001	4180	< .001
	Gamif.	209	98.0	85.4	5.9			.788	< .001		
Activity participation	Non-Gamif.	178	.106	.202	.016	0	1	.598	< .001	1732	< .001
	Gamif.	209	.777	.311	.022			.726	< .001		
Survey participation	Non-Gamif.	178	.657	.273	.020	0	1	.846	< .001	12934	< .001
	Gamif.	209	.777	.276	.019			.730	< .001		

Table 8.3: Summary of descriptive statistics, the Shapiro-Wilk normality test, and the Mann-Whitney test for investigating research question RQ8.2.

completed (see Table 8.3). Specifically, we ran the Mann-Whitney test ($\alpha = .05$) and the results rejected the null hypothesis of similarity for content creation, and the activity and survey completion dimensions (p-value=< .001). Therefore, significant differences were found in the impact on the participation rates of teenage users in the social network between the Gamified and the Non-Gamified configuration of the social network. Thus, RQ8.2 was supported.

8.4.3 Gender & Age behavior differences

Next, we analyze the privacy and engagement behavior of the participants in the social network regarding their gender and age, but only for the Gamified configuration. We

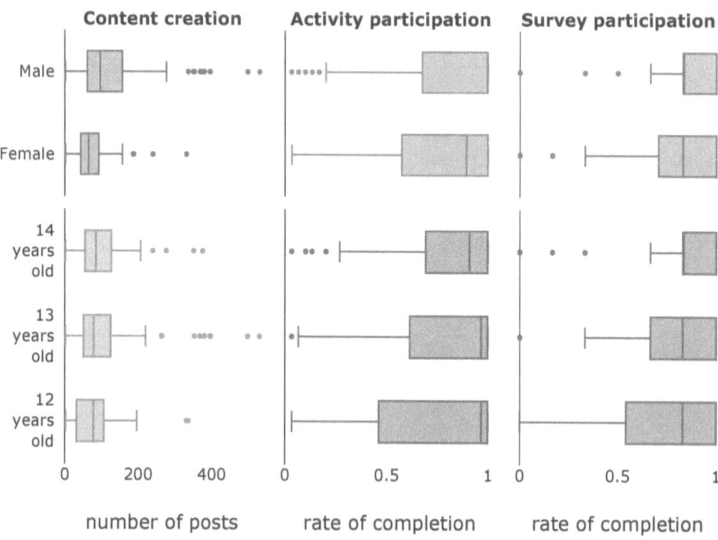

Figure 8.8: Participants' engagement split by gender and age for the Gamified Pesedia.

ferent way according to their gender and age. We analyze the same features as above
but split by gender and age. The collection was done for the duration of the experiment,
which was one month.

Figure 8.8 shows the distribution of the engagement of the participants in the social
network by gender and age for the Gamified configuration. We analyzed the features
to measure the engagement as we did in Section 8.4.2. The results obtained from the engagement distributions show slightly similar distributions for these features by gender
and age. There were only some differences in the engagement distributions by gender.
The clearest difference can be seen in the amount of content created on the social network by the male participants, where they obtain the maximum values per participant
and also have a higher median than the female participants. No differences were found
for gender or age regarding privacy behavior.

Research questions RQ8.3a, RQ8.3b, RQ8.4a, and RQ8.4b were tested in order to determine whether or not there was a significant difference regarding privacy behavior
or engagement in the social network taking into account the gender and age of the
participants of the Gamified configuration. We used the features analyzed and normalized for each participant in the Gamified configuration. Due to the non-normality

Variable	Category	Descriptive statistics						Shapiro-Wilk test		Man-Whitney test	
		N	M	SD	SE	Min	Max	W	p-value	U	p-value
PSB: Profile privacy	Male	110	.389	.278	.026	0	1	.924	< .001	5380	.882
	Female	99	.354	.206	.021			.955	.002		
PSB: Settings privacy	Male	110	.085	.128	.012	0	1	.634	< .001	5149	.429
	Female	99	.095	.119	.012			.702	< .001		
PSB: Posting privacy	Male	110	.231	.208	.020	0	1	.899	< .001	4990	.297
	Female	99	.282	.263	.026			.896	< .001		
SNE: Content creation	Male	110	120.2	102.6	9.7	0	-	.820	< .001	3767	< .001
	Female	99	73.4	51.1	5.1			.879	< .001		
SNE: Activity participation	Male	110	.799	.308	.029	0	1	.682	< .001	4375	.014
	Female	99	.752	.314	.032			.769	< .001		
SNE: Survey participation	Male	110	.780	.270	.026	0	1	.725	< .001	5436	.983
	Female	99	.773	.284	.028			.734	< .001		
										(Kruskal-Wallis test χ^2)	
PSB: Profile privacy	12-year-old	48	.361	.194	.028	0	1	.947	.003	3.307	.347
	13-year-old	106	.397	.265	.025			.943	.002		
	14-year-old	55	.336	.249	.034			.905	.004		
PSB: Settings privacy	12-year-old	48	.089	.116	.017	0	1	.691	< .001	1.296	.730
	13-year-old	106	.094	.136	.013			.665	< .001		
	14-year-old	55	.085	.107	.015			.671	< .001		
PSB: Posting privacy	12-year-old	48	.251	.234	.034	0	1	.898	.006	2.487	.477
	13-year-old	106	.285	.264	.025			.895	< .001		
	14-year-old	55	.205	.166	.022			.928	.003		
SNE: Content creation	12-year-old	48	84.2	70.3	10.2	0	-	.819	< .001	.9516	.621
	13-year-old	106	102.8	94.6	9.1			.747	< .001		
	14-year-old	55	100.6	79.8	10.8			.858	< .001		
SNE: Activity participation	12-year-old	48	.763	.331	.048	0	1	.716	< .001	.4791	.787
	13-year-old	106	.779	.307	.030			.732	< .001		
	14-year-old	55	.783	.313	.042			.704	< .001		
SNE: Survey participation	12-year-old	48	.748	.290	.042	0	1	.776	< .001	.3587	.835
	13-year-old	106	.781	.271	.026			.740	< .001		
	14-year-old	55	.784	.279	.038			.661	< .001		

Table 8.4: Summary of descriptive statistics, the Shapiro-Wilk normality test, and the non-parametric tests of significance (Mann-Whitney and Kruskal-Wallis tests) for investigating research questions RQ8.3a, RQ8.3b, RQ8.4a, and RQ8.4b. PSB and SNE denote privacy-seeking behavior and social network engagement variables, respectively.

tests, we calculated the mid p-value since its Type I error rate is closer to the nominal level. We investigated the research questions taking into account the theory of the null hypothesis. In statistical hypothesis testing, a Type I error is the rejection of a true null hypothesis. Thus, we are able to reject the null hypothesis (H_0) to accept the alternative (H_1).

To answer the research questions about how the gender of the participants in the Gamified social network configuration influences privacy behavior (RQ8.3a) and engagement (RQ8.3b), we tested the mean differences between genders taking into account the variables shown in Table 8.4. Specifically, we ran the Mann-Whitney test ($\alpha = .05$), and the results rejected the null hypothesis of similarity only for content

icant differences were only found for the impact on the participation rates of teenage
users for the gender of the participants regarding content creation and activity participation. Thus, RQ8.3b was partially supported only for engagement.

To answer the research questions about how the age of the participants in the gamified social network configuration influences privacy behavior (RQ8.4a) and engagement (RQ8.4b), we tested the mean differences for three groups(12, 13, and 14-year-
olds) taking into account the variables shown in Table 8.4. Specifically, we ran the
Kruskal-Wallis test ($\alpha = .05$) and the results did not reject the null hypothesis of
similarity (p-value> .05). Therefore, no significant differences were found in the participants' privacy behavior or engagement in the social network by age. Thus, RQ8.4a
and RQ8.4b were not supported.

8.5   Discussion

The integration of gamification instruments in non-game contexts to teach people in
a practical way about dull, tedious or complex tasks is rising in popularity. The privacy concept, and especially users' privacy on social networks, is a challenge that is
highlighted in several research works [231, 5, 255]. Therefore, the use of gamification in
the context of social networks to teach users about privacy and privacy mechanisms
of the social network is a perfect match. This combination allows users to be aware of
their privacy, and thus be better able to manage complex scenarios to avoid possible
leaks of information or regrets. In this work, we have assessed the integration of gamification on a social network through the investigation of four research questions. The
aim of these research questions was to measure the effect of gamification on teenage
users regarding the learning of privacy and social network features, privacy awareness,
and social network engagement. PESEDIA is the social network where the gamification
instruments were integrated, which is similar to Facebook and has most of the privacy
mechanisms of Facebook. To do this, we carried out a short-term, one-month experiment where two configurations of the social network PESEDIA were used: one with the
gamification module enabled, and the other without it. The gamified social network
proposed in this work may be relevant and useful for educators who wish to develop
and enhance teenagers' privacy skills, or for a broader base of aspects related to the
development of digital competences and technology in education.

The direct benefits of using gamification to improve learning have numerous defend-
ers [76, 295], although there are some contexts or features where gamification produces

where the combination of gamification instruments with social network instruments is proposed, defend the extra benefits of this union. However, as far as we know, the application of social gamification has not been proven on the teenage population nor with the aim of improving the users' awareness and privacy-seeking behavior. In our work, the results suggest that the gamification designed and integrated into PESEDIA has a positive learning effect on teenagers. They improved their awareness and seeking behavior of privacy, and their interest in the social network was higher when the gamification module was enabled. Specifically, profile items, general setting options, and posts had privacy policies that were more appropriate, and the rate of activity and survey completion was also higher. We did not see any negative effects on teenage users' behavior due to the use of gamification instruments. Furthermore, the age and gender of teenagers did not have a relevant effect on how they were influenced by gamification, except in the case of male teenagers who created content slightly more actively than female teenagers. While some studies indicate that females engage more in gamified courses than males [254], our work has extracted the conclusions for a younger population (teenagers). Moreover, our work has also been assessed in a different context (a social network), where studies like [283] have highlighted that male teens disclose more information than female teens. However, testing the effect of gamification on social networks to teach users about privacy should be done by extending the participant population to include other age ranges.

The way gamification is designed and the instruments used can enhance the learning effect on people [110]. Although our results show more awareness of privacy and higher participation rates by teens when the gamification module is active, we do not know with certainty which privacy policies are the most appropriate for a publication. The lack of easy metrics to compute the most appropriate privacy policy for a publication (i.e., the privacy policy that maximizes the social benefit of the user and minimizes his/her loss of privacy) makes our goal an estimation between the usage of the privacy mechanisms and the privacy choice. Therefore, once there is a recognized way of assessing the appropriateness of a privacy policy for users' publications, it will be possible to design gamification instruments that focus on improving the privacy policies chosen for a publication, taking into account all of the factors involved. Some works try to define the best way to measure these factors and combine them [288, 233, 70]. An interesting next step would be to use them with gamification. Thus, it would be possible to maximize users' learning about privacy concepts through gamification instruments.

Other factors to consider are the time when gamification is used and/or its duration, and what/how many rewards should be designed. In our case, we limited the number

erful gamification reinforcement at the beginning of each on-site lesson (and during
the course experience) that introduced them to the social networks and accelerated
the learning curve [132]. Once the participants achieved the rewards designed in each
lesson, no more rewards were activated in the same lesson. Thus, after the learning
period (i.e., at the end of each lesson, between lessons, and at the end of the course),
the participants used the social network with the knowledge acquired from the activities. Other interesting approaches to be considered would be: varying the gamification
time of use to determine the most optimal application time for the participants' learning; or adding punishments/rewards for users when they make bad/good privacy policy
choices (e.g., in cases of sensitive information, or conflicts detected between users, etc.).
It should always be taken into account that there are different types of users with different social network goals [216].

Despite the valuable conclusions extracted, this study has several limitations. First,
the current research was conducted for one month. That is why only a short-term impact on users' privacy behaviors and social network engagement could be measured.
As we stated above, we do not know the consequences of long-term usage of gamification instruments and their impact on users' behaviors. It could happen that, after
a certain period of time, some users might ignore the knowledge acquired. While the
observed immediate effect of gamification was desirable, future research that extends
the period of usage could be interesting. Second, as we have highlighted in this work,
the lack of easy metrics to measure the appropriate privacy policy for a publication
makes us estimate the privacy-seeking behavior as the usage of the privacy mechanisms plus the privacy choice. Furthermore, we designed our gamification activities
and instruments based on this estimation. Therefore, having a metric that is capable
of measuring the appropriate privacy policy for a publication, we would be able to
effectively design the gamification elements and assess the effect for improving users'
concern, awareness, and seeking behavior on privacy. Finally, the participants considered for the experiments have a certain age distribution (approx. 12-14 years old).
Therefore, these results cannot be extrapolated to teenage users in general (approx. 12-
18 years old) to obtain a broader view of this group of social network users. In order
to be able to confirm whether the effects observed in this study are extrapolatable to
other populations, we plan to evaluate the performance of gamification for different
populations, that is, a more heterogeneous sample of participants with different age

8.6 Conclusion

This research work studied the capabilities of social networks and social gamification for educational purposes about the concepts of social networks, especially users' online privacy. We assessed two configurations (with/without gamification), focusing on teenagers' learning and engagement with the educational process. We also statistically compared the two approaches to determine which one provided better results. After a statistical analysis, the results illustrated the value of social gamification for the teaching/learning of privacy and engagement in OSNs. It has also shown that teenagers using the gamified OSN had behaviors that are more restrictive in information disclosure that potentially might reduce actions with negative consequences via practice in a real environment. For the social gamification configuration, we investigated differences in teenagers' learning and engagement taking into account individual characteristics of the participants such as age and gender. The study explored possible age and gender differences regarding the social gamification, depicting only a significant difference for gender (greater for male teenagers than for female teenagers) for the engagement with the educational process.

Our findings and the gamified social platform proposed in this work may be relevant and useful for educators who wish to develop and enhance teenagers' privacy skills, or for a broader base of aspects related to the development of digital competences and technology in education.

Part III

Discussion

## CHAPTER 9

GENERAL DISCUSSION OF THE RESULTS

9.1 Results on open research lines about privacy 216

9.2 Results of the definition of a privacy risk metric . . . 217

9.3 Results of the proposed sensitivity metric for social network publications 218

9.4 Results on users' benefit-cost trade-off in privacy decisions 220

9.5 Results on nudging users with privacy risk and sensitivity metrics 221

9.6 Results of educating teenage users about privacy with social gamification items 222

In this chapter, the main results achieved by each of the contributions that compose this book are discussed as well as the possible lines for future research. Section 9.1 discusses the open challenges found in the design of privacy mechanisms, which help users to choose the elements of online communication during the privacy decision-making process. Section 9.2 discusses the proposal of privacy risk metrics that calculate the potential risk raised from information re-sharing users' actions. These privacy metrics were tested in experiments using the most popular social network structural topologies and behavioral models based on epidemics. Section 9.3 discusses the proposal of a metric that provides a sensitivity value of a social network publication. This proposal is based on previous papers/approaches that assess the degree of sensitivity of information in several contexts such as legal, economic, and social networks. A research model that assesses the benefit-cost trade-off of users for the elements of online communication (channel, message, and receptors) and their factors is discussed in Section 9.4. Finally, Sections 9.5 and 9.6 describe different approaches for informing and educating users about their actions on social networks and how these have an impact not only on the privacy of their information but also on the information of other users.

and were tested with real users' activity and interactions.

9.1 Results on open research lines about privacy

Chapter 2 presents a deep review of the advances made on privacy mechanisms and solutions. The advances of the reviewed papers and articles have been sorted taking into account the requirement that meet (from the eleven identified requirements). To help readers to understand these requirements, the whole privacy decision-making process was depicted in a picture identifying the communication elements, their factors, and the potential privacy problems by steps. Furthermore, comparative tables are included for each of the requirement sections remarking the properties of the privacy mechanism solutions analyzed.

The contributions of this paper highlight the requirements that have been less worked out and/or not yet met. These requirements are 1) the development of metrics for measuring privacy risks; 2) the validation of a realistic behavioral model that can be used for automatic privacy decisions; 3) the design of privacy mechanisms and elements that inform and educate users about their privacy decisions or about privacy recommendations received; 4) the adaptation of privacy mechanisms to users' decisions for still meeting these requirements; 5) the existing gaps in multi-party privacy decisions such as defining and detecting the real owners of publication content, argumentation to solve privacy conflicts, etc.; and 6) the creation of new disclosure mechanisms in social networks with new play rules in privacy policies (e.g., *Instagram Stories* which content becomes totally private over time). This **book** work contributes to addressing the first three (1-3) of these six requirements. By addressing these three requirements, the **book** contributes to preserving the users' privacy during single privacy decisions through the awareness of the value of their data, the consequences/scope of their actions, and most especially the understanding of the privacy risks.

The rest of the identified requirements remain still open and are part of the future research work. Although there are advances in privacy mechanisms for deciding multi-party content privacy, there are no tools for detecting which publications have more than one owner. For example, the photo of a baby, this content could have as many owners as legal representatives. On the other hand, new social network disclosure mechanisms like *Instagram* or *WhatsApp Stories* with new privacy rules lack of research

9.2   Results of the definition of a privacy risk metric

Chapter 3 propose a metric based on information flows resulting from re-sharing actions in social networks to assess the user's privacy risk. Users are constantly sharing information on social networks and they are not totally aware of the scope of their actions. Moreover, not all users have the same perception of risk. In this paper, the Privacy Risk Score (PRS) metric was proposed in several ways, one as a global network scope metric, and the other as a scope metric by distance levels with the following main contributions:

(i) The PRS is oriented to estimating the reachability of users' sharing actions instead of being focused on the misalignment of their users' expected audience with the actual audience.

(ii) This measure is provided globally and in levels in order to be able to adjust to the user's perception of risk.

(iii) The PRS takes into account the paths that the publications follow in the social network without having to provide the information explicitly by the user.

(iv) Centrality metrics are proposed to provide an approximation of the PRS in social networking environments where detailed record of the information sharing activity is not available.

Then, it was empirically tested through simulated experiments and real information flows on Twitter. The simulated experiments used the most popular network topologies and epidemic models to understand the dissemination information process and quantify the scope of users' actions. Regarding real social information flows, this work tested the PRS metric using a dataset of information flows based on life cycles of rumors on Twitter.

The results of the experiment proved the validity of the PRS metric for estimating the users' scope in the network and the accuracy of estimating users' scope using global, local, and social centrality properties. Global centrality metrics obtain in general good accuracy results but the main disadvantage of these metrics is the complexity of their computation (they are not always computationally affordable). Regarding local and social centrality metrics, their accuracy results showed a better estimation with the degree local metric for the global PRS metric, while the degree social metric worked better for the PRS metric by distance levels. Local and social metrics are computa-

flows in the network. The analysis of the PRS metric and the PRS value of users in the rumors network showed that most users have low PRS values (i.e., values in the range [0,0.2]). These results match with the conclusions obtained by the paper that presents the dataset [297]. The results in real social networks confirm that local and social centrality metrics based on degree perform well in estimating a user's privacy risk and could be integrated in social network applications that offer limited access to information flows.

Chapter 4 presents metrics of privacy risk extending the previous PRS metric based on friendship layers. The concept of friendship layers allows us to provide information about user's privacy risk for different levels of risk perception. This work proposes two privacy risk metrics, *Reachability* and *Audience*. Reachability provides information to the user about the probability that a message that he/she publishes reaches a specific friendship layer or a specific number of users in that layer. Audience provides information to the user about the percentage of users in a specific layer who are likely to see a message that he/she published. These new metrics provide more easy and detailed explanations that could be shown to users about their privacy risks during privacy decisions. Both privacy metrics were tested through a set of experiments. The *effectiveness* centrality metric obtained better results for estimating the privacy metrics, *Reachability* and *Audience*, than other centrality metrics such as *degree* or *ego-betweenness*. Finally, this work proposes a common regression model based on the *effectiveness* value of agents to approximate Reachability and Audience values in different network models.

9.3 Results of the proposed sensitivity metric for social network publications

Another way of measuring privacy risks is related to the information content dimension. Considering the sensitivity of the content of a publication in a social network, Chapter 5 proposes a metric for evaluating the amount of the user's personal information that is revealed. For this study, several works that compute information sensitivity from different approaches were reviewed. Four different approaches were identified in the literature review. First, the approach based on law and regulation, which raises as a result of governments' limitation to companies' activities that collect, store, and manage personal data. Second, the approach based on market valuation, companies values information as economic resources. Third, the approach based on individuals' valuation, people are concerned about their information but everyone has a price for which

tics, the same words reveals more or less information according to how generic/specific words are. In addition to these approaches, we identified a new one that raises from the OSNs domain. This new approach emerged from the documented reasons for users' regrets available in the literature. This type of information sensitivity is focused on the effect of the information on users' reputation. For example, the use of swearwords might be inappropriate in some contexts such as family circles. Another example is posting content with a strong sentiment which caused several cases of high regret. As a consequence, this work made the following contributions:

(i) Providing a sensitivity value for each information type that might be present in the OSN domain based on an analysis of values assigned in previous approaches;

(ii) Proposing the representation of the total value of sensitivity for a publication, taking into consideration that multiple information types could appear in the same publication.

After the analysis and review of previous works that deal with the assignment of a sensitivity value to information types, we identified that some information types have small variability of value among the different works. Categories such as demographics and human characteristics have a high degree of agreement among works that evaluate this data as being of low sensitivity. Categories such as medical, legal, and personally identifiable data categories also have a high degree of agreement, evaluating this data as being highly sensitive. For information types with less agreement among approaches, we highlight user behaviors and intentions. These may be valuable to companies, but the other approaches (laws & regulations, and individuals' valuation) give them low sensitive value or they do not even assess the value of these types.

Regarding the proposal of estimating a sensitivity value for each information type, we decided to accumulate the values of all the works and calculate the mean value for each information type. We also included new information types from OSNs regrets. The final sensitivity value of a publication is an added value of all the types of information included in it. The results of our study showed a high relation between the 196 teenage users' perception of risky information with the estimation made using the proposed metric. Future work in this line that we have considered is the analysis of different ways of introducing this value to users (e.g., as a monetary value, as a color scale, etc.).

9.4 Results on users' benefit-cost trade-off in privacy decisions

With the goal of understanding the impact of receptors types and sensitivity of messages on privacy decisions, Chapter 6 develops and tests a research model. Unlike most of the works that try to analyze the reasons why users share or not information in social networks, this work tries to understand the interplay of the communication elements and their properties that end up with disclosure actions. Furthermore, the paper also tries to explain how the final disclosure action facilitates to building social capital and/or losing privacy. Once these relationships could be quantified, better strategies and privacy mechanisms can be designed.

The research model was tested with data from 400 respondents. Their responses were collected and analyzed using partial least squares modeling. We measure the *channel's factors* with 1) the users' trust in the OSN provider, and 2) the users' perceived control; the *message's factor* with 3) the sensitivity of the information; and the *receptor's factors* differentiating between 4) trusted receptors, 5) influencing receptors, and 6) most common social circles (family members, friends, coworkers, and unknown users).

The findings of this study demonstrated that disclosing personal information to different kinds of users had a significant difference in users' privacy calculus perception. Although the social circle of coworkers had a few pieces of evidence of regrets like in the family case, the study revealed a non-relevant effect on users' privacy concerns and a significant positive effect on bonding social capital. This behavior might be explained by the seeking of job satisfaction and/or the desire of strengthening ties with coworkers, with whom we spend a great deal of time every day. It is worth to mention that the social circle of friends had no significant effect on users' perceptions of benefit or risk. It could be that the friend social circle has become the most diverse-interpretative of them (e.g., Facebook collapse other context relationships within it). Moreover, disclosing personal information with influencing receivers had a significantly positive effect on bridging capital building, while there was an insignificant impact on users' privacy concerns. In this regard, users do not perceive risky disclosing their information with influencing-users. However, if they do not know this user (unknown users) and they disclose their personal information, the study has been shown that it has a significantly negative effect on their bonding capital. Taken all together, these findings reveal that too close relationships (family) or, the flip side, unknown relationships are perceived by users as none beneficial for users' privacy/reputation. Future research of this work is oriented towards the application and validation of our research model in a social network (e.g., in our prototype of social network called PESEDIA). The research model will

networks. In this regard, we will test our privacy mechanisms based on the validated model versus other privacy mechanisms considered in the literature.

9.5 Results on nudging users with privacy risk and sensitivity metrics

Once the above contributions of this Ph.D. book measure risks on social networks, in Chapter 7 several designs of privacy mechanisms that explain to users the potential consequences of their actions during privacy decisions are presented. The most appropriate way for informing users about the measured risks, assist them, and, in turn, cause an effect on their behaviors was with the use of soft-paternalistic mechanisms (i.e., nudges). Recent research showed the great benefits of nudge mechanisms for privacy context, which do not actually limit users' ability to choose freely (because of all options are still available), thus, preserving the users' freedom of choice.

Previous research had already tested the positive impact of nudge mechanisms regarding privacy decisions. In this work, the individual personalization of the nudge to the user was tested. Several nudge mechanisms were designed: two kinds of nudge mechanisms for the scope metrics, and another for the information sensitivity metric. For the scope metric, a visual type nudge (*picture* nudge) included the users' profiles pictures of potential receivers estimated with the scope metrics, while another textual type nudge (*number* nudge) included an estimated number of potential receptors. For the sensitivity metric, the sensitivity metric value of the publication was provided to users in a message such as the following: *"The sensitivity value of your publication is XX. The higher this value, the higher your privacy risk."*. The impact of nudge mechanisms on users' behaviors was tested for both types of metrics (scope metric and sensitivity metric) in separate empirical experiments with teenage participants. We aimed this target population because they are vulnerable novice/amateur users who are initiating in their usage and have limited abilities for self-regulation and complex decision-making.

For the experiment with users' scope metrics, a total of 42 teenage participants completed the experiment producing 848 privacy decisions. About two-thirds of the privacy decisions were made using the nudge mechanism. The findings revealed that there is significant evidence that users' privacy behavior for posting actions changed when the nudging mechanisms were activated. Independently of the mechanism used (i.e., *picture* or *number* nudge), when the nudging mechanisms were activated, the number of messages published with a private policy (i.e., only me, collections, or friends) was

be driven by the nudges.

For the experiment with the information sensitivity metric, a total of 196 teenage participants completed the experiment producing 5880 privacy decisions. Half of the privacy decisions were made using the nudge mechanism. The findings revealed that the teenagers of the experiment had some previous knowledge about the sensitivity of the information, because they chose restrictive privacy policies for the most sensitive posts when nudges were not activated. The results also showed that nudge messages about sensitivity had a positive effect on their behavior as well as the sensitivity level shown on the nudge message. The effect on teenagers' privacy behavior was more significant the greater the sensitivity value included in the nudge message. From the results, we conclude that the teenagers were able to understand the nudge message that contained information about the sensitivity of their publications. Participants used them to have less risky behaviors on social networks by choosing more restrictive privacy policies. For future research in this line, we plan to investigate the behavioral effect of nudges in a long-term experiment.

9.6 Results of educating teenage users about privacy with social gamification items

Finally, this book work has also investigated the integration of gamification elements in a social network for improving the users' understanding of social network features and users' privacy. The integration of gamification instruments in non-game contexts is been used to teach people in a practical way about dull, tedious or complex tasks. Because privacy matches this definition, the use of gamification in the context of social networks to teaching users about privacy and privacy mechanisms of the social network sounds interesting. The contributions of this work (presented in Chapter 8) are 1) to illustrate the value of social gamification for introducing the social network features to new users (reducing the "learning curve") and for learning and promoting the application of privacy behaviors that prevent users from performing actions that could have negative consequences; and 2) to explore the effects of social network gamification on teenagers by gender and age. Moreover, the social network PESEDIA is also a contribution that has allowed us to test and validate the book' hypotheses.

An experiment with 387 participants was made. From them, 178 participants used a social network without gamification and the rest of the participants (209) used a social network with gamification. Their actions and activities were monitored to measure the

the gamification designed and integrated into PESEDIA had a positive learning effect on teenage participants. They improved their awareness and seeking behavior of privacy, and their interest in the social network was higher when the gamification module was enabled. Specifically, profile items, general setting options, and posts had privacy policies that were more appropriate, and the rate of activity and survey completion was also higher. We did not see any negative effects on teenage users' behavior due to the use of gamification instruments.

## CHAPTER 10

Conclusions and Future Work

Online social networks are a powerful tool for getting a range of social benefits that traditional (offline) communication cannot off er. However, social networks are still not the most secure tools. Specifically, a lot of privacy issues have been reported about the users' actions on sharing information and privacy decisions. Therefore, advances in improving social networks, privacy mechanisms, and, in turn, the users' privacy decisions are required.

Current research lines in enhancing users' privacy in social networks have made advances in proposals of privacy mechanisms/solutions that align users' preferences to information sharing decisions in single and multi-party scenarios. All of these proposals primarily use automation for recommending privacy policies for privacy setting items, profile items, and/or sharing actions. Automation allows systems to individually evaluate information content type, relations strength, social norms, and other features of social networks to decide in a fine-grained way what users are the most appropriate to have access to a user's information and activity. However, the last research works stressed several issues that might detract validity to these proposals. First, the proposals do not assess the risks of users' privacy decisions when it has been shown that users have problems evaluating privacy risks [5]. An example of these privacy risks is the potential audience that finally has access to users' information as consequences of re-sharing actions. Another example is the reported regrets due to sharing too sensitive information. Second, the proposals do not capture the social idiosyncrasies considered by users in the real-life, and users' behavior is far from perfectly rational [117]. Studies in users' behaviors regarding information disclosure have been done but none have analyzed the relationship between the different online communication elements and the costs-benefit in disclosure actions. Finally, users do not understand the privacy recommendations of proposals due to the lack of explanation regarding the privacy solution computed [93].

In order to enhance the privacy mechanisms, this **book** tackles the following chal-

aspects to improve privacy decisions; (ii) the proposal of metrics to compute privacy risks on social networks from the perspectives of over exposition, visibility, and privacy loss of users in the network; (iii) the analysis of users' trade-off between costs and benefits in disclosure decisions regarding the factors of the communication elements; and (iv) the development of privacy mechanisms that explain the potential consequences and benefits of users' privacy decisions and raise the users' concern regarding privacy.

Privacy-preserving mechanisms require an assessment of privacy risks and consequences of users' actions. Privacy risks that emerged from users' activity are caused by the scope of users' sharing-actions and an over exposition of their information. In this **book**, how information spread, the visibility of a user's actions by his/her connections, and the users' position in a network has been analyzed to propose a privacy risk metric. The PRS metric is focused on estimating the potential audience of a sharing-action. The metric is provided globally and in levels in order to be able to adjust to the users' perception of risk. The testing of the proposed PRS metric was made through experiments with simulated networks based on the most popular behavioral epidemic models and with a Twitter-sampling social network based on rumors. The findings proved the validity of the PRS metric for estimating the users' scope in the network and the possibility to compute the PRS metric using local and social centrality metrics. On the other hand, an information sensitivity metric was proposed based on the information types and the wording used in publications. Information types have different grades of sensitivity because they reveal more or less personal data. The proposed metric combines work estimations from economical, legislative, linguistical, and individual approaches. Experiments with real users showed a correlation between users' perceptions and the proposed sensitivity metric for real social network publications.

Before using the proposed privacy metrics for recommending possible audiences that maximizes a specific utility function, this **book** work analyzed the conditions why, dur-ing disclosure actions, a representative population of 400 social network users makes the decision to share specific pieces of information (the message) with a particular user (the receptor). The findings revealed that disclosing personal information with too close or far social circles computes positively for increasing the users' privacy con-cerns, while trusted and influential users compute positively for building the social capital of transmitter-users.

Finally, this **book** work tested two ways to translate the previous results in privacy mechanisms that could argue and explain to users' the consequences of privacy decisions. On the one hand, soft-paternalistic interventions (nudges) that attempt to influence decision making to improve individual well-being, without actually limiting

metrics (the scope metric and the sensitivity metric) were included in nudging privacy mechanisms and tested with 42 and 196 teenage users, respectively. The results remarked an impact on users' privacy behaviors towards more restrictive and safer privacy policies. As we expected, the empowerment of users via explainable information had a significant effect on their privacy decisions. On the other hand, this book also tested the effect of integrating gamified elements in a social network and compare the privacy decisions in both configurations (with and without gamification). The goals of including gamification in the social network were introducing the social network features to new users (reducing the "learning curve"), and teaching users in a practical way about dull, tedious or complex tasks like online privacy. The results of 387 teenage participants showed the improvement of users' awareness and their seeking behavior of privacy while they used the gamified configuration. Furthermore, users' interest in the social network was higher when the gamification module was enabled. All of the mech-anisms developed and proposed in this book were integrated into the social network PESEDIA.

The results and contributions of this Ph.D. book are important advances in the improvement of privacy mechanisms. However, the privacy field in social networks is a wide area of research and some of the identified challenges are still far to be completely solved. Moreover, the challenges identified in Chapter 2 that were not addressed in this book work are susceptible to be investigated. One is the adaptability of privacy recom-mendations through an argued discussion between the privacy mechanism and the user who wants to share a post. In this regard, users might reach an agreed-on privacy so-lution that preserves their privacy as well as meets their motivations. These agreed-on privacy solutions could be reached through the use of computational argumentation, persuasive systems, and the research model developed in Chapter 6. Another challenge that could be improved is the negotiations/recommendations in multi-party privacy scenarios. Currently, these negotiations/recommendations are based on the computa-tion of matching the users' preferences while solving conflicts on privacy preferences. However, there is no assessment of the potential privacy risks of users' decisions and/or the final privacy solution. Hence, it would be interesting to apply the privacy risk met-rics developed in this book to the multi-party privacy scenarios. Furthermore, it would also be interesting to show arguments about the privacy risks of co-owners (e.g., via nudge mechanisms). In this way, the multi-party privacy conflicts might be avoided instead of trying to reach agreements to users' conflicts. Finally, interesting propos-als could be reached by researching and analyzing new privacy mechanisms and new types of privacy policies like *Instagram Stories* which content fades with time.